Books by Randall Jarrell

POETRY

The Rage for the Lost Penny	
(in *Five Young American Poets*)	1940
Blood for a Stranger	1942
Little Friend, Little Friend	1945
Losses	1948
The Seven-League Crutches	1951
Selected Poems	1955
The Woman at the Washington Zoo	1960
The Lost World	1965
The Complete Poems	1969

ESSAYS

Poetry and the Age	1953
A Sad Heart at the Supermarket	1962
The Third Book of Criticism	1969
The Complete Essays and Criticism	edition in preparation

FICTION

Pictures from an Institution	1954

CHILDREN'S BOOKS

The Gingerbread Rabbit   1964
The Bat-Poet   1964
The Animal Family   1965
Fly by Night   *edition in preparation*

TRANSLATIONS

*The Golden Bird and Other Fairy Tales
   of the Brothers Grimm*   1962
*The Rabbit Catcher and Other Fairy Tales
   of Ludwig Bechstein*   1962
The Three Sisters   1969
Faust, Part I   *edition in preparation*

ANTHOLOGIES

The Anchor Book of Stories   1958
The Best Short Stories of Rudyard Kipling   1961
The English in England (Kipling stories)   1963
In the Vernacular: The English in India
   (Kipling stories)   1963
Six Russian Short Novels   1963
Modern Poetry: An Anthology   *edition in preparation*

The Third Book of Criticism

Randall Jarrell

THE THIRD BOOK
OF CRITICISM

Farrar, Straus & Giroux

NEW YORK

The publisher wishes to acknowledge the sources of the quoted material in the various essays: *The Man Who Loved Children* by Christina Stead (copyright 1940 by Christina Stead), Holt, Rinehart and Winston, Inc.; the copyrighted works of Wallace Stevens, Alfred A. Knopf, Inc.; the copyrighted works of Robert Graves, *Poems 1938–45*, Farrar, Straus and Giroux, Inc., *Collected Poems*, Doubleday and Co., Inc., *Goodbye to All That*, Anchor Books, *The White Goddess*, Farrar, Straus and Giroux, Inc. (copyright © by Robert Graves, 1946; 1955, 1958, 1961; 1929, 1957; and 1948, respectively); the copyrighted works of W. H. Auden, Random House, Inc.; *Complete Poems of Robert Frost* by Robert Frost (copyright 1930, 1939 by Holt, Rinehart and Winston, Inc.; copyright renewed © 1958 by Robert Frost; copyright renewed © 1967 by Lesley Frost Ballantine), Holt, Rinehart and Winston, Inc.; *Confession* by Leo Tolstoy, translated by Aylmer Maude, Oxford University Press; *Collected Poems* by Marianne Moore (copyright 1935, 1941, 1944, 1951 by Marianne Moore; copyright renewed © 1963 by Marianne Moore and T. S. Eliot), The Macmillan Company; the copyrighted works of Ezra Pound, New Directions Publishing Corporation; "The Pardon" in *Ceremony and Other Poems* by Richard Wilbur, Harcourt, Brace and World, Inc.

Note

Not long before he died, Randall Jarrell wrote out by hand a list headed "3rd criticism book." He did not live to write two of the essays he listed, "The Best of Auden" and one on *The Three Sisters. The Third Book of Criticism,* following his *Poetry and the Age* (1953) and *A Sad Heart at the Supermarket* (1962), collects the other nine essays.

"An Unread Book" prefaced the 1965 reissue of Christina Stead's *The Man Who Loved Children* (Holt, Rinehart and Winston) ; an abridged version of this essay appeared in *The Atlantic Monthly* earlier that year.

"The Collected Poems of Wallace Stevens" and "Graves and the White Goddess" were first published in *The Yale Review:* the former in the Spring 1955 issue; part I of the latter in Winter 1956, part II in Spring 1956.

"Changes of Attitude and Rhetoric in Auden's Poetry" was first published in *The Southern Review*, Autumn 1941.

"Freud to Paul: The Stages of Auden's Ideology" was first published in *Partisan Review*, Fall 1945.

"Robert Frost's 'Home Burial'" first appeared in *The Moment of Poetry*, edited by Don Cameron Allen (The Johns Hopkins Press, 1962).

"Six Russian Short Novels" and "The English in England" were introductions to Anchor Books of the same titles (Doubleday and Company, Inc., both 1963).

"Fifty Years of American Poetry" was delivered as a lecture at the National Poetry Festival in Washington, D.C., on October 22, 1962, and was published in the Spring 1963 issue of *Prairie Schooner*.

CONTENTS

1 *An Unread Book*   3

2 *The Collected Poems of Wallace Stevens*   55

3 *Graves and the White Goddess*   77

4 *Changes of Attitude and Rhetoric in
      Auden's Poetry*   115

5 *Freud to Paul: The Stages of Auden's
      Ideology*   153

6 *Robert Frost's "Home Burial"*   191

7 *Six Russian Short Novels*   235

8 *The English in England*   279

9 *Fifty Years of American Poetry*   295

An Unread Book

A MAN ON A PARK BENCH has a lonely final look, as if to say: "Reduce humanity to its ultimate particles and you end here; beyond this single separate being you cannot go." But if you look back into his life you cannot help seeing that he is separated off, not separate—is a later, singular stage of an earlier plural being. All the tongues of men were baby talk to begin with: go back far enough and which of us knew where he ended and Mother and Father and Brother and Sister began? The singular subject in its objective universe has evolved from that original composite entity —half subjective, half objective, having its own ways and laws and language, its own life and its own death —the family.

The Man Who Loved Children knows as few books have ever known—knows specifically, profoundly, exhaustively—what a family is: if all mankind had been reared in orphan asylums for a thousand years, it could learn to have families again by reading *The Man Who Loved Children.* Tolstoy said that "each

unhappy family is unhappy in a way of its own"
—a way that it calls happiness; the Pollits, a very
unhappy family, are unhappy in a way almost
unbelievably their own. And yet as we read we keep
thinking : "How can anything so completely itself, so
completely different from me and mine, be, somehow,
me and mine?" The book has an almost frightening
power of remembrance; and so much of our earlier life
is repressed, forgotten, both in the books we read and
the memories we have, that this seems friendly of the
book, even when what it reminds us of is terrible. A
poem says, "O to be a child again, just for tonight!"
As you read *The Man Who Loved Children* it is
strange to have the wish come true.

When you begin to read about the Pollits you
think with a laugh, "They're wonderfully plausible." When you have read fifty or a hundred pages
you think with a desperate laugh, or none, that they
are wonderfully implausible—implausible as mothers
and fathers and children, in isolation, *are* implausible.
There in that warm, dark, second womb, the bosom of
the family, everything is carried far past plausibility : a family's private life is as immoderate and
insensate, compared to its public life, as our thoughts
are, compared to our speech. (O secret, satisfactory,
shameless things! things that, this side of Judgment
Day, no stranger ever will discover.) Dostoevsky
wrote : "Almost every reality, even if it has its own
immutable laws, nearly always is incredible as well
as improbable. Occasionally, moreover, the more real,
the more improbable it is." Defending the reality of

his own novels, he used to say that their improbable extremes were far closer to everyday reality than the immediately plausible, statistical naturalism of the books everyone calls lifelike; as a proof he would read from newspaper clippings accounts of the characters and events of a Dostoevsky novel. Since Christina Stead combines with such extremes an immediately plausible naturalism, she could find her own newspaper clippings without any trouble; but the easiest defense of all would be simply for her to say, "Remember?" We do remember; and, remembering, we are willing to admit the normality of the abnormal— are willing to admit that we never understand the normal better than when it has been allowed to reach its full growth and become the abnormal.

I I

INSIDE THE POLLIT FAMILY the ordinary mitigated, half-appreciative opposition of man and woman has reached its full growth. Sam and his wife Henny are no longer on speaking terms; they quarrel directly, but the rest of the time one parent says to a child what the child repeats to the other parent. They are true opposites: Sam's blue-eyed, white-gold-haired, pale fatness is closer to Henny's haggard saffron-skinned blackness than his light general spirit is to her dark particular one. The children lean to one side of the universe or the other and ask for understanding: "Sam's answers were always to the point, full of facts; while the more one heard of Henny's answer, the more intriguing it was, the less was understood. Beyond Sam stood the physical world, and beyond Henny—what?"

Like Henny herself are Henny's *treasure drawers*, a chaos of laces, ribbons, gloves, flowers, buttons, hairpins, pots of rouge, bits of mascara, foreign coins, medicines (Henny's own "aspirin, phenacetin, and pyramidon"); often, as a treat, the children are allowed to *look in the drawers*. "A musky smell always came from Henrietta's room, a combination of dust, powder, scent, body odors that stirred the children's blood, deep, deep." At the center of the web of odors is their *Mothering, Moth, Motherbunch*, "like a tall crane in the reaches of the river, standing with one leg crooked and listening. She would look fixedly at her vision and suddenly close her eyes. The child watching (there was always one) would see nothing but the huge eyeball in its glove of flesh, deep-sunk in the wrinkled skull-hole, the dark circle round it and the eyebrow far above, as it seemed, while all her skin, unrelieved by brilliant eye, came out in its real shade, burnt olive. She looked formidable in such moments, in her intemperate silence, the bitter set of her discolored mouth with her uneven slender gambler's nose and scornful nostrils, lengthening her sharp oval face, pulling the dry skinfolds. Then when she opened her eyes there would shoot out a look of hate, horror, passion, or contempt."

To the children she is "a charming, slatternly witch; everything that she did was right, right, her right: she claimed this right to do what she wished

because of all her sufferings, and all the children believed in her rights." She falls in a faint on the floor,
and the accustomed children run to get pillows, watch
silently "the death-like face, drawn and yellow
under its full black hair," the "poor naked neck with
its gooseflesh." She is nourished on "tea and an aspirin"; "tea, almost black, with toast and mustard
pickles"; a "one-man curry" of "a bit of cold meat, a
hard-boiled egg, some currants, and an onion"—as her
mother says, "All her life she's lived on gherkins and
chilies and Worcestershire sauce. . . . She preferred
pickled walnuts at school to candy." She sews, darns,
knits, embroiders. School had taught her only three
things: to play Chopin ("there would steal through
the listening house flights of notes, rounded as doves,
wheeling over housetops in the sleeping afternoon,
Chopin or Brahms, escaping from Henny's lingering,
firm fingers"), to paint watercolors, and to sew. It is
life that has taught her to give it "her famous *black
look*"; to run through once again the rhymes, rituals,
jokes, sayings, stories—inestimable stones, unvalued
jewels—that the children beg her for; to drudge at old
tasks daily renewed; to lie and beg and borrow and
sink deeper into debt; to deal the cards out for the
game she cheats at and has never won, an elaborate
two-decked solitaire played "feverishly, until her
mind was a darkness, until all the memories and the
ease had long since drained away . . . leaving her
sitting there, with blackened eyes, a yellow skin, and
straining wrinkles." Marriage, that had found Henny
a "gentle, neurotic creature wearing silk next to the

skin and expecting to have a good time at White House receptions," has left her "a thin, dark scarecrow," a "dirty cracked plate, that's just what I am." In the end, her black hair swiftly graying, she has turned into "a dried-up, skinny, funny old woman" who cries out, "I'm an old woman, your mother's an old woman"; who cries out, "Isn't it rotten luck? Isn't every rotten thing in life rotten luck?"

All Henny's particularities, peculiarities, sum themselves up into a strange general representativeness, so that she somehow stands for all women. She shares helplessly "the natural outlawry of womankind," of creatures who, left-handed, sidelong in the right-handed, upright world of men, try to get around by hook or by crook, by a last weak winning sexual smile, the laws men have made for them. Henny "was one of those women who secretly sympathize with all women against all men; life was a rotten deal, with men holding all the aces." Women, as people say, *take everything personally*—even Henny's generalizations of all existence are personal, and so living. As she does her "microscopic darning," sometimes a "small mouse would run past, or even boldly stand and inquisitively stare at her. Henny would look down at its monstrous pointed little face calmly and go on with her work." She accepts the "sooty little beings" as "house guests" except when she wakes to smell the "musky penetrating odor of their passage"; or when she looks at one and sees that it is a pregnant mother; or when the moralist her husband says that mice bring germs, and obliges her to kill them. She kills them; "nevertheless, though she despised animals, she felt involuntarily that the little marauder was much like herself, trying to get by." Henny is an involuntary, hysterical moralist or none; as her creator says, "Henny was beautifully, wholeheartedly vile: she asked no quarter and gave none to the foul world." And yet, and so, your heart goes out to her, because she is miserably what life has made her, and makes her misery her only real claim on existence. Her husband wants to be given credit for everything, even his mistakes—especially his mistakes, which are always well-meaning, right-minded ones that in a better world would be unmistaken. Henny is an honest liar; even Sam's truths are ways to get his own way.

But you remember best about Henny what is worst about Henny: her tirades. These are too much and (to tell the truth) too many for us; but if anything so excessive is to be truthfully represented, that is almost inevitable. These tirades are shameful, insensate, and interminable, including and exaggerating all that there is; looking at the vile world, her enemy, Henny cries: "Life is nothing but rags and tags, and filthy rags at that. Why was I ever born?" Before long the reader has impressed upon his shrinking flesh the essential formula of Henny's rhetoric. A magnifying word like *great* is followed by an intensive like *vile, filthy, rotten, foul:* Henny's nose has been shoved into the filth of things, so that she sees them magnified, consummately foul, as Swift saw the bodies and the physiological processes of the people of Brobding-

9

nag. At the "mere sight of the great flopping monster" her stepdaughter, Henny cries out: "She's that Big-Me all over again. Always with her eyes glued to a book. I feel like snatching the rotten thing from her and pushing it into her eyes, her great lolling head. . . . She crawls, I can hardly touch her, she reeks with her slime and filth—she doesn't notice! I beat her until I can't stand—she doesn't notice! When I fall on the floor, she runs and gets a pillow and at that I suppose she's better than her murderer of a father who lets me lie there."

The girl sewing a fine seam, the watercolor painter, the piano player has stepped from the altar into the filth of marriage and childbearing and child rearing; and forever after she can tell the truth about it—the naked, physiological, excremental truth—only in physiological, excremental terms. It is women who must clean up the mess men make, the mess everything makes; the hag Henny stares out at "the darn muck of existence," the foul marsh above which the dwellings of men rise on precarious stilts, and screams at it her daemonic tirades. She knows. Whatever men say, women know; as an old woman says chuckling, an accessory to the fact: "Life's dirty, isn't it, Louie, eh? Don't you worry what they say to you, we're all dirty." Sometimes even Henny absently consents to it: "she looked vaguely about, sniffing that familiar smell of fresh dirtiness which belongs to mankind's extreme youth, a pleasant smell to mothers."

When Henny is "defenseless, in one of those absences of hatred, aimless lulls that all long wars must have," she looks at us "strangely, with her great, brown eyes," and even her husband's "heart would be wrung with their unloving beauty." Our own hearts are wrung by Henny, when, "beginning to cry like a little girl, and putting the fold of her dressing gown to her face," she cries, "Ai, ai"; when she feels "a curious, dull, but new sensation," and awakening from "a sort of sullen absence . . . knew what was happening : her heart was breaking. That moment, it broke for good and all"; when, no longer able to "stand any of this life any longer," in a sort of murderous delirium she beats her favorite child "across the head, screaming at him, 'Die, die, why don't you all die and leave me to die or to hang; fall down, die; what do I care?' "—while her son, "not thinking of defending himself," cries "brokenly, in a warm, pleading voice, 'Mother, don't, don't, Mother, Mother, Mother, Mother, Mother, don't, please, please, Mother, Mother' "; when her love affair—an affair like a piece of dirty newspaper—reaches its abject public end; when, a few days after death, "the image of Henny started to roam . . . the window curtains flapped, the boards creaked, a mouse ran, and Henny was there, muttering softly to herself, tapping a sauce pan, turning on the gas. The children were not frightened. They would say, laughing, somewhat curious, 'I thought I heard Mothering,' and only Ernie or Tommy . . . would look a bit downcast; and perhaps Chappy missed her, that queer, gypsylike, thin, tanned, pointed face with big black eyes rolling above him"; and when, last of all, the storms of July thunder above her grave, and "it was as if Henny too had stormed, but in another room in the universe, which was now under lock and key."

I I I

THERE IS something grand and final, indifferent to our pity, about Henny: one of those immortal beings in whom the tragedy of existence is embodied, she looks unseeingly past her mortal readers. The absurdity and hypocrisy of existence are as immortal in her husband Sam.

All of us can remember waking from a dream and uselessly longing to go back into the dream. In Sam the longing has been useful: he has managed to substitute for everyday reality an everyday dream, a private work of art—complete with its own language, customs, projects, ideology—in which, occasionally pausing for applause, he goes on happily and foolishly and self-righteously existing. As he reads about Henny the reader feels, in awe, how terrible it must be to be Henny; as he reads about Sam he blurts, "Oh, please don't let me be like Sam!" Sam is more than human; occasionally he has doubts, and is merely human for a moment—so that our laughter and revulsion cease, and we uneasily pity him—but then the moment is over and he is himself again.

Often Henny, in defeated misery, plunges to rock bottom, and gropes among the black finalities of existence; up above, in the holy light, the busy Sam, "painting and scraping and singing and jigging from the crack of dawn," clambers happily about in the superstructure of life. There among his own children, his own speeches, his own small zoo, pond, rockery, aquaria, museum ("What a world of things he had to have to keep himself amused!"), the hobbyist, naturalist, bureaucrat, democrat, moralist, atheist, teetotaler, ideologue, sermonizer, sentimentalist, prude, hypocrite, idealist Sam can say, like Kulygin: "I am satisfied, I am satisfied, I am satisfied!" If he had not been married he would not have remembered that he was mortal. Sam "was naturally lighthearted, pleasant, all generous effusion and responsive emotion. . . . Tragedy itself could not worm its way by any means into his heart. Such a thing would have made him ill or mad, and he was all for health, sanity, success, and human love."

Sam's vanity is ultimate: the occasional objectivity or common decency that makes us take someone else's part, not our own, is impossible for Sam, who is right because he is Sam. It is becoming for Sam to love children so (Henny says in mockery, "The man who loves children!" and gives the book its title), since he himself is partly an adult and partly a spoiled child in his late thirties; even his playing with words, the grotesque self-satisfying language he makes for himself, is the work of a great child, and exactly right for children. After he has had to live among adults for eight months, he seems sobered and commonplace; but at home among the children, he soon is Sam again. At home "the children listened to every word he said, having been trained to him from the cradle." He addresses them "in that low, humming, cello voice and with that tender, loving face he had when beginning one of his paeans or dirges"; his speech has "a low insinuating humming that enchanted the sulky earguards and got straight to their softened brains." The children listen openmouthed; but Sam's mouth is open wider still, as he wonders at himself. "Were not his own children happy, healthy, and growing like weeds, merely through having him to look up to and through knowing that he was always righteous, faithful, and understanding?" It is wonderful to him that he originates independently the discoveries of the great: "The theory of the expanding universe . . . it came to me by myself. . . . And very often I have an idea and then find months, years later, that a man like our very great Woodrow Wilson or Lloyd George or Einstein has had it too."

Kim was the Little Friend of all the World; Sam is its Little Father. He wishes that he "had a black baby too. A tan or Chinese one—every kind of baby. I am sorry that the kind of father I can be is limited." A relative objects, to his not sending the children to Sunday school, "When they grow up they will have nothing to believe in." Sam replies: "Now they believe in their poor little Dad: and when they grow up they'll believe in Faraday, Clerk Maxwell, and Einstein." Their poor little Dad is for the Pollit children a jealous God, one who interferes with everything they do and still is not satisfied, but imports children from outside the family so that he can interfere with *them*. He makes each of the children tell him what the others are doing "in the secrecy of their rooms or the nooks they had made their own. With what surprise and joy he would seize on all this information of his loving spies, showing them traits of character, drawing a moral conclusion from everything!" Sam loves and enjoys the children, the children admire and enjoy Sam; and yet there is nothing too awful for him to do to them and feel that he is right to do to them—the worst things are so mean and petty, are full of such selfishness and hypocrisy, are so *impossible*, that even as you believe you cry, "It's unbelievable!"

We can bear to read about Sam, a finally exasperating man, only because he is absolutely funny and absolutely true. He is so entirely real that it surprises the reader when an occasional speech of his—for instance, some of his *Brave New World* talk about the future—is not convincing. Perhaps different parts of his speech have different proportions of imagination and fancy and memory: it doesn't seem that the same process (in Christina Stead, that is) has produced everything. But Sam is an Anglo-Saxon buffoon, hypocrite, quite as extraordinary as the most famous of Dostoevsky's or Saltykov-Shchedrin's Slavic ones. Sam asks for everything and with the same breath asks to be admired for never having asked for anything; his complete selfishness sees itself as a complete selflessness. When he has been out of work for many months, it doesn't bother him: "About their money, as about everything, he was vague and sentimental. But in a few months he would be earning, and in the meantime, he said, 'It was only right that the mother

too should fend for her offspring.' " One morning
there are no bananas. "Sam flushed with anger. 'Why
aren't there any bananas? I don't ask for much. I
work to make the Home Beautiful for one and all, and
I don't even get bananas. Everyone knows I like
bananas. If your mother won't get them, why don't
some of you? Why doesn't anyone think of poor
little Dad?' He continued, looking in a most pathetic
way round the table, at the abashed children, 'It isn't
much. I give you kids a house and a wonderful playground of nature and fish and marlin and everything,
and I can't even get a little banana.' " Sam moralizes,
rationalizes, anything whatsoever: the children feel
that they have to obey, *ought* to obey, his least
whim. There is an abject reality about the woman
Henny, an abject ideality about the man Sam; he is
so idealistically, hypocritically, transcendentally masculine that a male reader worries, "Ought I to be a
man?"

Every family has words and phrases of its own;
that ultimate family, the Pollits, has what amounts to
a whole language of its own. Only Sam can speak it,
really, but the children understand it and mix phrases
from it into their ordinary speech. (If anyone feels
that it is unlikely for a big grown man to have a little
language of his own, let me remind him of that great
grown man Swift.) Children's natural distortions of
words and the distortions of Artemus Ward and Uncle
Remus are the main sources of this little language of
Sam's. As we listen to Sam talking in it, we exclaim in
astonished veneration, "It's so!" Many of the words

and phrases of this language are so natural that we admire Christina Stead for having invented them at the same instant at which we are thinking, "No, nobody, not even Christina Stead, could have made *that* up!"—they have the uncreated reality of any perfect creation. I quote none of the language: a few sentences could show neither how marvelous it is nor how marvelously it expresses Sam's nature, satisfies his every instinct. When he puts his interminable objections and suggestions and commands into the joke terms of this unctuous, wheedling, insinuating language—what a tease the wretch is!—it is as if to make the least disagreement on the part of the children a moral impossibility.

His friend Saul says to Sam: "Sam, when you talk, you know you create a world." It is true; and the world he creates is a world of wishes or wish-fantasies. What Freud calls the primary principle, the pleasure principle, is always at work in that world—the claims of the reality principle, of the later ego, have been abrogated. It is a world of free fantasy: "Sam began to wonder at himself: why did he feel free? He had always been free, a free man, a free mind, a freethinker."

Bismarck said: "You can do anything with children if you will only play with them." All Bismarck's experience of mankind has been concentrated into knowledge, and the knowledge has been concentrated into a single dispassionate sentence. Sam has, so to speak, based his life on this sentence; but he has taken literally the *children* and *play* that are figurative in

Bismarck's saying. Children are damp clay which Sam can freely and playfully manipulate. Yet even there he prefers "the very small boys" and "the baby girls"; the larger boys, the girls of school age, somehow cramp his style. (His embryonic love affair is an affair not with a grownup but with the child-woman Gillian.) He reasons and moralizes mainly to force others to accept his fantasy, but the reasoning and moralizing have become fantastic in the process.

In psychoanalytical textbooks we read of the mechanism of denial. Surely Sam was its discoverer: there is no reality—except Henny—stubborn enough to force Sam to recognize its existence if its existence would disturb his complacency. We feel for Sam the wondering pity we feel for a man who has put out his own eyes and gets on better without them. To Sam everything else in the world is a means to an end, and the end is Sam. He is insensate. So, naturally, he comes out ahead of misunderstanding, poverty, Henny, anything. Life itself, in Johnson's phrase, *dismisses him to happiness:* " 'All things work together for the good of him that loves the Truth,' said the train to Sam as it rattled down towards the Severn, 'all things—work—together—for the good—of him —that loves—the TRUTH!' "

Sam is one of those providential larger-than-life-size creations, like Falstaff, whom we wonder and laugh at and can't get enough of; like Queen Elizabeth wanting to see Falstaff in love, we want to see Sam in books called *Sam at School, Sam in the Arctic, Grandfather Sam.* About him there is the grandeur of completeness: beyond Sam we cannot go. Christina Stead's understanding of him is without hatred; her descriptions of his vilest actions never forget how much fun it is to be Sam, and she can describe Sam's evening walk with his child in sentences that are purely and absolutely beautiful: "Pale as a candle flame in the dusk, tallow-pale, he stalked along, holding her hand, and Louie looked up and beyond him at the enfeebled stars. Thus, for many years, she had seen her father's head, a ghostly earth flame against the heavens, from her little height. Sam looked down on the moon of her face; the day-shine was enough still to light the eyeballs swimming up to him."

I V

A DESCRIPTION of Louie ought to begin with *Louie knew she was the ugly duckling*. It is ugly ducklings, grown either into swans or into remarkably big, remarkably ugly ducks, who are responsible for most works of art; and yet how few of these give a truthful account of what it was like to be an ugly duckling!— it is almost as if the grown, successful swan had repressed most of the memories of the duckling's miserable, embarrassing, magical beginnings. (These memories are deeply humiliating in two ways: they remind the adult that he once was more ignorant and gullible and emotional than he is; and they remind him that he once *was*, potentially, far more than he is.) Stumbling through creation in awful misery, in oblivious ecstasy, the fat, clumsy, twelve- or thirteen-year-old Louie is, as her teacher tells her, one of those who "will certainly be famous." We believe this because the book is full of the evidence for it: the poems and plays Louie writes, the stories she tells, the lines she quotes, the things she says. The usual criticism of a novel about an artist is that, no matter how real he is as a man, he is not real to us as an artist, since we have to take on trust the works of art he produces. We do not have to take on trust Louie's work, and she is real to us as an artist.

Someone in a story says that when you can't think of anything else to say you say, "Ah, youth, youth!" But sometimes as you read about Louie there *is* nothing else to say: your heart goes out in homesick joy to the marvelous inconsequential improbable reaching-out-to-everything of the duckling's mind, so different from the old swan's mind, that has learned what its interests are and is deaf and blind to the rest of reality. Louie says, "I wish I had a Welsh grammar." Sam says, "Don't be an idiot! What for?" Louie answers: "I'd like to learn Welsh or Egyptian grammar; I could read the poetry Borrow talks about and I could read *The Book of the Dead.*"

She starts to learn *Paradise Lost* by heart ("Why? She did not know really"); stuffs the little children full of La Rochefoucauld; in joyful amazement discovers that *The Cenci* is about her father and herself; recites,

A yellow plum was given me and in return a topaz fair
 I gave,

No mere return for courtesy but that our friendship
  might outlast the grave,

indignantly insisting to the grownups that it *is* Con-
fucius; puts as a motto on her wall, *By my hope and
faith, I conjure thee, throw not away the hero in
your soul*; triumphantly repeats to that little tyrant
of her fields, Sam-the-Bold :

> The desolator desolate,
> The tyrant overthrown;
> The arbiter of other's fate,
> A suppliant for his own!

Louie starts out on her own *Faust*, a "play, called
Fortunatus, in which a student, sitting alone in his
room in the beaming moon, lifts his weary head from
the book and begins by saying,

> The unforgotten song, the solitary song,
> The song of the young heart in the age-old world,
> Humming on new May's reeds transports me back
> To the vague regions of celestial space. . . ."

For the teacher whom she loves Louie creates "a magnificent project, the Aiden cycle . . . a poem of
every conceivable form and also every conceivable
meter in the English language," all about Miss Aiden.
She copies the poems into an out-of-date diary, which
she hides; sometimes she reads them to the children in
the orchard "for hours on end, while they sat with
rosy, greedy faces upturned, listening." As Henny
and Sam shriek at each other downstairs, Louie tells
the children, lying loosely in bed in the warm night,

the story of *Hawkins, the North Wind*. Most of Louie's writings are so lyrically funny to us that as we laugh we catch our breath, afraid that the bubble will break. At *Hawkins*, a gruesomely satisfying story different from any story we have read before, we no longer laugh, nor can we look down at the storyteller with a grownup's tender, complacent love for a child: the story is dark with Louie's genius and with Christina Stead's.

Best of all is *Tragos: Herpes Rom (Tragedy: The Snake-Man)*. Louie writes it, and the children act it out, for Sam's birthday. It is written in a new language Louie has made up for it; the language maker Sam says angrily, "Why isn't it in English?" and Louie replies, "Did Euripides write in English?" Not only is the play exactly what Louie would have written, it is also a work of art in which the relations between Louie and her father, as she understands them, are expressed with concentrated, tragic force. Nowhere else in fiction, so far as I know, is there so truthful and satisfying a representation of the works of art the ugly duckling makes up, there in the morning of the world.

Louie reads most of the time—reads, even, while taking a shower: "her wet fingers pulped the paper as she turned." Her life is accompanied, *ostinato*, by *always has her nose stuck in a book . . . learn to hold your shoulders straight . . . it will ruin your eyes*. Louie "slopped liquids all over the place, stumbled and fell when carrying buckets, could never stand straight to fold the sheets and tablecloths from the

22

wash without giggling or dropping them in the dirt, fell over invisible creases in rugs, was unable to do her hair neatly, and was always leopard-spotted yellow and blue with old and new bruises. . . . She acknowledged her unwieldiness and unhandiness in this little world, but she had an utter contempt for everyone associated with her, father, stepmother, even brothers and sister, an innocent contempt which she never thought out, but which those round her easily recognized." The Louie who laconically holds her scorched fingers in the candle flame feels "a growling, sullen power in herself. . . . She went up to bed insulted again. 'I will repay,' she said on the stairs, halting and looking over the banisters, with a frown." When the world is more than she can bear she screams her secret at it: " 'I'm the ugly duckling, you'll see,' shrieked Louie."

Most of the time she knows that she is better and more intelligent than, different from, the other inhabitants of her world; but the rest of the time she feels the complete despair—the seeming to oneself wrong, *all* wrong, about everything, *everything*—that is the other, dark side of this differentness. She is a force of nature, but she is also a little girl. Heartbroken when her birthday play is a shameful failure, like so much of her life at home, Louie "began to squirm and, unconsciously holding out one of her hands to Sam, she cried, 'I am so miserable and poor and rotten and so vile [the words *rotten* and *vile* are natural, touching reminiscences of Henny's tirade style] and melodramatic, I don't know what to do. I don't know what to do. I can't bear the daily misery. . . .' She was bawling brokenly on the tablecloth, her shoulders heaving and her long hair, broken loose, plastered over her red face. 'No wonder they all laugh at me,' she bellowed. 'When I walk along the street, everyone looks at me, and whispers about me, because I'm so messy. My elbows are out and I have no shoes and I'm so big and fat and it'll always be the same. I can't help it, I can't help it. . . . They all laugh at me: I can't stand it any more. . . .' Coming to the table, as to a jury, she asked in a firmer voice, but still crying, 'What will become of me? Will life go on like this? Will I always be like this?' She appealed to Sam, 'I have always been like this: I can't live and go on being like this?' "

And Sam replies: "Like what? Like what? I never heard so much idiotic drivel in my born days. Go and put your fat head under the shower."

To Louie the world is what won't let her alone. And the world's interferingness is nothing to Sam's: Sam— so to speak—wakes her up and asks her what she's dreaming just so as to be able to make her dream something different, and then tells her that not every little girl is lucky enough to have a Sam to wake her up. To be let alone! is there any happiness that compares with it, for someone like Louie? Staying with her mother's relatives in the summer, she feels herself inexplicably, miraculously given a little space of her own—is made, for a few weeks, a sort of grownup by courtesy. And since Louie has "a genius for solitude," she manages to find it even at home. Henny may scold her and beat her, but Henny does leave her alone ("It is a rotten

24

shame, when I think that the poor kid is dragged into all our rotten messes"), and Louie loves her for it—when Sam talks to Louie about her real mother, Louie retorts, "Mother is my mother," meaning Henny.

At school Louie "was in heaven, at home she was in a torture chamber." She never tells anyone outside "what it is like at home . . . no one would believe me!" To the ordinary misery of differentness is added the misery of being the only one who sees the endless awful war between Henny and Sam for what it is: "Suddenly she would think, *Who can see aught good in thee / Soul-destroying misery?* and in this flash of intelligence she understood that her life and their lives were wasted in this contest and that the quarrel between Henny and Sam was ruining their moral natures." It is only Louie who tries to do anything about it all: with a young thing's fresh sense and ignorance and courage she tries to save the children and herself in the only way that she knows—what she does and what she can't quite make herself do help to bring the book to its wonderful climax. It is rare for a novel to have an ending as good as its middle and beginning: the sixty or seventy pages that sum up *The Man Who Loved Children*, bring the action of the book to its real conclusion, are better than even the best things that have come before.

As he looks at Louie, Sam "can't understand what on earth caused this strange drifting nebula to spin." By the time we finish the book we have been so thoroughly in sympathy and in empathy with Louie that we no longer need to understand—we are used to being Louie. We think about her, as her teacher thinks: "It's queer to know everything and nothing at the same time." Louie knows, as she writes in her diary, that "everyday experience which is misery degrades me"; she mutters aloud, "If I did not know I was a genius, I would die: why live?"; a stranger in her entirely strange and entirely familiar family, she cries to her father: "I know something, I know there are people not like us, not muddleheaded like us, better than us." She knows that soon she will have escaped into the world of the people better than us, the great objective world better than Shakespeare and Beethoven and Donatello put together—didn't they all come out of it? Louie is a potentiality still sure that what awaits it in the world is potentiality, not actuality. That she is escaping from some Pollits to some more Pollits, that she herself will end as an actuality among actualities, an accomplished fact, is an old or middle-aged truth or half-truth that Louie doesn't know. As Louie's story ends she has gone for a walk, "a walk around the world"; she starts into the future accompanied by one of those Strauss themes in which a whole young orchestra walks springily off into the sunshine, as though going away were a final good.

v

As you read *The Man Who Loved Children* what do you notice first? How much life it has, how natural and original it is; Christina Stead's way of seeing and representing the world is so plainly different from anyone else's that after a while you take this for granted, and think cheerfully, "Oh, she can't help being original." The whole book is different from any book you have read before. What other book represents—tries to represent, even—a family in such conclusive detail?

Aristotle speaks of the pleasure of recognition; you read *The Man Who Loved Children* with an almost ecstatic pleasure of recognition. You get used to saying, "Yes, that's the way it is"; and you say many times, but can never get used to saying, "I didn't know *anybody* knew that." Henny, Sam, Louie, and the children—not to speak of some of the people outside the family—are entirely real to the reader. This may not seem much of a claim: every year thousands of reviewers say it about hundreds of novels. But what they say is conventional exaggeration—reality is rare in novels.

Many of the things of the world come to life in *The Man Who Loved Children:* the book has an astonishing sensory immediacy. Akin to this is its particularity and immediacy of incident; it is full of small, live, characteristic, sometimes odd or grotesque details that are at once surprising enough and convincing enough to make the reader feel, "No, nobody could have made that up." And akin to these on a larger scale are all the "good scenes" in the book: scenes that stand out in the reader's memory as in some way remarkable—as representing something, summing something up, with real finality. There is an extraordinary concentration of such scenes in the pages leading up to the attempted murder and accomplished suicide that is the climax of the book: Ernie's lead, Louie's play, Louie's breakdown after it, Ernie's money box, Ernie's and Louie's discoveries before Miss Aiden comes, Miss Aiden's visit, Henny's beating of Ernie, the end of Henny's love affair, Henny's last game of solitaire, the marlin, Sam and the bananas, the last quarrel. That these scenes come where they do is evidence of Christina Stead's gift for structure; but you are bewildered by her regular ability to make the scenes that matter most the book's best-imagined and best-realized scenes.

Without its fairly wide range of people and places, attitudes and emotions, *The Man Who Loved Children* might seem too concentrated and homogeneous a selection of reality. But the people outside the Pollit household are quite varied: for instance, Louie's mother's family, Sam's and Henny's relatives, some of the people at Singapore, Henny's Bert Anderson, the "norphan" girl, Louie's friend Clare. There are not so many places—Washington, Ann Arbor, Harper's Ferry, Singapore—but each seems entirely different and entirely alive. As he reads about Louie's summers the reader feels, "So this is what Harper's Ferry looks like to an Australian!" European readers are used to being told what Europe looks like to an American or Russian of genius; we aren't, and we enjoy it. (Occasionally Christina Stead has a kind of virtuoso passage to show that she is not merely a foreign visitor, but a real inhabitant of the United States; we enjoy, and are amused at, it.) Because *The Man Who Loved*

Children brings to life the variety of the world outside the Pollit household, the happenings inside it—terrible as some of them are—do not seem depressing or constricted or monotonous to the reader: "within, a torment raged, day and night, week, month, year, always the same, an endless conflict, with its truces and breathing spaces; out here were a dark peace and love." And, too, many of the happenings inside the family have so much warmth and habitual satisfaction, are so pleasant or cozy or funny, are so *interesting*, that the reader forgets for a moment that this wonderful playground is also a battlefield.

Children-in-families have a life all their own, a complicated one. Christina Stead seems to have remembered it in detail from her childhood, and to have observed it in detail as an adult. Because of this knowledge she is able to imagine with complete realism the structures, textures, and atmosphere of one family's spoken and unspoken life. She is unusually sensitive to speech styles, to conversation structures, to everything that makes a dialogue or monologue a sort of self-propagating entity; she knows just how family speech is different from speech outside the family, children's speech different from adults'. She gives her children the speeches of speakers to whom a word has the reality of a thing: a thing that can be held wrong side up, played with like a toy, thrown at someone like a toy. Children's speechways—their senseless iteration, joyous nonsense, incremental variation, entreaties and insults, family games, rhymes, rituals, proverbs with the force of law, magical mistakes, occa-

sional uncannily penetrating descriptive phrases—are
things Christina Stead knows as well as she knows the
speechways of families, of people so used to each other
that half the time they only half say something,
imply it with a family phrase, or else spell it out in
words too familiar to be heard, just as the speaker's
face is too familiar to be seen. The book's household
conversations between mother and child, father and
child, are both superficially and profoundly different
from any conversation in the world outside; reading
such conversations is as satisfying as being given some
food you haven't tasted since childhood. (After making your way through the great rain forest of the
children's speech, you come finally to one poor
broomstick of a tree, their letters: all the children—as
Ernie says, laughing—"start out with 'Dear Dad, I
hope you are well, I am well, Mother is well,' and
then they get stuck.") The children inherit and em-
ploy, or recognize with passive pleasure, the cultural
scraps—everything from Mozart to *Hiawatha*—that
are a part of the sounds the grownups make. Father
and Mother are gods but (it is strange!) gods who will
sometimes perform for you on request, taking part in
a ritual, repeating stories or recitations, pretending to
talk like a Scot or a Jew or an Englishman—just as,
earlier, they would pretend to be a bear.

Christina Stead knows the awful eventfulness of
little children's lives. That grownups seldom cry,
scream, fall, fight each other, or have to be sent to bed
seems very strange to someone watching children: a
little child pays its debt to life penny by penny.

Sam is able to love a life spent with children because he himself has the insensate busyness of a child. Yet, wholly familiar as he is, partly childlike as he is, to the children he is monstrous—not the singular monster that he is to us, but the ordinary monster that any grownup is to you if you weigh thirty or forty pounds and have your eyes two feet from the floor. Again and again the reader is conscious of Christina Stead's gift for showing how different *anything* is when looked at from a really different point of view. Little Evie, "fidgeting with her aunt's great arm around her, seemed to be looking up trustfully with her brown eyes, but those deceptive eyes were full of revolt, mistrust, and dislike"; she averts her gaze from her aunt's "slab cheeks, peccary skin . . . the long, plump, inhuman thigh, the glossy, sufficient skirt, from everything powerful, coarse, and proud about this great unmated mare. . . . 'Oh,' thought Evie to herself, 'when I am a lady with a baby, I won't have all those bumps, I won't be so big and fat, I will be a little woman, thin like I am now and not fat in front or in the skirt.' "

One of the most obvious facts about grownups, to a child, is that they have forgotten what it is like to be a child. The child has not yet had the chance to know what it is like to be a grownup; he believes, even, that being a grownup is a mistake he will never make— when *he* grows up he will keep on being a child, a big child with power. So the child and grownup live in mutual love, misunderstanding, and distaste. Children shout and play and cry and want candy; grownups

say *Ssh!* and work and scold and want steak. There is
no disputing tastes as contradictory as these. It is not
just Mowgli who was raised by a couple of wolves;
any child is raised by a couple of grownups. Father
and Mother may be nearer and dearer than anyone
will ever be again—still, they are members of a
different species. God is, I suppose, what our parents
were; certainly the giant or ogre of the stories is so
huge, so powerful, and so stupid because that is the
way a grownup looks to a child.

Grownups forget or cannot believe that they seem
even more unreasonable to children than children seem
to them. Henny's oldest boy Ernie (to whom money
is the primary means of understanding and changing
the world; he is a born economic determinist, someone
with absolute pitch where money is concerned) is one
of Christina Stead's main ways of making us remember how mistaken and hypocritical grownups seem to
children. Ernie feels that he sees the world as it is, but
that grownups are no longer able to do this: their
rationalization of their own actions, the infinitely
complicated lie they have agreed to tell about the
world, conceals the world from them. The child sees
the truth, but is helpless to do anything about it.

The Pollit children are used to the terrible helplessness of a child watching its parents war. There over
their heads the Sun and the Moon, God the Father and
the Holy Virgin, are shouting at each other, striking
each other—the children contract all their muscles,
try not to hear, and hear. Sometimes, waked in darkness by the familiar sounds, they lie sleepily listen-

ing to their parents; hear, during some lull in the quarrel, a tree frog or the sound of the rain.

Ernie feels the same helpless despair at the poverty of the family; thinking of how *many* children there already are, he implores, "Mothering, don't have another baby!" (Henny replies, "You can bet your bottom dollar on that, old sweetness.") But he does not really understand what he is saying: later on, he and the other children look uncomprehendingly at Henny, "who had again queerly become a large woman, though her hands, feet, and face remained small and narrow." One night they are made to sleep downstairs, and hear Henny screaming hour after hour upstairs; finally, at morning, she is silent. "They had understood nothing at all, except that mother had been angry and miserable and now she was still; this was a blessed relief." Their blank misunderstanding of what is sexual is the opposite of their eager understanding of what is excremental. They thrill to the inexplicably varying permissiveness of the world: here they are being allowed to laugh at, as a joke, what is ordinarily not referred to at all, or mentioned expediently, in family euphemisms!

The book is alive with their fights, games, cries of "You didn't kiss me!"—"Look, Moth, Tommy kissed you in the glass!" But their great holidays so swiftly are gone: the "sun was going down, and Sunday-Funday was coming to an end. They all felt it with a kind of misery: with such a fine long day and so many things to do, how could they have let it slip past like this?" And summer vacation is the same: the indefinite, almost infinite future so soon is that small, definite, disregarded thing, the past!

On a winter night, with nothing but the fire in the living room to warm the house, the child runs to it crying, "Oo, gee whiz, is it cold; jiminy, I'm freezing. Moth, when are we going to get the coal?" (Anyone who remembers his childhood can feel himself saying those sentences—those and so many more of the book's sentences.) And as the child grows older, how embarrassing the parent is, in the world outside: "Louie looked stonily ahead or desperately aside." And, home again, the parent moralizes, sermonizes—won't he *ever* stop talking?—to the child doing its homework, writing, writing, until finally the parent reads over the child's shoulder what is being written on the page of notebook paper: *Shut up, shut up, shut up, shut up.* . . . The book follows the children into the cold beds they warm, goes with them into their dreams: when you read about Louie's hard-soft nightmare or the horseman she hears when she wakes in the middle of the night, you are touching childhood itself.

V I

THERE IS a bewitching rapidity and lack of self-consciousness about Christina Stead's writing; she has much knowledge, extraordinary abilities, but is too engrossed in what she is doing ever to seem conscious of them, so that they do not cut her off from the world but join her to it. How literary she makes most writers seem! Her book is very human, and full of humor of an unusual kind; the spirit behind it doesn't try to be attractive and is attractive. As you read the book's climactic and conclusive pages you are conscious of their genius and of the rightness of that genius: it is as though at these moments Christina Stead's mind held in its grasp the whole action, the essential form, of *The Man Who Loved Children*.

Say that you read: "As Henny sat before her teacup and the steam rose from it and the treacherous foam gathered, uncollectible round its edge, the thousand storms of her confined life would rise up before her, thinner illusions on the steam. She did not laugh at the words 'a storm in a teacup.' " You feel an astonished satisfaction at the swift and fatal conclusiveness, the real poetry—the concentration of experience into a strange and accurate, resonant image—of such a passage. Doesn't one feel the same satisfaction with, wonder at, some of the passages I have already quoted? But quotation gives no idea of what is most important in Christina Stead's style, its simple narrative power—she tells what happens so that it happens, and to you. The direct immediate life of most of her sentences is in extraordinary contrast to the complicated uneasy life of others; as her content varies, her style varies. Ordinary styles have the rhythmical and structural monotony of a habit, of something learned and persisted in. A style like Christina Stead's, so remarkable for its structural variety, its rhythmical spontaneity, forces you to remember that a style can be a whole way of existing, so that you exist, for the moment, in perfect sympathy with it: you don't read it so much as listen to it as it sweeps you along—fast enough, often, to make you feel a blurred pleasure in your own speed. Often a phrase or sentence has the uncaring unconscious authority—how else could you say it?—that only a real style has. But few such styles have the spontaneity of Christina Stead's; its own life carries it along, here rapid and a little rough, here good-humoredly, grotesquely incisive, here purely beautiful—and suddenly, without ever stopping being natural, it is grand.

Her style is live enough and spontaneous enough to be able to go on working without her; but, then, its life is mechanical. When her style is at its worst you have the illusion that, once set in motion, it can rattle along indefinitely, narrating the incidents of a picaresque, Pollit-y universe with an indiscriminate vivacity that matches theirs. (You remember, then, that where everybody's somebody, nobody's anybody—that Christina Stead is, on her father's side, a Pollit.) But, normally, you listen to "the breeze, still brittle, not fully leaved"; see a mountain graveyard, "all grass and long sights"; have a child raise to you its "pansy kitten-face"; see a ragged girl fling out her arms in "a gesture that somehow recalled the surf beating on a coast, the surf of time or of sorrows"; see that in the world outside "clouds were passing over, swiftly staining the garden, the stains soaking in and leaving only bright light again." You read: "Bonnie stayed upstairs sobbing, thinking she had a broken heart, until she heard soft things like the hands of ghosts rubbing her counterpane and soft ghostly feet unsteadily shifting on her rug; and, looking up, she saw Evie and Isabel staring at her with immense rabbit eyes. In a little crockery voice, Isabel asked, 'What are you crying for?' " Louie's dying uncle tells her the story of *Pilgrim's Progress;* "and occasionally he would pause, the eyes would be fixed on her, and suddenly he would smile with his long dark lips; the face would no longer be the face of a man dying of consumption, with its burning eyes, but the ravishment of love incarnate, speaking through voiceless but not secret signs to the child's nature." Sometimes one of her long descriptive sentences lets you see a world at once strange and familiar, Christina Stead's and your own : the romantic Louie looks out at the shabby old Georgetown of the 1930's and sees "the trees of the heath round the Naval Observatory, the lamplight falling over the wired, lichened fence of the old reservoirs, the mysterious, long, dim house that she yearned for, the strange house opposite, and below, the vapor-blue city of Washington, pale, dim-lamped, under multitudinous stars, like a winter city of Africa, she thought, on this night at this hour." As you look at the landscapes—houses and yards and trees and birds and weathers—of *The Man Who Loved Children,* you see that they are alive, and yet you can't tell what has made them come to life—not the words exactly, not even the rhythm of the words, but something behind both : whatever it is that can make the landscapes live and beautiful, but that can make Ernie sobbing over his empty money box, and Henny beginning to cry, "Ugh-ugh," with her face in her hands, more beautiful than any landscape.

V I I

CHRISTINA STEAD can perfectly imitate the surface of existence—and, what is harder, recognize and reproduce some of the structures underneath that surface, and use these to organize her book. You especially notice, in her representation of life, two structural processes: (1) A series of similar events, of increasing intensity and importance, that leads to a last event which sums up, incarnates, all the events that have come before. It is easy to recognize and hard to make up such an event; Christina Stead has an uncanny ability to imagine an event that will be the necessary but surprising sum of the events before it. (2) A series of quantitative changes that leads to a qualitative change: that is, a series of events leading to a last qualitatively different event that at once sums up and contradicts the earlier events, and is the beginning of a new series. And Christina Stead depends almost as much on the conflict of opposites—for instance, of Sam with Henny, the male principle with the female principle, the children with the grownups, the ugly duckling with the ducks. She often employs a different principle of structure, the principle that a different point of view makes everything that is seen from that point of view different. Her book continually shows the difference between children's and adults' points of view, between men's and women's, between Henny's relatives' and Sam's relatives', between Sam's and anybody else's, between Louie's and anybody else's, between Henny's and anybody else's—when Henny comes home from shopping and tells what happened on the trip, the people and events of the story seem to the children part of a world entirely different from their own, even if they have been along with Henny on the trip. A somewhat similar principle of organization is the opposition between practice and theory, between concrete fact and abstract rationalization, between what people say things are and what they are. And Christina Stead, like Chekhov, is fond of having a character tell you what life is, just before events themselves show you what it is.

The commonest and most nearly fundamental principle of organization, in serial arts like music and literature, is simply that of repetition; it organizes their notes or words very much as habit organizes our lives. Christina Stead particularly depends on repetition, and particularly understands the place of habit in our lives. If she admits that the proverb is true— *Heaven gives us habits to take the place of happiness* —she also admits that the habits *are* happiness of a sort, and that most happiness, after all, is happiness of a sort; she could say with Yeats that in Eden's Garden "no pleasing habit ends."

Her book, naturally, is full of the causal structures in terms of which we explain most of life to ourselves. Very different from the book's use of these is its use of rhythm as structure, atmosphere as structure: for instance, the series of last things that leads up to Henny's suicide has a dark finality of rhythm and atmosphere that prepares for her death as the air before a thunderstorm prepares for the thunderstorm. Kenneth Burke calls form the satisfaction of an expectation; *The Man Who Loved Children* is full of such satisfactions, but it has a good deal of the deliberate disappointment of an expectation that is also form.

A person is a process, one that leads to death: in *The Man Who Loved Children* the most carefully worked-out, conclusive process is Henny. Even readers who remember themselves as ugly ducklings (and take a sort of credulous, incredulous delight in Louie) will still feel their main humanness identify itself with Henny: the book's center of gravity, of tragic weight, is Henny. She is a violent, defeated process leading to a violent end, a closed tragic process leading to a conclusion of all potentiality, just as Louie is an open process leading to a "conclusion" that is pure potentiality. As the book ends, Henny has left, Louie is leaving, Sam stays. Sam is a repetitive, comic process that merely marks time: he gets nowhere, but then he doesn't want to get anywhere. Although there is no possibility of any real change in Sam, he never stops changing: Sam stays there inside Sam, getting less and less like the rest of mankind and more and more like Sam, Sam squared, Sam cubed, Sam to the nth. A man who repeats himself is funny; a man who repeats himself, *himself*, HIMSELF, is funnier. The book dignifies Henny in death, dismisses Sam with: *And he lived happily ever after*. The Pollits' wild war of opposites, with Henny dead, becomes a tame peace. Even Louie, the resistance, leaves, and Sam-the-Bold, the Great I-Am, the Man Who Loved Children, is left to do as he pleases with the children. *For a while:* Sam has laid up for himself treasures that moth and rust can't corrupt, but that the mere passage of the years destroys. Children don't keep. In the end Sam will have to love those hard things to love, grownups; and, since this is impossible for Sam, Sam won't despair, won't change, but will simply get himself some more children. He has made the beings of this world, who are the ends of this world, means; when he loses some particular means what does it matter?—there are plenty of other means to that one end, Sam.

The process the book calls Louie is that of a child turning into a grownup, a duckling turning into a swan, a being that exists in two worlds leaving the first world of the family for the world outside. The ugly duckling loves the other pretty ducklings and tries to save them from the awful war between the father duck and the mother duck—though the war is ended by Henny's act, not Louie's. Yet Louie knows that they are not really her brothers and sisters, not really her parents, and serenely leaves them for the swan world in which, a swan, she will at least be reunited to her real family, who are swans. Or do swans have families? Need families? Who knows? Louie doesn't know and, *for a while*, doesn't need to care.

The last fourth of the book makes Ernie, the child closest to Henny, a queer shadow or echo of Henny.

The episodes of Ernie's lead, Ernie's money box, and Ernie's beating bring him to a defeated despair like Henny's, to a suicide-in-effigy: he makes a doll-dummy to stand for himself and hangs it. But all this is only a child's "as if" performance—after Henny's death the penniless Ernie is given some money, finds some more money, forgets Henny, and starts out all over again on the financial process which his life will be.

The attempted murder and accomplished suicide that are the conclusion of Henny and the climax of *The Man Who Loved Children* are prepared for by several hundred events, conversations, speeches, phrases, and thoughts scattered throughout the book. Henny's suicide- or murder-rhetoric; the atmosphere of violence that hangs around her, especially where Sam and Louie are concerned; the conversation in which she discusses with her mother and sister the best ways to kill oneself, the quickest poisons: these and a great many similar things have established, even before the sixty or seventy pages leading directly to Henny's death, a situation that makes plausible—requires, really—her violent end. And yet we are surprised to have it happen, this happening as thoroughly prepared for as anything I can remember in fiction.

It is no "tragic flaw" in Henny's character, but her character itself, that brings her to her end: Henny is her own fate. Christina Stead has a Chinese say, "Our old age is perhaps life's decision about us"—or, worse, the decision we have made about ourselves without ever realizing we were making it. Henny's old age may be life's decision about Henny; her suicide is the decision she has made about herself—about life—without ever knowing she was making it. She is so used to thinking and saying: *I'll kill myself! Better kill myself!* that when Louie gives her the chance she is fatally ready to take it. The defeated, despairing Henny has given up her life many times, before that drinking of the breakfast cup of tea with which she gives it up for good. What life has made of Henny, what Henny most deeply is, drinks—she is never more herself than when she destroys herself.

Many things in her life are latent or ultimate causes of Henny's death; but its immediate, overt causes—the series of extraordinarily imagined and accomplished finalities that leads to this final finality, that demands as its only possible conclusion Henny's death—all occur in the sixty or seventy pages before that death. At the beginning of the series, there is finality in the episode in which Henny feels her heart break "for good and all"; in the episode in which the aging Henny becomes, suddenly, "a dried-up, skinny, funny old woman." Miss Aiden's visit makes the reader see that this family sinking into poverty has become, without his realizing it, *poor*, abjectly, irretrievably poor. Everything valuable is gone, Henny's dearest possessions have been sold or pawned: the treasure drawers are empty.

Next day Ernie finds his money box empty, blankly sobs, and Henny, who has stolen the money, cries "Ugh-ugh" and tries to comfort him. She has stolen, from the child she loves most, the one thing

RANDALL JARRELL

that is indispensable to him. When Henny, later on, begins to beat Ernie over the head, and goes on hysterically beating him until she faints, it is as if she felt so guilty about him that it is unbearable to her to have him exist at all. The life in which what has happened can happen is more than Henny can endure—she tries to obliterate Ernie and life, and then faints, momentarily obliterating herself.

The awful end of her affair with Bert Anderson is a kind of final, public, objective degradation of Henny; she begs for a last trifle, nothing almost, and the world refuses her even that. The long nightmarish episode of the rendering of the marlin into oil is the final incarnation of all the senseless busynesses with which Sam has tormented her: "one marlin had been enough, with their kneading, manuring, trotting about, plastering, oiling, and dripping, to give Spa House a scent of its own for many years to come." But nothing else in *The Man Who Loved Children* has the empty finality of Henny's last game of solitaire. She has played it her whole life and never once won; now she wins. "The game that she had played all her life was finished; she had no more to do; she had no game." And, a little later, Henny breaks down as she has never broken down before: " 'Ai, ai,' cried Henny, beginning to cry like a little girl, and putting the dressing gown to her face, 'ai, ai!' " The world has been too much for Henny, the old woman has changed back into a child. As there has never before been anything childlike about Henny, the scene has a pitiable finality. The quarrel with Sam which follows

44

(a quarrel monotonous with Henny's repetitions of *kill everybody, kill myself*) is the last, the worst, and the most violent of their quarrels. The next morning Henny admits to Ernie that she will never be able to pay him back, and says with a perplexed, wondering conclusiveness: "I don't know what to do." Ernie is Henny's main connection to life, her only connection to hope and to the future: when life makes her steal his money, beat him until she faints, and then tell him that she can never pay him back, what is there left to her but the "All right, I will!" that is her last word to life?

V I I I

AFTER YOU have read *The Man Who Loved Children* several times you feel that you know its author's main strengths and main weakness. The weakness is, I think, a kind of natural excess and lack of discrimination: she is most likely to go wrong by not seeing when to stop or what to leave out. About most things—always, about the most important things—she is not excessive and does discriminate; but a few things in *The Man Who Loved Children* ought not to be there, and a few other things ought not to be there in such quantities.

When you look at these passages that—it seems to you—ought not to be there, it is as if you were seeing an intrusion of raw reality into the imagined reality of the book: some actual facts are being rapidly, scrappily, and vivaciously described. You don't feel that these had to go into the book, nor do you feel that they have been through the process of being created all over again that the rest of the material of the book has been through. They are, so to speak, God's creation, not Christina Stead's; and Christina Stead's fairly effective reporting of this first creation is a poor substitute for her own second creation. Such accidental realities seem to have slipped into the book unquestioned —or perhaps, when a part of the author questioned them, another part answered, "But that's the way it really was." (One of the most puzzling things about a novel is that "the way it really was" half the time is, and half the time isn't, the way it ought to be in the novel.) Another sort of unrequired and consequently excessive passage seems to be there because the author's invention, running on automatically, found it easy to imagine it that way; such a passage is the equivalent, in narrative, of a mannered, habitual, easily effective piece of rhetoric.

Isn't there a little too much of the Pollits' homecoming party, of Henny's tirades, of Sam's dream sermons? Aren't these slightly excessive representations of monstrously excessive realities? Aren't there a few too many facts about Annapolis and Harper's Ferry, about Henny's more remote relatives? When Christina Stead is at her worst—in *The Man Who Loved Children* she never is—you feel that there is just too much of Christina Stead. At its worst her writing has a kind of vivacious, mechanical overabundance: her observation and invention and rhetoric, set into autonomous operation, bring into existence a queer picaresque universe of indiscriminate, slightly disreputable incidents. Reading about them is like listening to two disillusioned old automata gossiping over a cup of tea in the kitchen.

Ruskin says that anyone who expects perfection from a work of art knows nothing of works of art. This is an appealing sentence that, so far as I can see, is not true about a few pictures and statues and pieces of music, short stories and short poems. Whether or not you expect perfection from them, you get it; at least, there is nothing in them that you would want changed. But what Ruskin says is true about novels: anyone who expects perfection from even the greatest novel knows nothing of novels. Some of the faults of *The Man Who Loved Children* are the faults a large enough, live enough thing naturally has; others (those I have been discussing) are the faults a book of Christina Stead's naturally has—they are, really, the other side of her virtues. An occasional awkwardness or disparity is the result of her having created from an Australian memory an American reality; but usually you are astonished at how well acclimated, re-created, these memories are. Two or three Joyce-ish sentences—one seems consciously and humorously Joyce-ish—make you remember that the rest of the sentences in the book are pure Stead. What Louie reads and quotes and loves is more what she would have read in 1917 than in 1937; but objecting to *that* is like objecting to Tolstoy's making the characters in *War and Peace* his own contemporaries, not Napoleon's—Christina Stead understands that it is only her own realities, anachronistic or not, that can give Louie the timeless reality that Louie has.

A reader of *The Man Who Loved Children* naturally will want to know something about Christina Stead. I know only what I have found in reference books or guessed from her novels. Let me repeat some of the first: it will have for the reader the interest of showing where Sam and Louie (and, no doubt, Henny) began.

Christina Stead was born in Australia, in 1902. Her mother died soon afterwards, her father remarried, and she "became the eldest of a large family." Her father was a rationalist, a Fabian socialist, and a naturalist in the Government Fisheries Department. As a girl she was particularly interested in "fish, natural history, Spencer, Darwin, Huxley . . . the sea. . . . I had plenty of work with the young children, but I was attached to them, and whenever I could, told them stories, partly from Grimm and Andersen, partly invented."

She went to Teachers' College, disliked teaching, took a business course at night, went to London in 1928 and worked there, went to Paris in 1929 and worked there for several years. She had been a public-school teacher, a teacher of abnormal children, a demonstrator in the psychology laboratory of Sydney University, and a clerk in a grain company; in Paris she was a clerk in a banking house. She lived in the United States during the late thirties and early forties, and now lives in England. Her husband is William Blake, the author of several novels and of the best and most entertaining textbook of Marxian economics that I know. In 1934 Christina Stead published *The Salzburg Tales;* in 1935, *Seven Poor Men of Sydney;* in 1936, *The Beauties and the Furies;* in 1938, *House of All Nations;* in 1940, *The Man Who Loved Children;* in 1944, *For Love Alone;* in 1946, *Letty Fox, Her Luck;* in 1948, *A Little Tea, a Little Chat;* in 1952, *The People with the Dogs.*

Her books have had varying receptions. *House of All Nations* was a critical success and a best seller; *The Man Who Loved Children* was a failure both with critics and with the public. It has been out of print for many years, and Christina Stead herself is remembered by only a few readers. When the world rejects, and then forgets, a writer's most profound and imaginative book, he may unconsciously work in a more limited way in the books that follow it; this has happened, I believe, to Christina Stead. The world's incomprehension has robbed it, for twenty-five years, of *The Man Who Loved Children;* has robbed it, forever, of what could have come after *The Man Who Loved Children.*

I X

WHEN WE think of the masterpieces that nobody praised and nobody read, back there in the past, we feel an impatient superiority to the readers of the past. If we had been there, we can't help feeling, *we'd* have known that *Moby Dick* was a good book—why, how could anyone help knowing?

But suppose someone says to us, "Well, you're here now: what's our own *Moby Dick?* What's the book that, a hundred years from now, everybody will look down on *us* for not having liked?" What do we say then?

But if I were asked something easier—to name a good book that we don't read and that the people of the future will read— I'd be less at a loss. In 1941 I bought two copies of *The Man Who Loved Children*, one to read and the other to lend. In the long run a borrower of one died and a borrower of the other went abroad, so that I have nothing left but a copy from the library. Lending a favorite book has its risks; the borrower may not like it. I don't know a better novel than *Crime and Punishment*—still, every fourth or fifth borrower returns it unfinished: it depresses him; besides that, he didn't believe it. More borrowers than this return the first volume of *Remembrance of Things Past* unfinished: they were bored. There is no book you can lend people that all of them will like.

But *The Man Who Loved Children* has been a queer exception. I have lent it to many writers and more readers, and all of them thought it good and original, a book different from any other. They could see that there were things wrong with it—a novel is a prose narrative of some length that has something wrong with it—but they felt that, somehow, the things didn't matter.

To have this happen with a book that was a failure to begin with, and that after twenty-five years is unknown, is strange. Having it happen has helped me to believe that it is one of those books that their own age neither reads nor praises, but that the next age thinks a masterpiece.

But I suppose I'd believe this even if every borrower had told me it was bad. As Wordsworth and Proust say, a good enough book in the long run makes its own readers, people who believe in it because they can't help themselves. Where *The Man Who Loved Children* is concerned, I can't help myself; it seems to me as plainly good as *War and Peace* and *Crime and Punishment* and *Remembrance of Things Past* are plainly great. A few of its less important parts are bad and all of its more important parts are good: it is a masterpiece with some plain, and plainly negligible, faults.

I call it a good book, but it is a better book, I think, than most of the novels people call great; perhaps it would be fairer to call it great. It has one quality that, ordinarily, only a great book has: it does a single thing better than any other book has ever done it. *The Man Who Loved Children* makes you a part of one family's immediate existence as no other book quite does. When you have read it you have been, for a few hours, a Pollit; it will take you many years to get the sound of the Pollits out of your ears, the sight of the Pollits out of your eyes, the smell of the Pollits out of your nostrils.

The Collected Poems of

Wallace Stevens

B ACK IN THE STACKS, in libraries; in bookcases in
people's living rooms; on brick-and-plank book-
shelves beside studio couches, one sees big books in dark
bindings, the *Collected Poems* of the great poets. Once,
long ago, the poems were new: the book went by
post—so many horses and a coach—to a man in a
country house, and the letter along with it asked him
to describe, evaluate, and fix the place in English
literature, in 12,000 words, by January 25, of the
poems of William Wordsworth. And the man did.

It is hard to remember that this is the way it was;
harder to remember that this is the way it is. The
Collected Poems still go out—in this century there
have been Hardy's and Yeats's and Frost's and Eliot's
and Moore's, and now Stevens's—and the man who is
sent them still treats them with rough, or rude, or wild
justice; still puts them in their place, appreciates their
virtues, says, *Just here thou ail'st*, says, *Nothing I can
say will possibly* . . . and mails the essay off.

It all seems terribly queer, terribly risky; surely,

by now, people could have thought of some better way? Yet is it as different as we think from what we do to the old *Poems* in the dark bindings, the poems with the dust on them? Those ruins we star, confident that we are young and they, they are old—they too are animals no one has succeeded in naming, young things nothing has succeeded in aging; beings to which we can say, as the man in Kafka's story says to the corpse: "What's the good of the dumb question you are asking?" They keep on asking it; and it is only our confidence and our innocence that let us believe that describing and evaluating them, fixing their places—in however many words, by whatever date—is any less queer, any less risky.

The *Collected Poems* of such a poet as Stevens— hundreds and thousands of things truly observed or rightly imagined, profoundly meditated upon—is not anything one can easily become familiar with. Setting out on Stevens for the first time would be like setting out to be an explorer of Earth. Fortunately, I knew some of the poems well, and the poems I didn't know at all—the new ones in "The Rock"—I fell in love with. I have spent a long time on the book, and have made lists (of what seemed to me the best poems, and the poems almost as good) that I hope will be of help to those who want to get to know Stevens's poetry, and of interest to those who already know it. But I too want to say, *Nothing I can say will possibly* . . . before I mail my essay off.

This *Collected Poems* is full of extraordinary things, and the most extraordinary of all is the section of twenty-eight new—truly new—poems called "The Rock." One begins:

It makes so little difference, at so much more
Than seventy, where one looks, one has been there
before.

Wood-smoke rises through trees, is caught in an upper
flow
Of air and whirled away. But it has been often so.

In "Seventy Years Later," Stevens can feel that "It is an illusion that we were ever alive"; can feel that the old, free air "is no longer air"—that we, the houses, our shadows, their shadows, "The lives these lived in the mind are at an end. / They never were." To him, now, "The meeting at noon at the edge of the field seems like / An invention, an embrace between one desperate clod / And another in a fantastic consciousness, / In a queer assertion of humanity. . . ." Custom, the years, lie upon the far-off figures, and the man remembering them, *with a weight / Heavy as frost, and deep almost as life;* and this weight and depth are in the poems, but transfigured, transcendent —are themselves a part of the poems' life. When Stevens says, as he looks at an old man sleeping, that "The two worlds are asleep, are sleeping now. / A dumb sense possesses them in a kind of solemnity," the motion of his words is as slow and quiet as the sleep of the worlds. These are poems from the other side of existence, the poems of someone who sees things in steady accustomedness, as we do not, and who sees their accustomedness, and them, as about to perish. In some of the poems the reader feels over everything the sobering and quieting, the largening presence of death. The poems are the poems of a very old man, "a citizen of heaven though still of Rome"; many of their qualities come naturally from age, so that the poems are appropriately and legitimately different from other people's poems, from Stevens's own younger poems. These poems are magnanimous, compassionate, but calmly exact, grandly plain, as though they themselves had suggested to Stevens his "Be orator but with an accurate tongue / And without eloquence"; and they seem strangely general and representative, so that we could say of them, of Stevens, what Stevens himself says "To an Old Philosopher in Rome":

> . . . each of us
> Beholds himself in you, and hears his voice
> In yours, master and commiserable man. . . .

How much of our existence is in that "master and commiserable man"! When we read even the first stanzas of this long poem,

> On the threshold of heaven, the figures in the street
> Become the figures of heaven, the majestic movement
> Of men growing small in the distances of space,
> Singing, with smaller and still smaller sound,
> Unintelligible absolution and an end—
>
> The threshold, Rome, and that more merciful Rome
> Beyond, the two alike in the make of the mind.

58

> It is as if in a human dignity
> Two parallels become one, a perspective, of which
> Men are part both in the inch and in the mile.
>
> How easily the blown banners change to wings . . .
> Things dark on the horizons of perception,
> Become accompaniments of fortune, but
> Of the fortune of the spirit, beyond the eye,
> Not of its sphere, and yet not far beyond,
>
> The human end in the spirit's greatest reach,
> The extreme of the known in the presence of the extreme
> Of the unknown . . .

it seems to us that we are feeling, as it is not often possible for us to feel, what it is to be human; the poem's composed, equable sorrow is a kind of celebration of our being, and is deeper-sounding, satisfies more in us, than joy; we feel our own natures realized, so that when we read, near the end of the poem,

> It is a kind of total grandeur at the end
> With every visible thing enlarged, and yet
> No more than a bed, a chair and moving nuns . . .
>
> Total grandeur of a total edifice,
> Chosen by an inquisitor of structures
> For himself. He stops upon this threshold . . .

we feel that Santayana is Stevens, and Stevens ourselves—and that, stopping upon this threshold, we are participating in the grandeur possible to man.

This is a great poem of a new kind. The completeness and requiredness of the poem's working-out, the held-back yet magically sure, fully extended slowness with which these parallel worlds near each other and meet remind one of the slow movements of some of Beethoven's later quartets and sonatas. But poems like these, in their plainness and human rightness, remind me most of a work of art superficially very different, Verdi's *Falstaff*. Both are the products of men at once very old and beyond the dominion of age; such men seem to have entered into (or are able to create for us) a new existence, a world in which everything is enlarged and yet no more than itself, transfigured and yet beyond the need of transfiguration.

When Stevens writes, in "The World as Meditation," of Penelope waiting for Ulysses, it is not Penelope and Ulysses but Stevens and the sun, the reader and the world—"two in a deep-founded sheltering, friend and dear friend." At dawn "a form of fire approaches the cretonnes of Penelope," a "savage presence" awakes within her her own "barbarous strength." Has Ulysses come? "It was only day. / It was Ulysses and it was not. Yet they had met, / Friend and dear friend and a planet's encouragement"; and she combs her hair, "repeating his name with its patient syllables."

Some of the phrases of the poems describe the poems better than any I can invent for them. "St. Armorer's Church from the Outside" shows us the stony majesty of the past, man's settled triumphs:

> St. Armorer's was once an immense success.
> It rose loftily and stood massively; and to lie

In its churchyard, in the province of St. Armorer's,
Fixed one for good in geranium-colored day . . .

but it leaves them for "the chapel of breath," for "that which is always beginning because it is part / Of that which is always beginning, over and over," for the new creation that seems to us "no sign of life but life, / Itself, the presence of the intelligible / In that which is created as its symbol." And the poems' wish for themselves, at the end——"It was not important that they should survive. / What mattered was that they should bear / Some lineament or character, / Some affluence, if only half-perceived, / In the poverty of their words, / Of the planet of which they were part" ——is touching as Keats's "writ in water" is touching, and endears them to us more than our own praise.

Stevens has always looked steadily at the object, but has looked, often, shortly and with a certain indifference, the indifference of the artist who——as Goethe says——"stands above art and the object; he stands above art because he utilizes it for his purpose; he stands above the object because he deals with it in his own manner." But now that the unwanted, inescapable indifference of age has taken the place of this conscious indifference, Stevens is willing to be possessed by "the plain sense of things," and his serious undeviating meditation about them seems as much in their manner as in his. His poetry has had "the power to transform itself, or else / And what meant more, to be transformed." The movement of his poetry has changed; the reader feels in it a different presence, and is touched by all that is no longer there. Stevens's late-nineteenth-century orchestration has been replaced, most of the time, by plain chords from a few instruments—the stir and dazzle of the parts is lost in the sense of the whole. The best of these late poems have a calm, serious certainty, an easiness of rightness, like well-being. The barest and most pitiable of the world's objects—"the great pond, / The plain sense of it, without reflections, leaves, / Mud, water like dirty glass, expressing silence / Of a sort, silence of a rat come out to see"—have in the poems "the naked majesty . . . of bird-nest arches and of rain-stained-vaults," a dignity and largeness and unchangeableness; on the winter day "the wind moves like a great thing tottering."

I had meant to finish this section on "The Rock" by quoting the marvelously original "Prologues to What Is Possible," but it is too long; I had better quote "Madame La Fleurie," a particularly touching treatment of a subject that is particularly Stevens's:

Weight him down, O side-stars, with the great weightings of the end.
Seal him there. He looked in a glass of the earth and thought he lived in it.
Now, he brings all that he saw into the earth, to the waiting parent.
His crisp knowledge is devoured by her, beneath a dew.

Weight him, weight, weight him with the sleepiness of the moon.
It was only a glass because he looked in it. It was nothing he could be told.

It was a language he spoke, because he must, yet did not
    know.
It was a page he had found in the handbook of heart-
    break.

The black fugatos are strumming the blacknesses of
    black . . .
The thick strings stutter the finial gutturals.
He does not lie there remembering the blue-jay, say the
    jay.
His grief is that his mother should feed on him, himself
    and what he saw,
In that distant chamber, a bearded queen, wicked in her
    dead light.

When the reader comes to aberrant poems like
"Page of a Tale" and "A Rabbit as King of the
Ghosts," he realizes how little there is in Stevens, ordinarily, of the narrative, dramatic, immediately active
side of life, of harried actors compelled, impelled, in
ignorant hope. But how much there is of the man who
looks, feels, meditates, in the freedom of removedness,
of disinterested imagining, of thoughtful love! As we
read the poems we are so continually aware of Stevens
observing, meditating, creating, that we feel like saying that the process of creating the poem is the poem.
Surprisingly often the motion of qualification, of concession, of logical conclusion—a dialectical motion in
the older sense of *dialectical*—is the movement that
organizes the poem; and in Stevens the unlikely tenderness of this movement—the one, the not-quite-that,
the other, the not-exactly-the-other, the real one, the
real other—is like the tenderness of the sculptor or

draftsman, whose hand makes but looks as if it caressed.

Few poets have made a more interesting rhetoric out of just fooling around: turning things upside down, looking at them from under the sofa, considering them (and their observer) curiously enough to make the reader protest, "That were to consider it too curiously." This rhetoric is the rhetoric of a kaleidoscope, a kaleidoscope of parts; and when it is accompanied, as it sometimes is, by little content and less emotion, it seems clear, bright, complicated, and inhuman. When the philosopher is king, his subjects move like propositions. Yet one is uneasy at objecting to the play—to the professional playfulness, even—of a large mind and a free spirit.

I have written, in another essay, about the disadvantages of philosophizing (in verse) as inveterately and interminably as Stevens has philosophized. But his marvelous successes with his method, in its last bare anomalous stages in "The Rock," make me feel that the hand of the maker knows better than the eye of the observer, at least if it's my eye. Without his excesses, his endless adaptations and exaggerations of old procedures, how could he ever have learned these unimaginable new ways of his? A tree is justified in its fruits: I began to distrust my own ways, and went back to the poems (in *The Auroras of Autumn*) that had seemed to me monumental wastes; transcendental, all too transcendental études; improvisations preserved for us neither by good nor by bad, but by middle fortune. I read them over and over, relishing in

anticipation the pleasures of an honest reformation. I
could see how much familiarity this elaborate, almost
monotonously meditative style requires of the reader;
I managed, after a while, to feel that I had not been as
familiar with the poems, or as sympathetic to the
poems, as I ought to have been. And there I stuck.
Whatever is wrong with the poems or with me is as
wrong as ever; what they seemed to me once, they
seem to me still.

Stevens's poetry makes one understand how valuable it can be for a poet to write a great deal. Not too
much of that great deal, ever, is good poetry; but out
of quantity can come practice, naturalness, accustomed mastery, adaptations and elaborations and re-
versals of old ways, new ways, even—so that the poet
can put into the poems, at the end of a lifetime, what
the end of a lifetime brings him. Stevens has learned to
write at will, for pleasure; his methods of writing, his
ways of imagining, have made this possible for him as
it is impossible for many living poets—Eliot, for instance. Anything can be looked at, felt about, meditated upon, so Stevens *can* write about anything; he
does not demand of his poems the greatest concentration, intensity, dramatic immediacy, the shattering
and inexplicable rightness the poet calls inspiration.
(Often it is as if Stevens didn't want the poetic equivalent of sonata form, and had gone back to earlier
polyphonic ways, days when the crescendo was still
uninvented.) His good poems are as inspired as anybody else's—if you compare *The Auroras of Autumn* with "The Rock," you will decide that the last

poems come from a whole period of the most marvelous inspiration; but Stevens does not think of inspiration (or whatever you want to call it) as a condition of composition. He too is waiting for the spark from heaven to fall—poets have no choice about this—but he waits writing; and this—other things being equal, when it's possible, if it's possible—is the best way for the poet to wait.

Stevens's rhetoric is at its worst, always, in the poems of other poets; just as great men are great disasters, overwhelmingly good poets are overwhelmingly bad influences. In Stevens the reign of the dramatic monologue—the necessity to present, present! in concentrated dramatic form—is over, and the motion of someone else's speech has been replaced by "the motion of thought" of the poet himself. Ordinarily this poet's thought moves (until "The Rock") in unrhymed iambic pentameter, in a marvelously accomplished Wordsworthian blank verse—or, sometimes, in something akin to Tennyson's bland lissome adaptation of it. If someone had predicted to Pound, when he was beginning his war on the iambic foot; to Eliot, when he was first casting a cold eye on post-Jacobean blank verse; to both, when they were first condemning generalization in poetry, that in forty or fifty years the chief—sometimes, I think in despair, the only—influence on younger American poets would be this generalizing, masterful, scannable verse of Stevens's, wouldn't both have laughed in confident disbelief? And how many of the youngest English poets seem to want to write like Cowper! A great revolution is hardest of all on the great revolutionists.

At the bottom of Stevens's poetry there is wonder and delight, the child's or animal's or savage's—man's —joy in his own existence, and thankfulness for it. He is the poet of well-being: "One might have thought of sight, but who could think / Of what it sees, for all the ill it sees?" This sigh of awe, of wondering pleasure, is underneath all these poems that show us the "celestial possible," everything that has not yet been transformed into the infernal impossibilities of our everyday earth. Stevens is full of the natural or Aristotelian virtues; he is, in the terms of Hopkins's poem, all windhover and no Jesuit. There is about him, under the translucent glazes, a Dutch solidity and weight; he sits surrounded by all the good things of this earth, with rosy cheeks and fresh clear blue eyes, eyes not going out to you but shining in their place, like fixed stars—or else he moves off, like the bishop in his poem, "globed in today and tomorrow." If he were an animal he would be, without a doubt, that rational, magnanimous, voluminous animal, the elephant.

As John Stuart Mill read Wordsworth, to learn to feel, so any of a thousand logical positivists might read Stevens, to learn to imagine: "That strange flower, the sun, / Is just what you say. / Have it your way. / The world is ugly, / And the people are sad. / That tuft of jungle feathers, / That animal eye, / Is just what you say. / That savage of fire, / That seed, / Have it your way. / The world is ugly, / And the people are sad." But such a poem does more than imagine—it sees, it knows; so perhaps imagining is a part of seeing and knowing. Stevens finishes "Tea at the Palaz of Hoon" by admitting that it has all been imaginary, that his ears have made the hymns they heard, that "I was the world in which I walked, and what I saw / Or heard or felt came not but from myself; / And there I found myself more truly and more strange" —he has seen his own being, in truth and in strangeness, as he could never have seen it if he had looked at it directly.

When I read the first two lines of a poem, "Place-bound and time-bound in evening rain / And bound by a sound which does not change"; or of something "in which / We believe without belief, beyond belief"; or of the people of the future beginning to "avoid our stale perfections, seeking out / Their own, waiting until we go / To picnic in the ruins that we leave"; or that "Time is a horse that runs in the heart, a horse / Without a rider on a road at night"; or of "armies without / Either drums or trumpets, the commanders mute, the arms / On the ground, fixed fast in a profound defeat," these low grave notes are more to me, almost, than any of the old bright ones. But then I remember that some of the old ones were as grave: "The Snow Man" or "The Death of a Soldier" or that haunting poem no one seems haunted by, "Autumn Refrain":

> The skreak and skritter of evening gone
> And grackles gone and sorrows of the sun,
> The sorrows of sun, too, gone . . . the moon and moon,

The yellow moon of words about the nightingale
In measureless measures, not a bird for me
But the name of a bird and the name of a nameless air
I have never—shall never hear. And yet beneath
The stillness of everything gone, and being still,
Being and sitting still, something resides,
Some skreaking and skrittering residuum,
And grates these evasions of the nightingale
Though I have never—shall never hear that bird.
And the stillness is in the key, all of it is,
The stillness is all in the key of that desolate sound.

But how charming Stevens's jokes are, too! When he uses little cultural properties unexpectedly, with mocking elegiac humor; when we—so to speak—discover that the part of the collage we thought a washrag is really a reproduction of the Laocoön, we are pleased just as we are in Klee. This Dawn *is* one of Klee's little watercolor operas, isn't it?

An opening of portals when night ends,
A running forward, arms stretched out as drilled.
Act I, Scene 1, at a German Staats-Oper.

And when Stevens begins, "O that this lashing wind was something more / Than the spirit of Ludwig Richter!"; when he thinks, looking out upon a prospect of the Alps, "Claude has been dead a long time / And apostrophes are forbidden on the funicular"; when he says of "Lions in Sweden" that he too was once

A hunter of those sovereigns of the soul
And savings banks, Fides, the sculptor's prize,
All eyes and size, and galled Justitia,

6 9

> Trained to poise the tables of the law,
> Patientia, forever soothing wounds,
> And mighty Fortitudo, frantic bass . . .

—when Stevens does all this, I am delighted; and I am more delighted with these souvenirs, these ambiguous survivals, because in other poems the other times and the other peoples, the old masters and the old masterpieces, exist in fresh and unambiguous magnificence.

Stevens does seem a citizen of the world. The other arts, the other continents, the other centuries are essential not merely to his well-being but to his own idea of himself, his elementary identity. Yeats called Keats a schoolboy with his nose pressed against the window of a sweetshop; we Americans stand with our noses pressed against the window of the world. How directly, in *The Cantos* and *The Waste Land*, Pound and Eliot appropriate that world! Stones from the Coliseum, drops of water from the Jordan, glitter from the pages like a built mirage. (The only directer procedure would have been to go to Europe and stay there.) If Stevens could stay home, except for trips, it was because he had made for himself a Europe of his own, a past of his own, a whole sunlit—and, in the end, twilight—world of his own. It is an extremely large world, the world that an acute mind, varied interests and sympathies, and an enormous vocabulary can produce. (I know what an abject, basely material anticlimax that *enormous vocabulary* is; but the bigger a poet's effective, natural vocabulary is, the larger his world will seem.) And Stevens has an extraordinarily original imagination, one that has created for us—so to speak—many new tastes and colors and sounds, many real, half-real, and nonexistent beings.

He has spoken, always, with the authority of someone who thinks of himself as a source of interest, of many interests. He has never felt it necessary to appeal to us, make a hit with us, nor does he try to sweep us away, to overawe us; he has written as if poems were certain to find, or make, their true readers. Throughout half this century of the common man, this age in which each is like his sibling, Stevens has celebrated the hero, the capacious, magnanimous, excelling man; has believed, with obstinacy and good humor, in all the heights which draw us toward them, make us like them, simply by existing. A few weeks ago I read, in Sacheverell Sitwell, two impressive sentences: "It is my belief that I have informed myself of nearly all works of art in the known world. . . . I have heard most of the music of the world, and seen nearly all the paintings." It was hard for me to believe these sentences, but I wanted Sitwell to be able to say them, liked him for having said them—I believed. While I was writing this essay the sentences kept coming back to me, since they seemed to me sentences Stevens would say if he could. In an age when almost everybody sold man and the world short, he never did, but acted as if joy *were* "a word of our own," as if nothing excellent were alien to us.

I should like, now, to give a list of eighteen or twenty of Stevens's best poems, and a list of twenty or thirty of his better. Reading the poems in these lists will give anyone a definite—dazzlingly definite—idea of the things I think exceptional about Stevens's poetry, and the lists can be of help to people just beginning to make, from this big *Collected Poems*, a *Selected Poems* of their own. Some of his best poems are, I think: "The Snow Man," "To an Old Philosopher in Rome," "Esthétique du Mal," "The World as Meditation," "Peter Quince at the Clavier," "Autumn Refrain," "Angel Surrounded by Paysans," "Sunday Morning," "The Death of a Soldier," "Prologues to What Is Possible," "Madame La Fleurie," "Sea Surface Full of Clouds," "The Man on the Dump," "Some Friends from Pascagoula," "The Brave Man" —but now I begin to be very confused about where the best ends and the better begins—"Dutch Graves in Bucks County," "Seventy Years Later," "The Comedian as the Letter C," "The Emperor of Ice Cream," "Mrs. Alfred Uruguay," "Page from a Tale," "The Common Life," "Sailing after Lunch," "Le Monocle de Mon Oncle." And now I begin, however uneasily, on my second list: "To the One of Fictive Music," "St. Armorer's Church from the Outside," "Disillusionment of Ten O'Clock," "The Plain Sense of Things," "The Good Man Has No Shape," "Lions in Sweden," "Gubbinal," "Sonatina to Hans Christian," "The American Sublime," "A Quiet Normal Life," "Tea at the Palaz of Hoon," "Bantams in Pinewoods," the first of "Six Significant Landscapes," Part IX of "Credences of Summer," "A Lot of People Bathing in a Stream," "Metaphors of a Magnifico," "Cy Est Pourtraicte, Madame Ste Ursule, et Les Unze

Mille Vierges," "The Idea of Order at Key West,"
"Anecdote of the Prince of Peacocks," "No Possum,
No Sop, No Taters," "Martial Cadenza," "Anglais
Mort à Florence," "Mozart, 1935," "A Rabbit as
King of the Ghosts," "Poetry as a Destructive Force,"
"A Woman Sings a Song for a Soldier Come Home,"
"Less and Less Human, O Savage Spirit."

Stevens has spoken with dignity and elegance and
intelligence—with eloquence—of everything from
pure sensation to pure reflection to pure imagination,
from the "elephant-colorings" of tires to the angel of
reality, the "necessary angel" in whose sight we "see
the earth again, / Cleared of its stiff and stubborn,
man-locked set"—the angel who asks as he departs:

> Am I not
> Myself, only half of a figure of a sort,
> A figure half seen, or seen for a moment, a man
> Of the mind, an apparition apparelled in
> Apparels of such lightest look that a turn
> Of my shoulder and quickly, too quickly, I am gone?

These lines, so pure and light and longing, remind me
of the other figures which, in the second of the *Duino
Elegies,* touch us lightly on the shoulder before they
turn and go. "A man / Of the mind": in this end of
one line and beginning of another, and in the suspension between them, the angel has spoken an epitaph
for Stevens.

Graves and

the White Goddess

AT THE BEGINNING of Robert Graves's *Collected Poems* [1955] there is a list of thirty-three books and three translations. The list makes it seem foolish to talk only of the poems, and if you think of *Goodbye to All That* and *The White Goddess*, it seems foolish to talk only of the writing: there is a great deal of Graves's life in what he has written, and a great deal of his writing seems plausible—explicable, even —only in terms of his life. I want to write, in the first half of this essay, about what his poetry seems to me; and later, about how his life (all I know of it comes from him) has made his poetry and his understanding of the world into the inimitable, eccentric marvels that they are.

Looking along his list, I see that I have read two of the translations and twenty-nine and a half of the books—three haven't got to me yet, and I quit in the middle of *Homer's Daughter*—but I have read three or four of the books Graves doesn't list. And I have read *I, Claudius* (a good book singular enough to be immortal) and its slightly inferior continuation three or four times; *King Jesus*, a wonderfully imagined, adequately written novel, three times; *The White Goddess*, that erudite, magical (or, as Eliot calls it, "prodigious, monstrous, stupefying, indescribable") masterwork of fantastic exposition, twice; the poems scores or hundreds of times. In two months I have had time to read *The Greek Myths* only once, but it is, both in matter and in manner, an odd rare classic that people will be rereading for many years. And they will be reading, I think, the book with which, in 1929, I began: the thirty-three-year-old Robert Graves's autobiography, *Goodbye to All That*. If you are interested in Graves—and how can anyone help being interested in so good and so queer a writer?—there is no better place to begin. No better, except for the *Collected Poems*: that, with Graves, is where one begins and ends.

For Graves is, first and last, a poet: in between he is a Graves. "There is a coldness in the Graveses which is anti-sentimental to the point of insolence," he writes. The Graveses have good minds "for examinations . . . and solving puzzles"; are loquacious, eccentric individualists "inclined to petulance"; are subject to "most disconcerting spells of complete amnesia . . . and rely on their intuition and bluff to get them through"; and, no matter how disreputable their clothes and friends, are always taken for gentlemen. This is a fine partial summary of one side of Robert von Ranke Graves: of that professional, matter-of-fact-to-the-point-of-insolence, complacent, prosaic competence of style and imagination that weighs down most of his fiction, gives a terse, crusty, Defoe-esque plausibility to even his most imaginative nonfiction, and is present in most of his poetry only as a shell or skeleton, a hard lifeless something supporting or enclosing the poem's different life. Graves has spoken of the "conflict of rival sub-personalities," of warring halves or thirds or quarters, as what makes a man a poet. He differentiates the two sides of his own nature so sharply that he speaks of the first poem "I" wrote and the first poem "I wrote as a Graves"; he calls his prose "potboiling"—much of it is—and puts into his autobiography a number of his mother's sayings primarily to show how much more, as a poet, he owes to the von Rankes than to the Graveses. (One of these sayings was, "There was a man once, a Frenchman, who died of grief because he could never become a mother." I find it delightful to think of the mother bending to the child who was to become the excavator or resurrector of the White Goddess, and repeating to him this Delphic sentence.)

The sincere and generous von Rankes, with their castles, venison, blind trout, and black honey; their women who "were noble and patient, and always kept their eyes on the ground when out walking"; their great historian of whom Graves says, "To him I owe my historical method"—a tribute that must have made Leopold von Ranke's very bones grow pale—the von Rankes are certainly, as Graves considers them, the more attractive side of himself. He speaks of his "once aquiline, now crooked nose" as being "a verti-

cal line of demarcation between the left and right sides
of my face, which are naturally unassorted—my
eyes, eyebrows, and ears all being notably crooked
and my cheek-bones, which are rather high, being on
different levels." I do not propose to tell you which is
the Graves, and which the von Ranke, eye, eyebrow,
ear, and cheekbone, but I am prepared to do as much
for almost any sentence in Robert Graves—to tell
you whether it was written by the cold, puzzle-solving, stamp-collecting, logic-chopping Regimental Explainer; or by the Babe, Lover, and Victim howling,
in dreadful longing, for the Mother who bears, possesses, and destroys; or, as happens sometimes, by
both. But I am being drawn, not much against my
will, into the second part of this essay; let me get back
to the poetry.

Graves's poems seem to divide naturally into six or
seven types. These are: mythical-archaic poems,
poems of the White Goddess; poems about extreme
situations; expressive or magical landscapes; grotesques; observations—matter-of-fact, tightly organized, tersely penetrating observations of types of
behavior, attitude, situation, of the processes and categories of existence; love poems; ballads or nursery
rhymes.

These last are early poems, and disappear as soon as
Graves can afford to leave "what I may call the folk-
song period of my life," the time when "country
sentiment," childlike romance, were a refuge from
"my shellshocked condition." The best of these poems
is his grotesquely and ambiguously moving, faintly
Ransomesque ballad of the Blatant Beast, "Saint."

Some others are "Frosty Night," "Apples and Water," "Richard Roe and John Doe," "Allie," "Henry and Mary," "Vain and Careless," "The Bedpost," and the beautiful "Love without Hope":

> Love without hope, as when the young bird-catcher
> Swept off his tall hat to the Squire's own daughter,
> So let the imprisoned larks escape and fly
> Singing about her head, as she rode by.

The young birdcatcher might have stepped from "Under the Greenwood Tree" or "Winter Night in Woodland (Old Time)"—and in all Italy where is there a halo like his, made from such live and longing gold?

Graves has never forgotten the child's incommensurable joys; nor has he forgotten the child's and the man's incommensurable, irreducible agonies. He writes naturally and well—cannot keep himself from writing—about bad, and worse, and worst, the last extremities of existence:

> Walls, mounds, enclosing corrugations
> Of darkness, moonlight on dry grass.
> Walking this courtyard, sleepless, in fever;
> Planning to use—but by definition
> There's no way out, no way out—
> Rope-ladders, baulks of timber, pulleys,
> A rocket whizzing over the walls and moat—
> Machines easy to improvise.
>
> > No escape,
> No such thing; to dream of new dimensions,
> Cheating checkmate by painting the king's robe
> So that he slides like a queen;

Or to cry, "Nightmare, nightmare!"
Like a corpse in the cholera-pit
Under a load of corpses;
Or to run the head against these blind walls,
Enter the dungeon, torment the eyes
With apparitions chained two and two,
And go frantic with fear—
To die and wake up sweating in moonlight
In the same courtyard, sleepless as before.

This poem, "The Castle," and such poems as "Haunted House," "The Pier-Glass," "Down," "Sick Love," "Mermaid, Dragon, and Fiend," "The Suicide in the Copse," "The Survivor," "The Devil at Berry Pomeroy," "The Death Room," and "The Jealous Man" are enough to make any reader decide that Graves is a man to whom terrible things have happened.

At the end of the First World War, Graves says, "I could not use a telephone, I was sick every time I travelled in a train, and if I saw more than two new people in a single day it prevented me from sleeping. . . . Shells used to come bursting on my bed at midnight even when Nancy was sharing it with me; strangers in daytime would assume the faces of friends who had been killed." Graves has removed from his *Collected Poems* any poem directly about the war; only the generalized, decade-removed "Recalling War" remains. When he had said *Goodbye to All That* he had meant it—meant it more than he had known, perhaps. The worst became for him, from then on, a civilian worst, and his thoughts about war dried

and hardened into the routine, grotesque professional-
ism that is the best way of taking for granted, cancel-
ing out, the unbearable actualities of war. Who would
have believed that the author who wrote about these,
in *Goodbye to All That*, with plain truth, would in a
few years be writing such a G. A. Henty book as
Count Belisarius?

To Graves, often, the most extreme situation is
truth, the mere seeing of reality; we can explain
away or destroy the fabulous, traditional mermaids
or dragons or devils of existence, but the real "mermaids will not be denied / The last bubbles of our
shame, / The dragon flaunts an unpierced hide, / The
true fiend governs in God's name." In "A jealous
Man" Graves writes with this truth about another war
in which he has fought—writes about it in night-
marishly immediate, traditional, universal terms. The
objectively summarizing, held-in, held-back lines
seem, in Hopkins's phrase, to "wince and sing" under
the hammering of this grotesque, obscene, intolerable
anguish—an anguish that ends in untouched, indifferent air :

> To be homeless is a pride
> To the jealous man prowling
> Hungry down the night lanes,
>
> Who has no steel at his side,
> No drink hot in his mouth,
> But a mind dream-enlarged,
>
> Who witnesses warfare,
> Man with woman, hugely
> Raging from hedge to hedge :

The raw knotted oak-club
Clenched in the raw fist,
The ivy-noose well flung,

The thronged din of battle,
Gaspings of the throat-snared,
Snores of the battered dying,

Tall corpses, braced together,
Fallen in clammy furrows,
Male and female,

Or, among haulms of nettle
Humped, in noisome heaps,
Male and female.

He glowers in the choked roadway
Between twin churchyards,
Like a turnip ghost.

(Here, the rain-worn headstone,
There, the Celtic cross
In rank white marble.)

This jealous man is smitten,
His fear-jerked forehead
Sweats a fine musk;

A score of bats bewitched
By the ruttish odor
Swoop singing at his head;

Nuns bricked up alive
Within the neighbouring wall
Wail in cat-like longing.

Crow, cocks, crow loud!
Reprieve the doomed devil,
Has he not died enough?

Now, out of careless sleep,
She wakes and greets him coldly,
The woman at home,

She, with a private wonder
At shoes bemired and bloody—
His war was not hers.

Often these poems of extreme situation, like those of
observation, are grotesques—this neither by chance
nor by choice, but by necessity. Much of life comes
to Graves already sharpened into caricature: "another
caricature scene" and "plenty of caricature scenes"
are ordinary remarks in his autobiography. ("Another caricature scene to look back on," he writes of his
wedding.) The best of his grotesques have a peculiar
mesmeric power, shock when touched, since they are
the charged caricatures of children, of dreams, of the
unconscious:

All horses on the racecourse of Tralee
    Have four more legs in gallop than in trot—
    Two pairs fully extended, two pairs not;
And yet no thoroughbred with either three
    Or five legs but is mercilessly shot.
I watched a filly gnaw her fifth leg free,
Warned by a speaking mare since turned silentiary.

Somewhere in Kafka there is a man who is haunted by
two bouncing balls; living with this poem is like being
haunted by a Gestalt diagram changing from figure
to ground, ground to figure, there in the silent dark-

ness, until we get up and turn on the light and look at it, and go back to sleep with it ringing—high, hollow, sinister, yet somehow lyric and living—in our dream-enlarged ears. One can say about this poem of Graves's, as about others: "If I weren't looking at it I wouldn't believe it." According to Stalky and Company, the impassioned Diderot burst forth, "O Richardson, thou singular genius!" When one reads "It Was All Very Tidy," "The Worms of History," "Ogres and Pygmies," "Lollocks," "The Laureate," "The Death Room," one feels just like Diderot; nor is one willing to dismiss grotesques like "Song: Lift-Boy," "The Suicide in the Copse," "Grotesques" II, "The Villagers and Death," "Welsh Incident," "Wm. Brazier," "General Bloodstock's Lament for England," "Vision in the Repair Shop," and "Front Door Soliloquy" with a mere "Singular, singular!"

Sometimes these grotesques are inspired hostile observations, highly organized outbursts of dislike, revulsion, or rejection: where these observations (and much else) are concerned, Graves is the true heir of Ben Jonson, and can give to his monstrosities, occasionally, the peculiar lyric magnificence Jonson gives them in *The Alchemist*. It is easy for him to see God or Death as grotesque monsters; and the White Goddess, with all her calm, grave, archaic magnificence, is monstrous. But sometimes Graves writes grotesques of local color, traditional properties, comfortable-enough types, and these can be good-humored—are even, once, wistful:

86

Even in hotel beds the hair tousles.
But this is observation, not complaint—
"Complaints should please be dropped in the complaint-
    box"—
"Which courteously we beg you to vacate
In that clean state as you should wish to find it."

And the day after Carnival, today,
I found, in the square, a crimson cardboard heart:
"Anna Maria," it read. Otherwise, friends,
No foreign news—unless that here they drink
Red wine from china bowls; here anis-roots
Are stewed like turnips; here funiculars
Light up at dusk, two crooked constellations. . . .

"It is not yet the season," pleads the Porter,
"That comes in April, when the rain most rains."
Trilingual Switzer fish in Switzer lakes
Pining for rain and bread-crumbs of the season,
In thin reed-beds you pine!

                In bed drowsing,
(While the hair slowly tousles) uncomplaining. . . .
Anna Maria's heart under my pillow
Evokes no furious dream. Who is this Anna?
A Switzer maiden among Switzer maidens,
Child of the children of that fox who never
Ate the sour grapes: her teeth not set on edge.

The reader can murmur: "Why—why, this is life."
But Graves—as mercilessly good a critic of his own
poetry as he is a mercilessly bad critic of everybody
else's—has here had a most disconcerting spell of complete amnesia: "Hotel Bed" isn't included in his new

Collected Poems. "My poetry-writing has always been a painful process of continual corrections and corrections on top of corrections and persistent dissatisfaction," he writes. He is the only one who can afford to be dissatisfied with the process or the poems it has produced: he is the best rewriter and corrector of his own poetry that I know. Lately I have gone over the new, and old, and very old versions of all the poems in *Collected Poems,* and I am still dazzled by the magical skill, the inspiration apparently just there for use when needed, with which Graves has saved a ruined poem or perfected a good one. Usually the changes are so exactly right, so thoroughly called for, that you're puzzled at his ever having written the original; it grieves me that I have no space in which to quote them.

About sixty of Graves's collected poems are what one might call Observations—observations of types, functions, states; of characteristic strategies and attitudes, people's "life-styles"; of families, genetic development in general; of the self; of well-known stories or characters; of good reasons and real reasons; of dilemmas; of many of the processes and categories of existence. Ordinarily these observations are witty, detailed, penetrating, disabused, tightly organized, logical-sounding, matter-of-fact, terse: Graves sounds, often, as if he were Defoe attempting to get his Collected Works into the "Sayings of Spartans." Frequently an observation is put in terms of landscape or grotesque, organized as an approach to a limit or a *reductio ad absurdum;* sometimes a set of observations (for instance, "To Bring the Dead to Life" and "To Evoke Posterity") reminds one of a set of non-Euclidean geometries, differing assumptions rigorously worked out. Such a poem seems an organized, individual little world, this and no other. Finishing one we may feel, as in Graves's dry masterpiece, that It Was All Very Tidy—tidier, certainly, than life and our necessities; we feel about it a gnawing lack, the lack of anything lacking, of a way out—between the inside of the poem and the great outside there is no communication, and we long for an explosion or an implosion, we are not sure which. But these local actions, limited engagements, punitive expeditions; these poems which do, with elegance and dispatch, all that they set out to do; these bagatelles—on occasion Beethoven bagatelles; these complete, small-scale successes, are poems in which Graves excels. Few poets have written more pretty-good poems: "Midway," "The Devil's Advice to Story Tellers," "The Fallen Tower of Siloam," "The Reader over My Shoulder," "To Bring the Dead to Life," "To Walk on Hills," "The Persian Version," "The Furious Voyage," "The Climate of Thought," and "The Shot" are some examples of notably successful "observations," but there are many more; and the grotesques and landscapes and love poems are full of such small successes.

Landscapes have always been of particular importance to Graves; shell-shocked, he spent an entire leave walking through some favorite country, and went back to France half cured. When he writes about landscapes he puts into them or gets out of them meanings, attitudes, and emotions that Poets rarely get from Poetic landscapes; like Wordsworth, he is not interested in landscape as landscape. Some of the best of these poems describe magical landscapes—inside-out, box-inside-a-box, infinite regress—that seem to express, or correspond to, emotional or physiological states in Graves that I am not sure of, and that Graves may not be sure of: "Warning to Children," "Interruption," and, especially, "The Terraced Valley" are better than I can explain, and I listen to

> . . . Neat outside-inside, neat below-above,
> Hermaphrodizing love.
> Neat this-way-that-way and without mistake:
> On the right hand could slide the left glove.
> Neat over-under: the young snake
> Through an unyielding shell his path could break.
> Singing of kettles, like a singing brook,
> Made out-of-doors a fireside nook.

> . . . I knew you near me in that strange region,
> So searched for you, in hope to see you stand
> On some near olive-terrace, in the heat,
> The left-hand glove drawn on your right hand,
> The empty snake's egg perfect at your feet—

with, at the climax, a kind of rapt uneasy satisfaction.

But Graves's richest, most moving, and most consistently beautiful poems—poems that almost deserve the literal *magical*—are his mythical-archaic pieces, all those the reader thinks of as "White Goddess poems": "To Juan at the Winter Solstice," "Theseus and Ariadne," "Lament for Pasiphaë," "The Sirens'

Welcome to Cronos," "A Love Story," "The Return
of the Goddess," "Darien," and eight or ten others.
The best of these are different from anything else in
English; their whole meaning and texture and motion
are different from anything we could have expected
from Graves or from anybody else. "The Sirens'
Welcome to Cronos," for instance, has a color or taste
that is new because it has been lost for thousands of
years. In the second part of this essay I mean to
discuss exactly what these poems are, and how they
got to be that, along with the more ordinary love
poems which form so large a part of Graves's work;
but here I should like simply to quote the poem that
represents them best, "To Juan at the Winter Solstice":

> There is one story and one story only
> That will prove worth your telling,
> Whether as learned bard or gifted child;
> To it all lines or lesser gauds belong
> That startle with their shining
> Such common stories as they stray into.
>
> Is it of trees you tell, their months and virtues,
> Or strange beasts that beset you,
> Of birds that croak at you the Triple will?
> Or of the Zodiac and how slow it turns
> Below the Boreal Crown,
> Prison of all true kings that ever reigned?
>
> Water to water, ark again to ark,
> From woman back to woman:
> So each new victim treads unfalteringly

The never altered circuit of his fate,
Bringing twelve peers as witness
Both to his starry rise and starry fall.

Or is it of the Virgin's silver beauty,
All fish below the thighs?
She in her left hand bears a leafy quince;
When, with her right she crooks a finger smiling,
How may the King hold back?
Royally then he barters life for love.

Or of the undying snake from chaos hatched,
Whose coils contain the ocean,
Into whose chops with naked sword he springs,
Then in black water, tangled by the reeds,
Battles three days and nights,
To be spewed up beside her scalloped shore?

Much snow is falling, winds roar hollowly,
The owl hoots from the elder,
Fear in your heart cries to the loving-cup:
Sorrow to sorrow as the sparks fly upward.
The log groans and confesses
There is one story and one story only.

Dwell on her graciousness, dwell on her smiling,
Do not forget what flowers
The great boar trampled down in ivy time.
Her brow was creamy as the crested wave,
Her sea-blue eyes were wild
But nothing promised that is not performed.

Graves's best poems, I think, are "To Juan at the
Winter Solstice," "A Jealous Man," "Theseus and
Ariadne," "Lament for Pasiphaë," "The Sirens' Wel-

come to Cronos," "Ogres and Pygmies," "The Worms of History," "It Was All Very Tidy," "Saint," "The Terraced Valley," "The Devil at Berry Pomeroy," "Lollocks"; poems like "The Laureate," "The Castle," "Hotel Bed," "A Love Story," and "The Death Room" might end this list and begin a list of what seem to me Graves's next-best poems: "Interruption," "Warning to Children," "The Young Cordwainer," "Down," "Reproach," "Recalling War," "Song: Lift-Boy" (with the old coda), "The Bards," and "The Survivor." Quite as good as some of these are the best of Graves's slighter poems, delicate or witty or beautiful pieces without much weight or extent of subject and movement: "Love without Hope," "She Tells Her Love While Half Asleep," "Advocates," "Dawn Bombardment," "Sick Love," "Grotesques" II and VI, "The Suicide in the Copse," "Like Snow," "An English Wood," "The Shot," "On Dwelling," "The Portrait"; and I have already listed what seem to me some of his best grotesques and observations.

Graves is a poet of varied and consistent excellence. He has written scores, almost hundreds, of poems that are completely realized, different either from one another or from the poems of any other poet. His poems have to an extraordinary degree the feeling of one man's world, one man's life: what he loves and loathes; what he thinks and feels and doesn't know that he feels; the rhythms of his voice, his walk, his gestures. To meet Robert Graves is unnecessary: all his life has transformed itself into his poetry. The

limitations of his poetic world come more from limitations of temperament than from limitations of gift or
ability—anything Graves is really interested in he
can do. He writes, always, with economical strength,
with efficient distinction. Both the wording and the
rhythm of his verse are full of personal force and impersonal skill: the poems have been made by a craftsman, but a craftsman whose heart was in his fingers.
His wit; terseness; matter-of-factness; overmastering
organizational and logical skill; penetrating observation; radical two-sidedness; gifts of skewness, wry-
ness, cater-corneredness, sweet-sourness, of "English
eccentricity," of grotesque humor, of brotherly acceptance of the perverse random contingency of the
world; feeling for landscapes and for Things; gifts of
ecstasy, misery, and confident command; idiosyncratic encyclopedic knowledge of our world and the
worlds that came before it; the fact that love—everyday, specific, good-and-bad, miraculous-and-disastrous
love, not the Love most writers write about—is the
element he is a native of; his—to put it in almost
childish terms—invariable *interestingness*, are a few
of the many qualities that make Graves extraordinary.

Later on I should like to discuss Graves's limitations,
which are as interesting as any of his qualities—
which are, so to speak, the grotesque shadow of his
qualities. His poems seem to me in no sense the work of
a great poet; when you compare Graves with Wordsworth or Rilke, you are comparing a rearrangement
of the room with a subsidence of continents. But

Graves's poems are a marvel and a delight, the work of a fine poet who has managed, by the strangest of processes, to make himself into an extraordinary one. In the "Fiend, Dragon, Mermaid" that is not included in this last *Collected Poems*, Graves tells how he escaped from the monstrous fiend, dragon, mermaid, each dying—and how, quit of them, "I turned my gaze to the encounter of / The later genius, who of my pride and fear / And love / No monster made but me." This is true: he is, now, somewhat of a monster, a marvelous and troubling one, and it is by means of this "later genius," the White Goddess, the monstrous Muse, that he has made himself into what he is. In the second half of this essay I shall try to show how it was done.

I I

"THERE IS one story and one story only," Graves writes; all poems have the same theme. "The theme," he says in *The White Goddess*, "is the antique story . . . of the birth, life, death, and resurrection of the God of the Waxing Year; the central chapters concern the God's long battle with the God of the Waning Year for love of the capricious and all-powerful Threefold Goddess, their mother, bride, and layer-out. The poet identifies himself with the God of the Waxing Year and his muse with the Goddess; the rival is his blood-brother, his other self, his weird. All true poetry— true by Housman's practical test—celebrates some incident or scene in this very ancient story, and the main characters are so much a part of our racial inheritance that they not only assert themselves in poetry but recur on occasions of emotional stress in the form of dreams, paranoiac visions and delusions. . . . The Goddess is a lovely, slender woman with a hooked nose, deathly pale face, lips red as rowanberries, startlingly blue eyes and long fair hair; she will suddenly transform herself into sow, mare, bitch, vixen, she-ass, weasel, serpent, owl, she-wolf, tigress, mermaid or loathsome hag. . . . I cannot think of any true poet from Homer on who has not independently recorded his experience of her. . . . The reason why the hairs stand on end, the skin crawls and a shiver runs down the spine when one writes or reads a true poem is that a true poem is necessarily an Invocation of the White Goddess, or Muse, the Mother of All Living, the ancient power of fright and lust—the female spider or the queen-bee whose embrace is death.

". . . The true poet must always be original, but in a simpler sense: he must address only the Muse— not the King or Chief Bard or the people in general— and tell her the truth about himself and her in his own passionate and peculiar words. . . . Not that the Muse is ever completely satisfied. Laura Riding has summed her up in three memorable lines:

> Forgive me, giver, if I destroy the gift:
> It is so nearly what would please me
> I cannot but perfect it."

The Muse or Triple Goddess "was a personification of primitive woman—woman the creatress and destructress. As the New Moon or Spring she was girl; as the Full Moon or Summer she was woman; as the Old Moon or Winter she was hag. . . . The revolutionary institution of fatherhood, imported into Europe from the East, brought with it the institution of individual marriage. . . . Once this revolution had occurred, the social status of women altered: man took over many of the sacred practices from which his sex had debarred him, and finally declared himself head of the household." Graves describes with disgust the progressive degradation of this patriarchal world, as it moved farther and farther from its matriarchal beginnings, and as the "female sense of orderliness" was replaced by "the restless and arbitrary male will." This "female sense of orderliness" seems a rationalization or secondary elaboration: usually Graves speaks, without any disguise, of "the cruel, capricious, incontinent White Goddess," and values above all things the prospect of being destroyed by her. *Though she slay me, yet will I trust in her* is his motto, almost; if one substitutes *if* and *then* for *though* and *yet*, the sentence exactly fits his attitude.

One sees both from *The White Goddess* and the lectures recently published in England that almost no poets seem "true poets" to Graves; most of the poets of the past belonged to the Apollonian or "Classical homosexual" tradition, and most modern poets have ceased "to make poetic, prosaic, or even pathological sense." Woman "is not a poet: she is either a Muse or she is nothing." (One of his poems to Laura Riding is dedicated "To the Sovereign Muse": of all the poets who erstwhile bore the name, he says, "none bore it clear, not one"; she is the first to do so.) A woman should "either be a silent Muse" or "she should be the Muse in a complete sense; she should be in turn Arianrhod, Blodenwedd and the Old Sow of Maenawr Penarrd who eats her farrow." For the poet "there is no other woman but Cerridwen and he desires one thing above all else in the world: her love. As Blodenwedd, she will gladly give him her love, but at only one price: his life. . . . Poetry began in the matriarchal age. . . . No poet can hope to understand the nature of poetry unless he has had a vision of the Naked King crucified to the lopped oak, and watched the dancers, red-eyed from the acrid smoke of the sacrificial fires, stamping out the measure of the dance, their bodies bent uncouthly forward; with a monotonous chant of 'Kill! kill! kill!' and 'Blood! blood! blood!' "

But the reader before now will have interrupted this summary of Graves's world picture with an impatient "Why repeat all this to me? It's an ordinary wish fantasy reinforced with extraordinary erudition—a kind of family romance projected upon the universe. Having the loved one the mother is the usual thing. Of course, some of the details of this Mother-Muse, female spider, are unusual: she always *has* to kill, so that she is called cruel, capricious, incontinent, and yet is worshipped for being so; she—but case histories always are unusual. Let's admit that it's an unusual, an extraordinary fantasy; still, why quote it to me?"

I quote it for two reasons:

(1) It is the fantastic theory that has accompanied a marvelous practice: some of the best poems of our time have been written as a result of this (I think it fair to say) objectively grotesque account of reality. If the Principle of Indeterminacy had been discovered as a result of Schrödinger or Heisenberg's theory that the universe is a capricious, intuitive Great Mother whose behavior must always rightfully disappoint the predictions of her prying son—*a fingering slave, / One that would peep and botanize / Upon his mother's grave*—the theory would have an extrinsic interest that it now lacks. Because of the poems it enabled Yeats to write, many of us read *A Vision*. That Graves's astonishing theories should be so necessary to him, so right and proper for him, that by means of them he could write "To Juan at the Winter Solstice," "Theseus and Ariadne," "The Sirens' Welcome to Cronos," is a thing worthy of our admiration and observation.

(2) Graves's theories, so astonishing in themselves, are—when we compare them with Graves's life and with psychoanalytical observation of lives in general, of the Unconscious, of children, neurotics, savages, myths, fairy tales—not astonishing at all, but logical and predictable; are so *natural* that we say with a tender smile, "Of course!" We see, or fancy that we see, why Graves believes them and why he is helped by believing them. Few poets have made better "pathological sense." I wish to try to explain these theories in terms of Graves's life; I shall try as far as possible to use Graves's own words.

In *Goodbye to All That* Graves cannot speak with enough emphasis of the difference between the side of him that is Graves and the side that is von Ranke. He writes with rather patronizing exactness of the Graveses, who are made to seem dry English eccentrics, excellent at puzzle solving, but writes with real warmth of the "goodness of heart" of his mother and the von Rankes; he seems to associate her idealism and *Gemütlichkeit*, her *Children, as your mother I command you* . . . with all that is spontaneous and emotional in his own nature—he has a heartfelt sentence telling "how much more I owe, as a writer, to my mother than to my father." His father was a poet. Graves writes: "I am glad in a way that my father was a poet. This at least saved me from any false reverence for poets. . . . Some of his songs I sing without prejudice; when washing up after meals or shelling peas or on similar occasions. He never once tried to teach me how to write, or showed any understanding of my serious work; he was always more ready to ask advice about his own work than to offer it for mine." Graves also says that "we children saw practically nothing of him except during the holidays." It is not difficult to see why, in Graves's myth of the world, it is a shadowy left-handed "blood-brother" or "other self," and not the father in his own form, against whom the hero struggles for the possession of the mother.

Graves's mother was forty, his father forty-nine, when he was born; she "was so busy running the household and conscientiously carrying out her obli-

gations as my father's wife that we did not see her
continuously"; he writes about his nurse: "In a practical way she came to be more to us than our mother. I
began to despise her at the age of twelve—she was
then nurse to my younger brothers—when I found
that my education was now in advance of hers, and
that if I struggled with her I was able to trip her up
and bruise her quite easily." Graves says that his religious training developed in him, as a child, "a great
capacity for fear (I was perpetually tortured by the
fear of hell), a superstitious conscience and a sexual
embarrassment." Graves's reading was "carefully
censored"; after two years of trench service he had
still been to the theater only twice, to children's
plays; his mother "allowed us no hint of its [hu-
manity's] dirtiness and intrigue and lustfulness, believing that innocence was the surest protection against
them." Two of his earlier memories seem particularly
important to him:

"And the headmaster had a little daughter with a
little girl friend, and I was in a sweat of terror whenever I met them; because, having no brothers, they
once tried to find out about male anatomy from me by
exploring down my shirt-neck when we were digging
up pig-nuts in the garden.

"Another frightening experience of this part of my
life was when I once had to wait in the school cloakroom for my sisters. . . . I waited about a quarter of
an hour in the corner of the cloakroom. I suppose I was
about ten years old, and hundreds and hundreds of girls
went to and fro, and they all looked at me and giggled

and whispered things to each other. I knew they hated me, because I was a boy sitting in the cloakroom of a girls' school, and when my sisters arrived they looked ashamed of me and quite different from the sisters I knew at home. I realized that I had blundered into a secret world, and for months and even years afterwards my worst nightmares were of this girls' school, which was filled with coloured toy balloons. 'Very Freudian,' as one says now.

"My normal impulses were set back for years by these two experiences. When I was about seventeen we spent our Christmas holidays in Brussels. An Irish girl stopping at the same *pension* made love to me in a way that I see now was really very sweet. I was so frightened I could have killed her.

"In English preparatory and public schools romance is necessarily homosexual. The opposite sex is despised and hated, treated as something obscene. Many boys never recover from this perversion. I only recovered by a shock at the age of twenty-one. For every born homosexual there are at least ten permanent pseudo-homosexuals made by the public school system. And nine of these ten are as honorably chaste and sentimental as I was."

His strained affection for Dick, a boy at his school, ended disastrously only after two years of military service. Graves went directly from what seemed to him the organized masculine nightmare of the public schools into the organized masculine nightmare of the First World War. He was an excellent soldier. His sense of professional tradition, of regimental loyalty,

was extreme ("we all agreed that regimental pride was
the greatest force that kept a battalion going as an
effective fighting unit, contrasting it particularly with
patriotism and religion"), but it led him only into
prolonged service at the front, murderous and routine
violence, wounds so serious that he was reported dead,
shell shock, neurosis, and an intense hatred for gov-
ernments, civilians, the whole established order of the
world. Jung says, in a sentence that might have been
written to apply specifically to Graves: "It is no light
matter to stand between a day-world of exploded
ideals and discredited values, and a night-world of apparently senseless fantasy. The weirdness of this
standpoint is in fact so great that there is nobody who
does not reach out for security, even though it be a
reaching back to the mother who shielded his childhood from the terrors of night."

When, on sick leave, he met a young artist, Nancy
Nicholson, Graves reached back. "Of course I also accepted the whole patriarchal system of things," he
writes. "It is difficult now to recall how completely I
believed in the natural supremacy of male over female. I never heard it even questioned until I met
Nancy, when I was about twenty-two, towards the
end of the war. *The surprising sense of ease* that I got
from her frank statement of equality between the
sexes was among my chief reasons for liking her.
. . . Nancy's crude summary: 'God is a man, so it
must be all rot,' *took a load off my shoulders*." [My
italics.]

Champagne was scarce at their wedding; "Nancy

said: 'Well, I'm going to get something out of this wedding, at any rate,' and grabbed a bottle. After three or four glasses she went off and changed into her land-girl's costume of breeches and smock. . . . The embarrassments of our wedding night were somewhat eased by an air-raid. . . . Nancy's mother was a far more important person to her than I was. . . . The most important thing to her was judicial equality of the sexes; she held that all the wrong in the world was caused by male domination and narrowness. She refused to see my experiences in the war as in any way comparable with the sufferings that millions of married women of the working-class went through. . . . Male stupidity and callousness became an obsession with her and she found it difficult not to include me in her universal condemnation of men.''

In country cottages; living from hand to mouth; ashamed of himself "as a drag on Nancy"; a friend, rather than a father, to Nancy's children; helping with the housework, taking care of the babies; so hauntedly neurotic that he saw ghosts at noon, couldn't use a telephone, couldn't see more than two new faces without lying awake all that night; writing child-poems or "country sentiment" poems to escape from his everyday reality, or else haunted nightmarish poems to express that everyday reality—so Graves spent the next six or eight years. (The keenest sense of the pathetic strangeness of that household comes to me when I read Graves's "I realized too that I had a new loyalty, to Nancy and the baby, tending to overshadow regimental loyalty now that the war was over.") "I had bad nights," Graves writes. "I thought that perhaps I owed it to Nancy to go to a psychiatrist to be cured; yet I was not sure. Somehow I thought that the power of writing poetry, which was more important than anything else I did, would disappear if I allowed myself to get cured; my *Pier-Glass* haunting would end and I would become a dull easy writer. It seemed to me less important to be well than to be a good poet. I also had a strong repugnance against allowing anyone to have the power over me that psychiatrists always seem to win over their patients." *Anyone*, here, means *any man*, I think; in the end Graves decided that he "would read the modern psychological books and apply them to my case," and "cure myself."

Their marriage, regretted by both husband and wife, ended after the two read an American poem and invited its author to come and live with them. Its author was a violent feminist, an original poet, a more than original thinker, and a personality of seductive and overmastering force. Judging from what Graves has written about her (in many poems, in some novels, and in his ecstatic epilogue to *Goodbye to All That*, in which he tells how he and she "went together to the land where the dead parade the streets and there met with demons and returned with the demons still treading behind us," speaks of the "salvation" that, through her, he has neared, and calls her a being essentially different from all others, a mystic savior "living invisibly, against kind, as dead, beyond event"), I believe that it is simplest to think of her as, so to speak, the White Goddess incarnate, the Mother-Muse in contemporary flesh. She seems to have had a radical influence on Graves's life, poetry, and opinions until 1939; and it was only after Graves was no longer in a position to be dominated by her in specific practice that he worked out his general theory of the necessary dominance of the White Goddess, the Mother-Muse, over all men, all poets.

Graves's theoretical picture of what life necessarily must be is so clearly related to what his life actually has been that it is possible to make summaries or outlines of the two, to put these outlines side by side, and to see that they match in every detail: this is what I have tried to do. (If the reader feels that he understands no better than before how and why Graves's world picture came into existence, either I have made very bad summaries or else I have deluded myself with an imaginary resemblance.) One does not need much of a psychoanalytical or anthropological background to see that Graves's world picture is a projection upon the universe of his own unconscious, of the compulsively repeated situation in which, alone, it is able to find satisfaction; or to see that this world picture is one familiar, in structure and in much detail, in the fantasies of children and neurotics, in dreams, in fairy tales, and, of course, in the myths and symbols of savages and of earlier cultures. Many details of case histories, much of Freud's theoretical analysis, are so specifically illuminating about Graves's myth that I would have quoted or summarized them here, if it had been possible to do so without extending this essay into a third issue of the *Review*. That all affect, libido, mana should be concentrated in this one figure of the Mother-Muse; that love and sexuality should be inseparably intermingled with fear, violence, destruction in this "female spider"—that the loved one should be, necessarily, the Bad Mother who, necessarily, deserts and destroys the child; that the child should permit against her no conscious aggression of any kind, and intend his *cruel, capricious, incontinent*, his *bitch, vixen, hag*, to be neither condemnation nor invective, but only fascinated description of the loved and worshipped Mother and Goddess, She-Who-Must-Be-Obeyed—all this is very interesting and very unoriginal. One encounters a rigorous, profound, and quite unparalleled understanding of such cases as Graves's in the many volumes of Freud; but one can read an excellent empirical, schematic description of them in Volume VII of Jung's *Collected Works*, in the second part of the essay entitled "The Relations between the Ego and the Unconscious." Anyone familiar with what Jung has written about the *persona* and *anima*, and what happens when a man projects this *anima* upon the world and identifies himself with it, will more than once give a laugh of astonished recognition as he goes through *The White Goddess*.

The double-natured Graves has continually written about this split in himself—thought of it, once, as the poet's necessary condition: "I regarded poetry as, first, a personal cathartic for the poet suffering from some inner conflict, and then as a cathartic for readers in a similar conflict." One side of Robert Graves was—

and is—the Graves or Father-of-the-Regiment side: the dry, matter-of-fact, potboiling, puzzle-solving, stamp-collecting, "anti-sentimental to the point of insolence" side, which notes, counts, orders, explains, explains away, which removes all affect from the world and replaces it by professional technique, pigeonholing, logic chopping. When this side is haunted or possessed by the childish, womanly, disorderly, emotional nightside of things, by the irresistible or inconsequential Unconscious—when the *dusty-featured Lollocks, by sloth on sorrow fathered, play hide and seek* among the *unanswered letters, empty medicine bottles* of *disordered drawers; plague little children* who cannot sleep; *are nasty together in the bed's shadow*, when *the imbecile aged are overlong in dying;* are invisible to, denied by, the men they torment; are visible to women, *naughty wives* who *slyly allow them* to lick their *honey-sticky fingers*—when all this happens, the dry masculine Ego can protect itself from them only by *hard broom and soft broom, / To well comb the hair, / To well brush the shoe, / And to pay every debt / So soon as it's due.* These measures—so Graves says—are *sovereign against Lollocks.*

And so they are, much of the day, a little of the night; that they are ever sovereign against "the Mother of All Living, the ancient power of fright and lust—the female spider or the queen-bee whose embrace is death," I doubt. The whole Tory, saddle-soap, regimental-song-singing side of Graves can only drug, quiet temporarily, disregard as long as routine and common sense have power, the demands, manifestations, and existence of Graves's other side, the side that says: "Oh, *him!* He's just something I fool people with in the daytime."

Yet we should be foolish to believe its remark—to insist, with Graves's unconscious, that the male principle is without all affect, libido, mana. (We can see from Graves's early life, from his public-school experiences, why it is necessary for *him* to insist that this is so.) It would be equally foolish to believe that the White Goddess does not exist: she is as real as the Unconscious which she inhabits and from which she has been projected, first upon actual women and later upon the universe. (A car's headlights can rest upon a deer until the deer moves away, but then the beam of light goes out to the sky beyond.) The usefulness of this projection, the therapeutic value of Graves's myth, is obvious: it has been able to bring into efficient and fairly amiable symbiosis the antagonistic halves of his nature.

Graves understands men far better than he understands women; has taken as his own *persona* or mask or life style the terse, professional, matter-of-fact, learned Head of the Regiment—Colonel Ben Jonson of the Royal Welch Fusiliers, so to speak. Men are as dry and as known to him as his own Ego; women are as unknown, and therefore as all-powerful and as all-attractive, as his own Id. Salvation, Graves has to believe, comes through Woman alone; regimented masculinity can work only for, by means of, everyday routine, unless it is *put into the service of Woman.*

Graves is willing to have the Ego do anything for the Id except notice that it *is* the Id, analyze it, explain it as subjective necessity; instead the Ego completely accepts the Id and then, most ingeniously and logically and disingenuously, works out an endless explanation of, justification for, every aspect of what it insists is objective necessity. (All of Graves's readers must have felt: "Here is a man who can explain anything.") Graves's Ego can dismiss any rebellion against the reign of Woman with a hearty matter-of-fact—next to the White Goddess, matter-of-factness is the most important thing in the world to Graves—"Nonsense! nonsense!"; can dryly, grotesquely, and cruelly satirize those who rebel; can pigeonhole them, explain them, explain them away—and all in the service of the Mother! No wonder that the once-torn-in-two Graves becomes sure, calm, unquestioning; lives in the satisfied certainty that he is right, and the world wrong, about anything, anything! He has become, so to speak, his own Laura Riding. *There is only one Goddess, and Graves is her prophet*—and isn't the prophet of the White Goddess the nearest thing to the White Goddess?

If you break your neck every time you climb over a stile, soon you will be saying that the necessary condition of all men is to break, not rib, not thigh, not arm, not shin, but always, without fail, THE NECK when climbing over stiles; by making the accidental circumstances of your life the necessary conditions of all lives, you have transformed yourself from an accident-prone analysand into an emblematic Oedipus.

Instead of going on thinking of himself, with shaky hope, as an abnormal eccentric, a "spiritual Quixote" better than the world, perhaps, in his own queer way, Graves now can think of himself as representing the norm, as being the one surviving citizen of that original matriarchal, normal state from which the abnormal, eccentric world has departed. The Mother whom he once clung to in personal shame ("childishly / I dart to Mother-skirts of love and peace / To play with toys until those horrors leave me")—what will the Fathers of the Regiment say?—turns out to be, as he can show with impersonal historical objectivity, the "real" Father of the Regiment: the Father-Principle, if you trace it back far enough, is really the Mother-Principle, and has inherited from the Primal Mother what legitimacy it has. Graves wants all ends to be Woman, and Man no more than the means to them. Everything has an original matriarchal core; all Life (and all "good" Death) comes from Woman. Authority is extremely important to Graves: by means of his myth he is able to get rid of the dry, lifeless, external authority of the father, the public school, the regiment, and to replace it with the wet, live, internal authority of the mother. All that is finally important to Graves is condensed in the one figure of the Mother-Mistress-Muse, she who creates, nourishes, seduces, destroys; she who saves us—or, as good as saving, destroys us—as long as we love her, write poems to her, submit to her without question, use all our professional, Regimental, masculine qualities in her service. Death is swallowed up in victory, said

111

St. Paul; for Graves Life, Death, everything that exists is swallowed up in the White Goddess.

Graves's poems will certainly seem to the reader, as they seem to me, a great deal more interesting than any explanation of their origin. This account is no more than a sketch: the psychoanalytically or anthropologically minded reader will find in the poems, in *Goodbye to All That*, in *The White Goddess*, many things that I should have liked to discuss, many that I should have liked to understand. Because of the White Goddess, some of the most beautiful poems of our time have come into existence. But our gratitude to her need not stop there: as we read Graves's account of her we can say to ourselves, "We *are* the ancients," for it furnishes an almost incomparably beautiful illustration of the truth of Freud's "The power of creating myths is not extinct, but still produces in the neuroses the same psychical products as in the most ancient times."

Changes of Attitude and

Rhetoric in Auden's Poetry

We never step twice into the same Auden.—Heraclitus

IN THE FIRST PART of this article I want to analyze
the general position Auden makes for himself in
his early poems, and to show how the very different
attitude of the later poems developed from it; in the
second part I shall describe the language of the early
poems and the rhetoric of the late, and try to show why
one developed from the other. I have borrowed several
terms from an extremely good book—Kenneth Burke's
Attitudes toward History—and I should like to make
acknowledgments for them.

I

THE DATE IS *c.* 1930, the place England. Auden (and
the group of friends with whom he identifies himself)
is unable or unwilling to accept the values and authority, the general world picture of the late-capitalist society in which he finds himself. He is conscious of a

profound alienation, intellectual, moral, and aesthetic
—financial and sexual, even. Since he rejects the established order, it is necessary for him to find or make a
new order, a myth by which he and his can possess
the world. Auden synthesizes (more or less as the
digestive organs synthesize enzymes) his own order
from a number of sources: (1) Marx—Communism
in general. (2) Freud and Groddeck: in general, the
risky and nonscientific, but fertile and imaginative,
side of modern psychology. (3) A cluster of related
sources: the folk, the blood, intuition, religion and
mysticism, fairy tales, parables, and so forth—this
group includes a number of semi-Fascist elements. (4)
The sciences, biology particularly: these seem to be
available to him because they have been only partially assimilated by capitalist culture, and because,
like mathematics, they are practically incapable of being corrupted by it. (5) All sorts of boyish sources of
value: flying, polar exploration, mountain climbing,
fighting, the thrilling side of science, public-school
life, sports, big-scale practical jokes, "the spies' career," etc. (6) Homosexuality: if the ordinary sexual values are taken as negative and rejected, this can
be accepted as a source of positive revolutionary
values.

Auden is able to set up a We (whom he identifies
himself with—rejection loves company) in opposition
to the enemy They; neither We nor They are the
relatively distinct or simple entities one finds in political or economic analyses, but are tremendous clusters
of elements derived from almost every source: Auden

is interested in establishing a dichotomy in which one side, naturally, gets all the worst of it, and he wants this *all the worst* to be as complete as possible, to cover everything from imperialism to underlining too many words in letters. A reader may be indifferent to some or most of Their bad points, but They are given so many that even the most confirmed ostrich will at some point break down and consent to Auden's rejection. Auden wants a total war, a total victory; he does not make the political mistake of taking over a clear limited position and leaving to the enemy everything else. Sometimes his aptitude for giving all he likes to Us, all he doesn't like to Them, passes over from ingenuity into positive genius—or disingenuousness. I am going to treat this We-They opposition at the greatest length—a treatment of it is practically a treatment of Auden's early position; and I shall mix in some discussion of the sources of value I have listed.

Auden begins: The death of the old order is inevitable; it is already economically unsound, morally corrupt, intellectually bankrupt, and so forth. We=the Future, They=the Past. (So any reader tends to string along with Us and that perpetual winner, the Future.) Auden gets this from Marxism, of course; but never at any time was he a thorough Marxist: it would have meant giving up too much to the enemy. He keeps all sorts of things a Marxist rejects, and some of his most cherished doctrines—as the reader will see—are in direct contradiction to his Marxism. At the ultimate compulsive level of belief most of his Marxism drops away (and, in the last few years, *has* dropped away); his psychoanalytical, vaguely medical beliefs are so much more essential to Auden—"son of a nurse and doctor, loaned a dream" —that the fables he may have wanted to make Marxist always turn out to be psychoanalytical. But Marxism as a source of energy, of active and tragic insight, was invaluable; it was badly needed to counteract the passivity, the trust in Understanding and Love and God, that are endemic in Auden. Marxism has always supplied most of the terror in his poetry; in his latest poems all that remains is the pity—an invalid's diet, like milk toast.

Obviously They represent Business, Industrialism, Exploitation—and, worse than that, a failing business, an industrialism whose machines are already rusting. Auden had seen what happened to England during a long depression, and he made a romantic and beautifully effective extension of this, not merely into decadence, but into an actual breakdown of the whole machinery, a Wellsish state where commerce and transportation have gone to pieces, where the ships lie "long high and dry," where no one goes "further than railhead or the end of pier," where the professional traveler "asked at fireside . . . is dumb." The finest of these poems is XXV in *Poems:* history before the event, one's susceptible and extravagant heart tells one. (Incidentally, this vision is entirely non-Marxist.) Here Auden finds a symbol whose variants are obsessive for him, reasonably so for the reader, another machine's child: *grass-grown pitbank, abandoned seam, the silted harbors, derelict works*—these, and the wires that carry nothing, the rails over which no one comes, are completely moving to Auden, a boy who wanted to be a mining engineer, who "Loved a pumping-engine, / Thought it every bit as / Beautiful as you." The thought of those "beautiful machines that never talked / But let the small boy worship them," abandoned and rusting in the wet countryside—the early Auden sees even his machines in rural surroundings—was perhaps, unconsciously, quite as influential as some political or humanitarian considerations.

Auden relates science to Marxism in an unexpected but perfectly orthodox way: Lenin says somewhere that in the most general sense Marxism is a theory of evolution. Auden quite consciously makes this connection; evolution, as a source both of insight and image, is always just at the back of his earliest poems. (This, along with his countryishness—Auden began by writing poetry like Hardy and Thomas—explains his endless procession of birds and beasts, symbols hardly an early poem is without.) IV in *Poems* is nothing but an account of evolution—by some neo-Hardyish *I* behind it—and a rather Marxist extension of it into man's history and everyday life. The critical points where quantity changes into quality, the Hegelian dialectic, what Burke calls neo-Malthusian limits—all these are plain in the poem. There are many examples of this coalition of Marxism and biology; probably the prettiest is IX, a poem with the refrain, "Here am I, here are you: / But what does it mean? What are we going to do?" The *I* of the poem is supposed to be anonymous and typical, a lay figure of late capitalism; he has not retained even the dignity of rhetoric, but speaks in a style that is an odd blank parody of popular songs. He has finally arrived at the end of his blind alley: he has a wife, a car, a mother complex, a vacation, and no use or desire for any. All he can make himself ask for is some fresh tea, some rugs—this to remind you of Auden's favorite view of capitalism: a society where everyone is sick. Even his instincts have broken down: he doesn't want to go to bed with Honey, all the wires to the base in his spine are severed. The poem develops in this way up to the next to the last stanza: "In my veins there is a wish, / And a memory of fish: / When I lie crying on the floor, / It says, 'You've often done this before.' " The "wish" in the blood is the evolutionary will, the blind urge of the species to assimilate the universe. He remembers the fish, that at a similar impasse, a similar critical point, changed over to land, a new form of being. Here for the millionth time (the racial memory tells the weeping individual) is the place where the contradiction has to be resolved; where the old answer, useless now, has to be transcended; where all the quantitative changes are over, where the qualitative leap has to occur. The individual remembers all these critical points because he is the product of them. And the individual, in the last stanza, is given a complete doom ("I've come a very long way to prove / No land, no water, and no love"). But his bankruptcy and liquidation are taken as inevitable for the species, a necessary mode of progression: the destructive interregnum between the old form and the new is inescapable, as old

as life. The strategic value in Auden's joining of
Marxism and evolution, his constant shifting of terms
from one sphere to the other, is this: the reader will
tend to accept the desired political and economic
changes (and the form of these) as themselves inevitable, something it is as ludicrous or pathetic to
resist as evolution.

When compared with the folkish Us, They are
complicated, subtle in a barren Alexandrian-encyclo-
pedia way. They are scholarly introspective observ-
ers, We have the insight and natural certainty of the
naïve, of Christ's children, of fools, of the third sons in
fairy stories. They are aridly commercial, financial,
distributive; We represent real production, the soil.
They are bourgeois-respectable or perverted; We are
folk-simple, or else consciously Bohemian so as to
break up Their system and morale—there is also a
suggestion of the prodigal son, of being reborn
through sin. They represent the sterile city, We the
fertile country; I want to emphasize this, the surprisingly *rural* character of most of Auden's earliest
poems, because so far as I know everyone has empha-
sized the opposite. They are white-collar workers,
executives, or idlers—those who neither "make" nor
"do"; We are scientists, explorers, farmers, manual
laborers, aviators, fighters and conspirators—the real
makers and doers. Auden gets Science over on Our side
by his constant use of it both for insight and images,
by his admiration of, preoccupation with, the fertile
adventurous side of it; he leaves Them only the dec-

adent complexity of Jeans or "psychological" economics.

Since Auden has had to reject Tradition, he sets up a new tradition formed of the available elements (available because rejected, neglected, or misinterpreted) of the old. There are hundreds of examples of this process (particularly when it comes to appropriating old writers as Our ancestors); the process is necessary partly to reassure oneself, partly to reassure one's readers, who otherwise would have to reject Our position because accepting it necessitates rejecting too much else. One can see this working even in the form of Auden's early poetry: in all the Anglo-Saxon imitation; the Skeltonics; the Hopkins accentual verse, alliteration, assonance, consonance; the Owens rhymes; the use of the fairy story, parable, ballad, popular song— the folk tradition They have rejected or collected in Childs. Thus Auden has selected his own ancestors, made from the disliked or misprized his own tradition.

In *The Orators* Auden shows, by means of the regular Mendelian inheritance chart, that one's "true ancestor" may be neither a father nor a mother, but an uncle. (His true ancestor wasn't the Tradition, but the particular elements of it most like himself.) This concept is extremely useful to Auden in (1) family, (2) religious, and (3) political relations. (1) By this means he acquires a different and active type of family relationship to set up against the inertia of the ordinary bourgeois womanized family. (2) God is addressed and thought of as Uncle instead of Father: God as Uncle will help revolutionary Us just as naturally and appropriately as God as Father would help his legitimate sons, the Enemy. This Uncle has a Christlike sacrificial-hero representative on earth, who is surrounded with a great deal of early-Christian, secret-service paraphernalia. This hero is confused or identified with (3) the political leader, a notably un-political sort of fantasy Hitler, who seems to have strayed into politics with his worshippers only because he lives in an unreligious age. There is hardly more politics in early Auden than in G. A. Henty; what one gets is mostly religion, hero worship, and Ad-venture, combined with the odd Lawrence-Nazi folk mysticism that serves as a false front for the real politics behind it—which Auden doesn't treat.

When Auden occasionally prays to this Uncle he asks in blunt definite language for definite things: it is a personal, concrete affair. In his later poetry Auden is always praying or exhorting, but only to some abstract eclectic Something-or-Other, who is asked in vague exalted language for vague exalted abstractions. Once Auden wanted evils removed by revolutionary action, and he warned (*it is later than you think*). Today—when he is all ends and no means, and sees everything in the long run—he exhorts (*we all know how late it is, but with Love and Understanding it is not too late for us to* . . .) or prays (*Thou knowest —O save us!*). Most of this belongs to the bad half of what Burke calls secular prayer: the attempt, inside any system, to pray away, exhort away, legislate away evils that are not incidental but essential to the system. Auden used to satirize the whole "change of heart" point of view; "do not speak of a change of heart," he warned. He had a deceived chorus sing vacantly: "Revolutionary worker / I get what you (The reactionary intellectual's immediate revulsion within." He came to scoff, he remained to pray: for a general moral improvement, a spiritual rebirth, Love. Remembering some of the incredible conclusions to the later poems—*Life must live*, Auden's wish to *lift an affirming flame*—the reader may object that this sort of thing is sentimental idealism. But sentimental idealism is a necessity for someone who, after rejecting a system as evil, finally accepts it—even with all the moral reservations and exhortations possible. The sentimentality and idealism, the vague abstraction of such prayers and exhortations, is a *sine qua non:* we can fool ourselves into praying for some vague general change of heart that is going to produce, automatically, all the specific changes that even we could never be foolish enough to pray for. When Auden prays for anything specific at all; when he prays against the organization of the world that makes impossible the moral and spiritual changes he prays for, it will be possible to take the prayer as something more than conscience- and face-saving sublimation, a device ideally suited to make action un-urgent and its nature vague.

Swift believed—to quote Empson—that "everything spiritual and valuable has a gross and revolting parody, very similar to it, with the same name." Similarly, everything spiritual and valuable has a sentimental idealistic parody; and—by a horrible variant of Gresham's law—this parody replaces it with stupid people, discredits it with cleverer people. (The reactionary intellectual's immediate revulsion toward anything that even smells of "progress" or "humanitarianism" is an example of the operation of this law.) Auden's desire to get away from the negativism typical of so much modernist poetry has managed to make the worst sections of his latest lyrics not much more than well-meaning gush. These sentimental parodies are far more dangerous than any gross ones could possibly be. If we have wicked things to say, and say them badly, not even the Girl Guides are injured; but if we say badly what is "spiritual and valuable," we not only spoil it, but help to replace or discredit the already expressed good that we wish to preserve. Let me quote Auden against himself: "And what was livelihood / Is tallness, strongness / Words and longness, / All glory and all story / Solemn and not so good."

Just how did Auden manage to change from almost Communist to quite liberal? He did *not* switch over under stress of circumstance; long before any circumstances developed he was making his Progress by way of an old and odd route: mysticism. In Auden's middle period one finds a growing preoccupation with a familiar cluster of ideas: All power corrupts; absolute power corrupts absolutely. Government, a necessary evil, destroys the governors. All action is evil; the will is evil; life itself is evil. The only escape lies in the avoidance of action, the abnegation of the will. I don't mean that Auden wholly or practically accepted all this—who does? But he was more or less fascinated by such ideas (completely opposed to Marxism; fairly congenial with a loose extension of psychoanalysis), and *used* them: If all government is evil, why should we put our trust in, die for, a choice of evils? If all action is evil, how can we put our faith in doing anything? If the will itself is evil, why select, plan, do? Life is evil; surely the contemplation of ideal ends is better than the willing and doing of the particular, so-often-evil means.

The reader may object that the method of change I suggest is too crude. But let me quote against him the changer: "The windiest militant trash / Important Persons shout / Is not so crude as our wish. . . ." What is the mechanism of most changes of attitude?—the search for any reasons that will justify our believing what it has become necessary for us to believe. How many of us can keep from chorusing with Bolingbroke, *God knows, my son, by what bypaths and indirect crook'd ways I met this*—position? Marxism was too narrow, tough, and materialistic for the Essential Auden, who would far rather look dark with Heraclitus than laugh with Democritus. Auden's disposition itself (Isherwood says that if Auden had his way their plays would be nothing but choruses of angels); the fact that he was never a consistent or orthodox Marxist; the constant pressure of a whole society against any dangerous heresy inside it; Auden's strong "medical" inclinations, his fundamental picture of society as diseased, willing itself to be diseased (a case to be sympathized with, treated, and talked to *à*

la Groddeck) ; his increasing interest in metaphysics
and religion; the short-range defeatism, the compensa-
tory long-range optimism that kept growing during
the interminable defeat of the thirties—these, and
more, made Auden's change inevitable.

But let me return to We and They, the early
Auden. We are Love; They are hate and all the terrible perversions of love. There is an odd ambivalent
attitude toward homosexuality: in Us it is a quite
natural relationship shading off into comradeship (like
Greek homosexuality in Naomi Mitchison), in Them it
is just another decadent perversion. The reader can see
this plainly in *The Dog beneath the Skin:* the Cozy
Corner, where Jimmy "sent them crazy in his thick
white socks," belongs to Them; We have the vague
virtuous relationship between Alan and Francis, which
the reader rates very high, since he is forced to compare it with Alan's relations with Miss Iris Crewe and
Miss Lou Vipond. Such cultural homosexuality is an
alienation more or less forced upon certain groups of
Auden's society by the form of their education and
the nature of their social and financial conditions.
Where the members of a class and a sex are taught, in
a prolonged narcissistic isolation, to hero-worship
themselves—class and sex; where—to a different class
—unemployment is normal, where one's pay is inadequate or impossible for more than one; where
children are expensive liabilities instead of assets;
where women are business competitors; where most
social relationships have become as abstract, individu-
alistic, and mobile as the relations of the labor market,

homosexuality is a welcome asset to the state, one of the cheapest and least dangerous forms of revolution. One gets no such analysis in the early Auden, though a real uneasiness about Our condition is plain in the allegorical *Letter to a Wound*, implicit in the Airman's kleptomania. A contempt for women sometimes breaks out in little half-sublimated forms; "there is something peculiarly horrible about the idea of women pilots," writes the Airman, whose love for E. has not managed to give him any prejudice in her sex's favor. Sometimes this contempt is openly expressed. "All of the women and most of the men / Shall work with their hands and not think again" is the early Auden's lyrical premonition of the ideal State of the future. Words fail me here; this is not tactics, not sense, and certainly not Marxism: compare Engels's contempt at Dühring's ingenuous belief that the Ideal State would have professional porters. All this is related to a Lawrence–Hitler–*Golden Bough* folk mysticism— complete with Führer, folk, blood, intuition, "the carved stone under the oak-tree"—which crops up constantly; it is partly literary, partly real. What is wrong with it is too plain to say; what is right about it—the insistence on a real society, the dislike of the weird isolation and individualism, the helpless rejection, forced on so many of the members of our own society—may be worth mentioning. Auden has forgotten the good with the bad, and now takes the isolation of the individual—something that would have seemed impossible to almost any other society, that is a tragic perversion of ours—as necessary, an absolute that can only be accepted.

We are health, They are disease; everything Auden gets from Freud and Groddeck is used to put Them into the category of patients, of diseased sufferers who unconsciously will their own disease. This makes Our opposition not only good for Them but necessary—Our violence is the surgeon's violence, Their opposition is the opposition of madmen to psychiatrists. We are Life, They are Death. The death wish is the fundamental motive for all Their actions, Auden often says or implies; if They deny it, he retorts, "Naturally you're not *conscious* of it."

These earliest poems are soaked in Death : as the real violence of revolutionary action and as a very comprehensive symbol. Death is Their necessary and desired conclusion; often poems are written from Their increasingly desperate point of view. Death belongs to Us as martyrs, spies, explorers, tragic heroes—with a suggestion of scapegoat or criminal—who die for the people. It belongs to Us because We, Their negation, have been corrupted by Them, and must ourselves be transcended. But, most of all, it is a symbol for *rebirth:* it is only through death that We can leave the old for good, be finally reborn. I have been astonished to see how consistently most of the important elements of ritual (purification, rebirth, identification, etc.) are found in the early poems; their use often seems unconscious. The most common purification rituals (except that of purification by fire) are plain. There is purification through decay :

physical and spiritual, the rotting away of the machines and the diseased perversions of the men. There are constant glaciers, ice, northern exploration— enough to have made Cleanth Brooks consider the fundamental metaphorical picture of the early poems that of a new ice age. There is purification by water: in the second poem in *On This Island* a sustained flood metaphor shifts into parent-child imagery. There is some suggestion of purification through sin. There is mountain climbing: from these cold heights one can see differently, free of the old perspectives; one returns, like Moses, with new insights. This is akin to the constantly used parable of the fairy-tale search, the hero's dangerous labors or journey. And the idea of rebirth is plainest of all, extending even to the common images of ontogenetic or phylogenetic development; of the fetus, newborn infant, or child; of the discontinuities of growth. The *uncle* is so important because he is a new ancestor whom We can identify ourselves with (Auden recommends "ancestor worship" of the true ancestor, the Uncle); by this identification We destroy our real parents, our Enemy ancestry, thus finally abolishing any remaining traces of Them in us. These ideas and their extensions are worth tracing in detail, if one had the space. Here is a quotation in which rebirth through death is extremely explicit; seasonal rebirth and the womb of the new order are packed in also. Auden writes that love

> Needs death, death of the grain, our death,
> Death of the old gang; would leave them
> In sullen valley where is made no friend,

> The old gang to be forgotten in the spring,
> The hard bitch and the riding-master,
> Stiff underground; deep in clear lake
> The lolling bridegroom, beautiful, there.

I want my treatment of Auden's early position to be suggestive rather than exhausting, so I shall not carry it any further; though I hate to stop short of all the comic traits Auden gives the Enemy, wretched peculiarities as trivial as saying *I mean* or having a room called the Den. The reader can do his own extending or filling in by means of a little unusually attractive reading: Auden's early poems. My own evaluation of Auden's changes in position has been fairly plain in my discussion. There are some good things and some fantastic ones in Auden's early attitude; if the reader calls it a muddle I shall acquiesce, with the remark that the later position might be considered a more rarefied muddle. But poets rather specialize in muddles—and I have no doubt which of the muddles was better for Auden's poetry: one was fertile and usable, the other decidedly is not. Auden sometimes seems to be saying with Henry Clay, "I had rather be right than poetry"; but I am not sure, then, that he is either.

I I

IN CONSIDERING Auden's earliest poems one finds little to say about peculiar kinds of rhetoric, but a great deal to say about a peculiar language. (The opposite is true of the late poems.) One sees how effec-

tive the best of the early poems are—how concrete,
startling, and thoroughly realized their texture is; but
one finds, on analysis, that they are astonishingly
unrhetorical, that the tough magical effects that en-
chant one are not being accomplished by any elaborate rhetoric, but by a great variety of causes, the
most noticeable of which is the language—a concrete,
laconic, and eccentric variant of ordinary English. (It
is derived, probably, from the extension of certain
tendencies in Hopkins, Joyce, and Anglo-Saxon.)
Even when Auden is not using this private language,
his regular speech is tougher and terser because of it. I
offer a list of some of its more important characteristics: (1) The frequent omission of articles and demon-
strative adjectives. (2) The frequent omission of subjects—especially *I, you, he,* etc. (3) The frequent
omission of *there* and similar introductory words. (4)
The frequent omission of coordinate conjunctions, sub-
ordinating conjunctions, conjunctive adverbs, etc.
Even prepositions are sometimes omitted. (5) The
frequent omission of relative pronouns. (6) The frequent omission of auxiliary verbs. (7) Constant inversion, consciously effective changes of the usual
word order. (8) Unusual punctuation: a decided
underpunctuation is common. (9) To denote habitual
action, verbals are regularly preferred to nouns.
(10) The scarcity of adverbs, adjectives, or any
words that can possibly be dispensed with. On the
other hand, there are enormous numbers of verbs,
verbals, and nouns. The result is a very strong speech.
(11) Constant parataxis, often ungrammatical. In

these poems Auden is willing to stretch or break most rules of grammar or syntax. (12) The use of dangling participles and other dangling modifiers. (13) A sort of portmanteau construction—common to the Elizabethans—in which a qualifying phrase may refer both to what comes before and to what comes after. (14) Repetition or partial repetition of words; this is allied to the use of like-sounding or similarly constructed words. (15) The use of absolute constructions. (16) The constant use of alliteration, assonance, consonance, etc. (17) The use of normally uncoordinate elements as coordinates. (18) The use of unusual or unusually abrupt appositions. (19) The occasional use of archaic words or constructions. (20) Frequent ambiguity—usually effective, sometimes merely confusing. (21) Constant ellipses, sometimes enormous ones; similarly, there are frequent jumps in logic where one must make out a meaning without much help from the syntax. (22) The use of very long parallel constructions, generally elliptical; the elements may even be separated by periods. (23) The wide (sometimes very wide) separation of modifiers from what they modify. (24) The use of a homogeneous and somewhat specialized vocabulary. (25) The use of one part of speech for another: adjective for adverb, adverb for adjective, verb or preposition for noun, etc. (26) The insertion into a sentence of elements which have no orthodox syntactical relationship to any part of the sentence.

These are most of the more important characteristics. It is a list that obviously gives the reader no idea of the effect or value of the language; I hope that he will look up examples and minor characteristics himself—I have no space for them, nor for any thorough evaluation of the language and its effects. It seems to me generally successful; at its best, magnificent. It is easy to condemn it as an eccentric limitation of language; I am going to defend it as a creative extension. One can show, I think, that much of the early poems' strength and goodness—often original enough to seem positively magical—exist because of this language or because of its effect on Auden's regular language, and could not have been attained otherwise. The language fits what he has to say (or generates new and fitting things to say). It is original, not merely odd; it is "constructive," not merely *Transition* breaking-of-rules for breaking-of-rules' sake. Let me invoke for it the protecting aegis of the Elizabethans. (If the language of the early poems is unfamiliar to the reader, I beg him not to make any judgments on these remarks merely from my list of characteristics.)

In Auden's later poems the language becomes weaker. It is relatively passive and abstract; full of adverbs, adjectives, intransitive verbs, it seems pale and feeble by the side of his magnificently verb-y early speech. But the rhetoric becomes stronger. In the late poems there is a system of rhetorical devices so elaborate that Auden might list it under *Assets*, just as a firm lists its patents. I shall analyze a good many of these devices; and I shall sometimes give a good many examples of them, since I need to show that they are typical, and since I want the reader to appreciate the full weight and range of their use.

How much the texture of poetry depends on the poet's extreme sensitivity to different levels or ranges of words, to the juxtaposition, sometimes shocking and sometimes almost imperceptible, of words from different universes or way stations of discourse, can hardly be exaggerated; though if it can, reading Auden is the way to do it. Everyone recognizes such extreme cases as the Elizabethans' *gross and full of bread* formula and the Orators' Favorite—the insertion of a concrete word in an abstract context; but many of the nicer cases go unpraised and unanalyzed, though not unfelt. One of Auden's most thoroughly exploited rhetorical formulas (rhetoricians ought to distinguish it with his name) is an inversion of the Orators' Favorite: a surprisingly abstract word is put into a concrete "poetic" context—in general, unexpectedly abstract critical "nonpoetic" words, taken from relatively abstract technical "nonpoetic" universes of discourse, are substituted for their expected and concrete sisters. The consistent use of this device is one of the things that has got Auden's poetry attacked as relaxed or abstract. The device, like its opposite, is a variety of Effect by Incongruity. Here are some examples—a few from many; most of them will be rather obvious, since the less obvious depend too much on a largish context or established tone to be convenient for quotation:

The beauty's set cosmopolitan smile; love's fascinating biased hand; the baroque frontiers, the surrealist police; the shining neutral summer; the tree's clandestine tide; a new imprudent year; the small uncritical islands; and the indigenous figure on horseback / On the bridle-path down by the lake; the genteel dragon; the rare ambiguous monster; the luscious lateral blossoming of woe; weep the non-attached angels; their whorled unsubtle ears; the first voluptuous rectal sins; the band / Makes its tremendous statements; the hot incurious sun; and so on. In one stanza occur *the effusive welcome of the piers, the luxuriant life of the steep stone valleys,* and *the undiscriminating sea.* These last three are not very effective; I chose them to show how the method can degenerate into abstraction. The reader will have noticed that this device is often an inversion of the *gross and full of bread* formula, with the *and* omitted.

This sort of thing is not Auden's discovery, any more than accentual verse was Hopkins's; but its bureaucratization, its systematic use as a major principle of rhetoric, is new, I think. It is the opposite of poetic diction, where the abstract is thought of as the necessary and proper language of poetry; here the effect depends on the opposite idea, on the fact that the context of the poem (*ground* in relation to the expression's *figure*) is still concrete.

Another of Auden's usual formulas is the *juxtaposition of disparate coordinates:* this includes the Elizabethan adjective-formula and the extension of it to three or four not regularly coordinate terms. One finds many examples of the first (or of its common Shakespearean application to two nouns) : *remote and hooded; nude and fabulous epochs; your unique and*

*moping station; the noise and policies of summer;
dumb and voilet; deaf to prophecy or China's drum;
the flutes and laughter of the happily diverted; the
stoves and resignations of the frozen plains.* Here are
some examples of the second: *the enchanted, the
world, the sad;* (spoken of the sea) *the citiless, the
corroding, the sorrow; the friend, the rash, the
enemy / The essayist, the able; cold, impossible,
ahead; the melting friend, the aqueduct, the flower;
an illness, a beard, Arabia found in a bed, / Nanny
defeated, money; were they or he / The physician,
bridegroom, and incendiary?* See how beautifully a
variation of the device can describe Civilization As We
Know It:

> Certainly our city—with the byres of poverty down to
> The river's edge, the cathedral, the engines, the dogs;
>> Here is the cosmopolitan cooking
>> And the light alloys and the glass. . . .

When Auden began to use the capitalized personified abstraction, he was extremely conscious of what
he was doing, and meant for the reader to realize that:
the use is different and exciting, a virtuoso performance meant to make the reader exclaim, "Why, he
got away with it after all." One finds such things as
*ga-ga Falsehood; Scandal praying with her sharp
knees up; Lust . . . muttering to his fuses in a tunnel, "Could I meet here with Love, / I would hug him
to death."* But Auden was like someone who keeps
showing how well he can hold his liquor until he becomes a drunkard. At first he made all sorts of in-

genious variations: he made capitalized personified abstractions out of verbs, adverbs, pronouns, or whole phrases. But at last even his ingenuity disappears; he is like a man who will drink canned heat, rubbing alcohol, anything. There is a thirteen-line menagerie where I Will, I Know, I Am, I Have Not, and I Am Loved peer idiotically from behind their bars; nearby, gobbling peanuts, throng the Brothered-One, the Not-Alone, the Just, the Happy-Go-Lucky, the Filthy, hundreds of We's and They's and Their's and Our's and Me's, the Terrible Demon, the Lost People, the Great, the Old Masters, and the Unexpected; they feel Love and Hate and Lust and Things; above them hover all sorts of tutelary deities: the Present, the Past, the Future, the Just City, the Good Place, Fate, Pride, Charity, Success, Knowledge, Wisdom, Violence, Life and Art and Salvation and Matter and the Nightmare, Form, the State, Democracy, Authority, Duality, Business, Collective Man, the Generalized Life, the Meaning of Knowing, the Flower of the Ages, and Real Estate. Reading *Another Time* is like attending an Elks' Convention of the Capital Letters; all my examples come from it, and I had not even begun to exhaust the supply. (There are not a tenth as many in his previous book of poems.) The reader must manage for himself a list of noncapitalized personified abstractions; experience has taught me that all this is a squeamish business, a pilgrimage through some interminable Vegetarians' Cafeteria.

The terrible thing about such rhetorical devices, about any of the mechanisms and patented insights

that make up so much of any style, is that they are
habit-forming, something the style demands in ever-
increasing quantities. We learn subtle variations or
extensions we once would have thought impossible or
nonexistent; but we constantly permit ourselves excesses, both in quantity and quality, that once would
have appalled us. That is how styles—and more than
styles—degenerate. Stylistic rectitude, like any other,
is something that has to be worked at all the time,
a struggle—like sleeping or eating or living—that
permits only temporary victories; and nothing makes
us more susceptible to a vice than the knowledge
that we have already overcome it. (The fact that one
once used an argument somehow seems to give one the
right to ignore it.)

Everyone must have noticed all the *the*'s in Auden's
middle and late poems: *the this, the that, the other*—
all the thousands of categories into which beings are
flung. (Compare this with the early poems, where
the's are as far as possible omitted.) The bases of clas-
sification are thoroughly unsystematic, whatever
comes to hand in need. The device is a convenient
shorthand, shortcut, in which the type or trait is used
as the unit of analysis: it is a useful method for
handling the immense quantities and qualities of
difference that everyone sees everywhere today—
especially Auden, who took the world for his province
without much hesitation. (The constant use of this
method helps explain why Auden, in the plays, gets
efficient observed types, but no characters.) There is
plenty of journalism, fact as *summum bonum*, in

Auden; his *the* method has an illusive effect of merely pointing to the Facts, a reality effective in itself. But Auden has far more than the good journalistic sense of the typical or immediately differentiating detail; his differentiating characteristics seem at their best conclusive. Let me finish with the rueful commonplace that he has exploited this method for all it is worth. In his later verse one finds the most mechanical or exaggerated examples: poems that are mere masques of abstractions, gatherings not of the clans but of the classes.

Auden depends a good deal on periphrasis: *the neat man / To their east who ordered Gorki to be electrified; the naughty life-forcer in the Norfolk jacket; that lean hard-bitten pioneer* (there follow fourteen lines: Dante) ; *the German who / Obscure in gas-lit London, brought* (there follow fifty lines about Marx) ; etc. It is easy for the rhetorical heightening this represents —the substitution of an elegant or surprising allusiveness for the proper noun—to become a vice; not so easy, however, in didactic or expository verse, where a little formal gilding comforts the yawning traveler.

Auden fairly early began to use words like *lovely, marvelous, wonderful, lucky, wicked* (words that are all weight and no "presentation"; that are all attitude of subject and no description of object; that approach as a limit the semanticists' *meaningless emotional noises*) in a peculiarly sophisticated sense. Their use is highly conscious, and implies quite definitely an attitude that it is hard to state definitely, but that I shall paraphrase as: *How well I know such words as these are looked down on, by any schoolboy even, as simple-silly, naïve, wholly inadequate. Yet you and I know that all the most cunningly chosen figures, all the "objective" terms, all the "presentation," are in the end quite as inadequate—that real representation, especially of the states such words point at, is impossible. You know how much better I could do; but certainly that better would not be good enough; this time I shan't even try, the* lovely *is something we can tacitly consent to, an indulgent and shared secret. Besides, how much of the charm, the real freshness of the experience such a word retains; and there is a real shock about it, too, an undoubted rhetorical effectiveness about its lack either of rhetoric or effectiveness, here in the midst of so much of both.*

A good deal of the "early romanticism" in Auden has a vague root in some such attitude as this. I hope the tone of my paraphrase doesn't seem to deny its real and precarious effectiveness; this is one of the dangerous devices of decadence, but not less charming for that. The use of such words later degenerated into oblivious sentimentality; the same end was waiting for Auden's *love-dove rhymes*, which at first were small jokes that, in their contexts at the end of poems, had a deliberate and pathetic conclusiveness.

One of the conscious devices of the late poems is the use of a simile blunt, laconic, and prosaic enough to be startling : Housman *kept tears like dirty postcards in a drawer;* in Rimbaud *the rhetorician's lie / Burst like a pipe.* There are *the rooks / Like agile babies; Terrible Presences that like farmers have purpose and knowl-*

edge. Desire *like a policedog is unfastened; a phrase goes packed with meaning like a van*. As if to show how much on order this device is, Auden once uses it three times in five lines : poets are *encased in talent like a uniform . . . amaze us like a thunderstorm . . . dash forward like hussars*. This device is allied to the surprising and compressed metaphor, where no explanation is furnished, but where one is required—of the reader : *the beast of vocation, the bars of love, the stool of madness*, etc. And Auden will often insert slang or colloquialisms in an elevated or abstract context : he says in an idealistic sonnet about the Composer, *only your notes are pure contraption;* one finds *an invite with gilded edges; the identical and townee smartness; ga-ga Falsehood; the sexy airs of summer; lucky to love the new pansy railway;* and so on. All this is merely a special case of the insertion of the concrete word in the abstract context, which itself is a special case of Effect by Incongruity. These last are too common in any poet to need quotation here.

I now come to some formidable machinery which I am going to overwhelm with the even more formidable title of : The Bureaucratization of Perspective by Incongruity. Auden, who has a quick eye and an enormous range (of interests, information, and insight), was at the start plunged into the very blood of the world, the Incongruous; and he found even a drop of that blood, like Fafnir's, enough to make us see (the word is ambiguous here, standing for both perception and insight) what we could not possibly see without it. He began to make his poems depend on perspective by incongruity very much more than other modern poetry does; and he made them depend very much less on violence, forced intensity, emotional heightening, etc. But—if I may bureaucratize my own metaphor—so ingenious and conscious a mind was thoroughly dissatisfied with the random application of any drop or two of blood from that disreputable old dragon, the world. Why not rationalize the whole process? Why not mass together incongruities in a sort of blood bank, as ready as money, available for unlimited use in any emergency? Why not *synthesize* the Incongruous? and then (independent of natural sources, your warehouses groaning with the cheap blood poured out, in ever-increasing quantities, by that monopoly-creating secret) why not flood the world's markets, retire on the unlimited profits of the unlimited exploitation of—Incongruity?

I have been so extravagantly and mechanically incongruous because Auden has been; he has bureaucratized his method about as completely—and consequently as disastrously—as any efficiency expert could wish. It is a method that can be applied to any material : a patented process guaranteed to produce insights in any quantities. The qualities, unfortunately, cannot be guaranteed. The law of diminishing returns sets in very quickly; the poet's audience (one of the members of which is the poet) is as easily fatigued for incongruity as for an odor, and the poet has to supply larger and larger quantities that have less and less effect. The reader has seen in my earlier quotations many examples of Auden's use of this method; there exist enough examples for several generations of critics; I shall take the space for only one, a certain kind of spatial metaphor Auden uses for people.

Freud is a *climate, weather*. The *provinces* of Yeats's body revolted; *the squares of his mind were empty, / Silence invaded the suburbs, / The current of his feeling failed*. Matthew Arnold is a *dark disordered city*, completely equipped with *square, boulevard, slum, prison, forum, haphazard alleys, mother-farms, and a father's fond-chastising sky*—all this in twelve packed lines. Let me quote a poem, "Edward Lear," and italicize the unexpected or incongruous effects the poet and I want noticed. In some story a child keeps repeating, "I want to see the *weels* go round"; I hope no child will need to make such a remark here.

Left by his friend to breakfast alone on the white
Italian shore, his *Terrible Demon* arose
Over his shoulder; he wept to himself in the night,
A *dirty* landscape-painter who *hated his nose*.

The legions of cruel inquisitive *They*
Were *so many and big like dogs;* he was upset
By *Germans and boats;* affection was *miles away:*
But *guided by tears* he successfully *reached his Regret*.

How prodigious the welcome was. *Flowers took his hat*
And *bore him off* to *introduce him to the tongs;*
The demon's *false nose* made the *table laugh;* a *cat
Soon had him waltzing madly, let him squeeze her hand;
Words pushed him to the piano to sing comic songs;*

And children swarmed to him *like settlers*. He *became a
land*.

I shan't insult the reader with comment—though I should like to mention the dangling participle I couldn't italicize. No one could miss seeing how mechanical, how consciously *willed*, such a rhetorical process is; in italicizing these words I have done no one an injustice—they have already been italicized by the poet. And now my list of quotations comes to a magnificent climax, with a conceit in which Auden sees Man as two pages of English countryside. But—two pages! I shall have to conclude weakly, with a bare reference to *New Year Letter*.

This collection of lists must by now have suggested a generalization to the reader: that in his later poems Auden depends to an extraordinary extent on *devices*. I could now add to my lists the device of—lists; but I will leave to the reader the pleasure of discovering that Auden not only imitates Joyce, Whitman, *et cetera*, but even parodies a list of Chaucer's. Another extended device, not precisely rhetorical, has a decided effect on the rhetorical texture of a poem. It is what might be called the *set piece:* a poem conscientiously restricted to some appropriated convention. This may even arrive at its limit, the parody; in any case, the interplay between prototype and "copy" is consistently and consciously effective—if the reader does not realize that the poem depends upon the relations to a norm of deviations from a norm, the poem will be badly misunderstood. The poem exists on two levels, like counterpoint—that is, like a counterpoint in which one of the levels has to be supplied by the hearer. Auden, who has an acute sense of the special function and convention of a poem, and no trace of the delusion that a single poem can serve as a model for the poet's poems or for Poetry, often tries for these limited successes. When he writes a popular song, it is always a pleasure to see critics discovering that he is "influenced by popular songs"; which is like finding that Eliot's poems in French are "influenced by the French language," or like finding Tchaikovsky's *Mozartiana* "influenced by Mozart." Today we are not good at convention, and delight in nothing so much as demanding sermons from stones, books from brooks—from every poem the more-than-what-it-gives that is precisely what its convention precludes it from giving; if we are poets we even try to furnish the *more than.* Auden has eight or ten types of set pieces; the reader will remember most of them, so there is no need for another list. (A good deal of the incidental effectiveness of *New Year Letter,* even, comes from this source.) Another favorite and very noticeable device is the long, mechanically worked-out conceit.

Auden's effective rhetorical use of abstract diction sometimes degenerates, in the later poems, into the flatness and vagueness, the essayistic deadness, of bad prose. (Let me emphasize, however, that the relatively abstract—what most poets would reject or fear —is one of the principal sources of Auden's effectiveness.) *The major cause of our collapse / Was a distortion in the human plastic by luxury produced* is bad enough; later Rimbaud is *from lyre and weakness estranged*—I am surprised Auden didn't finish the list with *the fair sex;* finally there is *If he succeeded, why, the Generalized Life / Would become impossible, the monolith / Of State be broken, and prevented / The cooperation of avengers.* With *Imperialism's face / And the international wrong* we have left poetry for editorials; and *the Hitlerian monster* is like a parody of Churchill—if I am not making an Irish bull.

But this degeneration into abstraction was inescapable for Auden, the reflection of his whole development. Auden's development, to a critic who knows his work well, has so much causal unity, fits together so logically and becomingly, that the critic can hardly bear to break up the whole into fragments of analysis, and feels like saying with Schopenhauer: All this is a single thought. It was *necessary* for Auden to develop and depend upon all this rhetorical machinery, because his poetry, his thought itself, was becoming increasingly abstract, public, and prosaic. These rhetorical devices constitute a quasi-scientific method by which you can make rhetorically effective *any* material, by which even the dead or half living can be galvanized into a sort of animation. (The method is much better suited to didactic or expository poetry than to lyric poetry: so *New Year Letter* is much more successful than Auden's latest lyrics—he is working with a congenial subject and a congenial method.) The earliest poems do not need and do not have such a rhetoric.

Auden wished to make his poetry better organized, more logical, more orthodox, more accessible, and so on; with these genuinely laudable intentions, going in the right direction from his early work, he has managed to run through a tremendous series of changes so fast that his lyric poetry has almost been ruined. If I may speak in the loose figurative language that fits such feelings: this late technique and material seem appropriated, not earned—an empty rootless *goes after* without the *comes before* necessary to give it meaning. Many of the early poems seem produced by Auden's whole being, as much unconscious as conscious, necessarily made just as they are; the best of them have shapes (just as driftwood or pebbles do) that seem the direct representation of the forces that produced them. Most of the later poems represent just as directly the forces that produced *them:* the head, the head, the top of the head; the correct, reasoning, idealistic, sentimental Intelligence. Nietzsche has this terrible sentence: *Euripides as a poet is essentially an echo of his own conscious knowledge.* It is hard not to apply the judgment to most of Auden's latest poetry.

How conscious, rational, controlled is poetry? can poetry afford to be? Our answers are bad: the half-knowledge we keep comes mostly from personal experience—which differs—and is terribly corrupted by our desires. (Imagine trying to reconcile Winters's testimony with that of Dylan Thomas.) But I think one can safely say that Auden's later method is far too conscious and controlled; too Socratic, too Alexandrian—to borrow from Nietzsche again. This rational intelligence guides and selects, it does not produce and impose; we make our poetry, but we make it what we can, not what we wish. Freud has taught everyone what happens to us when we impose on ourselves unacceptable or unbearable restrictions. Poetry —which represents the unconscious (or whatever you want to call it) as well as the conscious, our lives as well as our thoughts; and which has its true source in the first and not the second—is just as easily and fatally perverted. The sources of poetry—which I, like you, don't know much about, except that they are delicate and inexplicable, and open or close for no reason we can see—are not merely checked, but dried up, by too rigorous supervision.

Auden has been successful in making his poetry more accessible; but the success has been entirely too expensive. Realizing that the best poetry of the twenties was too inaccessible, we can will our poetry into accessibility—but how much poetry will be left when we finish? Our political or humanitarian interests may make us wish to make our poetry accessible to large groups; it is better to try to make the groups accessible to the poetry, to translate the interests into political or humanitarian activity. The best of causes ruins as quickly as the worst; and the road to Limbo is paved with writers who have done everything—I am being sympathetic, not satiric—for the very best reasons. All this is a problem that disquiets most poets today; to write as good and plain a poem as you can, and to find it over the heads of most of your readers, is enough to make anyone cry. The typical solution of the twenties (modern poetry is necessarily obscure; if the reader can't get it, let him eat Browning) and the typical solution of the political poetry of the thirties (poetry must be made available to the People or it is

decadent escapism; poetry is Public Speech—to use
MacLeish's sickening phrase, so reminiscent of the
public prayer of the Pharisees) were inadequate sim-
plicities, absurd half-truths. A classically rational and
absurd solution is that of Winters and his school,
whose willed and scrupulously limited talking-down
has resulted in a kind of moral baby-talk. Auden's
more appealing solution has worked out much better;
it is too conscious, too thin, too merely rational: we
should distrust it just as we distrust any Rational (or
Rationalized) Method of Becoming a Saint. I am not
going to try to tell the reader what the solution should
be, but I can tell him where to find it: in the work of
the next first-rate poet. An essay like this may seem
an ungrateful return for all the good poetry Auden
has written; and I feel embarrassed at having furnished—even in so limited an article—so much
Analysis and so little Appreciation. But analyses,
even unkind analyses of faults, are one way of showing appreciation; and I hope at another time to try
another way.

Freud to Paul:

The Stages of Auden's Ideology

THERE ARE three stages of the works (and the ideas which are their sources or elaborated by-products) that we call Auden. In the beginning there is the Old Auden, the *Ur*-Auden. What should I call this stage? *Freud and Grettir? The Law of the Members?* Here everything of importance happens inside the Realm of Causal or Magical Necessity. Here—in *Poems*, in *Paid on Both Sides*, and in most of *The Orators*—is the world of the unconscious, the primitive, the childish, the animal, the natural : it is Genesis. The basic structural picture (in Wittgenstein's sense) underlying these poems is that of the long struggle of genetic development, of the hard, blind journey of the creature or its kind. Existence is an essentially dialectical evolution, presented with particular directness in Freudian or saga terms—*i.e.*, in terms succeeding or preceding those of the higher religions. The primary subject of the poems is the discontinuities of growth, the unrecognized or opposed Necessity that determines men and Man. The "change of heart" is meaningless except as a preliminary to change—is, generally, an evasion by which we avoid changing. But even the real choices, the continued-in changes, possess a deterministic pathos. Our fundamental activity is a guilty revolt against a guilty Authority, a revolt predetermined to immediate or eventual failure, a revolt by the neurotic and diseased (to the Auden of Stage I medicine is a branch of psychiatry, and all illness is functional) against a neurotic and diseased culture.

In Stage I morality is never the instant of choosing, but the years of doing. It is thought of not as a choice, a simple single act of the will or understanding, but as a long and almost impossibly difficult series of actions, a process of processes. True development and genuinely moral behavior have nothing to do with the systematic, disinterested abstraction of the moralist; they are what you yourself are mixed up in, puzzle out, and work at all your life, failing or succeeding only to fail. This is a narrative morality instead of a sermon morality; morality as particular, experienced practice instead of morality as general, vicarious theory. It is Job's morality opposed to that of his comforters, the morality of an endangered and confused participant speaking *to himself*. (Auden's later morality is that of a group adviser, abstract, sentimental, and *safe*—for the adviser, at least.)

These early poems effect a strange assimilation of machinery and the industrial world into a traditional, rural, almost feudal world; the new world view of expanding optimism rots away (as its machines rust to a halt, as its industry grinds down to perpetually lower and poorer levels) into the cyclic pessimism of an older view. The weight and concentration of the poems fall upon *things* (and those great things, animals and people), in their tough, laconic, un-get-pastable plainness: they have kept the stolid and dangerous inertia of the objects of the sagas—the sword that snaps, the man looking at his lopped-off leg and saying, "That was a good stroke." They gain an uncommon plausibility from the terse understated matter-of-factness of their treatment, the insistence (such as that found in the speech of children, in Mother Goose, in folk or savage verse, in dreams) upon the *thingness* of the words themselves. Things are vaguely tabooish, totemistic, animistic—everything is full of *mana*, especially the machines, rusting tutelary deities of the countryside in which everything occurs: if Jung had read the early Auden he would have decided that rusting machines in the country are Archetypal Images of the Racial Unconscious. Auden's early style is rooted in the English country; his later style, compared to it, is an air plant in a window box of the cloud city of the exiled *Wandervögel*. The early poems are in harmony with the more primitive levels of our experience, levels which—since they precede others in the life of the individual conscious—underlie the moralistic and rationalizing levels at which the later Auden is usually working. When we say that some patch of an early poem seems "magical," we sometimes mean that it works directly at levels which we are not accustomed to verbalize or scrutinize, often because they are taken for granted. But in our culture how much (like the flaying of Marsyas) goes on under—far under—the level gray gaze of Reason and Taste; just as Apollo, when he was not occupied with Knowledge, Art, and Light, slithered under the pillars of his temples in the person of a hunting snake, and was called by his worshippers the Mouse-Slayer.

In *Look, Stranger!* and *The Dog beneath the Skin* Auden changes over into a second, essentially transitional stage which continues until *New Year Letter*—itself a transition from the Moral Auden to the New Auden. It is easy to find titles or mottoes for this second stage: *The Moralist from the Machine; The Questing Beast; Reason as Agape, or The Saviour with the Vote.* Here everything important happens in the Realm of Logical Necessity. Here are free to choose—are implored or forced to choose, are told again and again that our choices are meaningful, that the right choice is predestined to success. A change of heart is a change of vote—what is meaningless about that? Existence has become a *problem* that Auden reasons about, advises us about, exhorts us to make the right choice about; it is categorized, rather than presented, in secular, liberal, humanitarian, sentimental, metaphorically scientific terms. The typical poems are problem poems. The political moralist raids a generalized, popularized Science for the raw materials and imagery of a morality which he constructs to satisfy the demands of the self and of the age, but which he implies is Scientific: a favorable mutation becomes for him "a morally good act," and even Destiny presents itself (as it does to his father-in-law) in political terms, to be voted for or spoken against. Animals, misguided former voters bogged down in the partial but final solutions brought them by their wasted votes, are patronizingly condemned by the political adviser because they are not free, like us, to go on voting (and being advised). Auden's ethics appear in an abstract, virtuous, and interminable Volume II, all the particulars of which are derived from a Volume I that consists of a single sentence: *We must do something about Hitler.* We are all guilty, the will itself is evil (the judgment is a bitter pill with a sugar-and-morphine center); but we can, practically speaking, escape our guilt by recognizing it, by *willing* a sort of Popular Front of the Universe. The quoted *Freedom is the recognition of necessity* (originally, in the purely deterministic Spinoza, the recognition that there is no freedom except the "freedom" of acting according to the conditions of our being, of knowing and consequently loving the universe we are helpless to change) changes, through the growingly optimistic determinism of Hegel and Engels, into Auden's consolatory fable: *To recognize necessity is to have escaped it.* Thus the fundamental structural picture underneath the poems is that of the *fairy-tale quest* (and the assimilated Quest of the Grail, temptations of the Buddha or the Messiah, etc.) : so much so that genetic development, the underlying structural picture of the first stage, is itself expressed in terms of the quest. Success is no longer struggled for interminably and found at last a failure, but is won, in an instant, by choosing correctly—*i.e.*, voting. Good will *is* Grace:

in this ideally democratic fable the third son—a humble
and unexceptional hero distinguished from his able
and eager brothers by his amorphous generalization,
his fetalization—tramps goodheartedly, selflessly,
will-lessly over the conditions of the universe, choosing, choosing, up to a final choice: a choice rewarded
by an external, causally unrelated, paradoxical "success." Actually his normal state is its own reward, his
real reward. "Success" is merely the morphological
stamp of approval necessary to impress the undiscern-
ing hearers of the parable; it is truly success only
insofar as it resembles the state it rewards. Thus the
third son, in his most developed and Audenish, his
truest form, sits happily at home, already successful,
and reads indifferently the love letters of his more
primitive forebear, trudging unnecessarily over the
tundra or gasping on the peak.

There is only one real name for Auden's latest
period: *Paul;* but it is hard to resist *Grace Abounding;
The Teleological Suspension of Ethics; Waiting for
the Spark from Heaven to Fall.* Here everything that
is important happens in the Realm of Grace. The
fundamental structural picture underlying the poems
is that of *waiting humbly for Grace;* man's ultimate
accomplishment is *sitting still.* We are damned not
merely for what we do, but for doing anything at all—
and properly damned, for what *we* do is necessarily
evil: *Do not, till ye be done for* is our only possible
slogan. In Stage II action and the will are evil, in Stage
III everything (except the Wholly Other, God) is evil;
Auden, like a backward Cato, leaves no speech without
its *Carthage has fallen*—for he, like Niebuhr, accepts

the Fall not merely as a causal myth but as the observed essence of all experience. But the speeches no longer support any Universal Popular Front; who are we to help out God's world? (Better wait it out instead.) The earlier *We must do something about Hitler* has become *We must realize that we* ARE *Hitler*. There is no more choice—we are chosen; the elections of the free voter, the man of good will and good works, have been succeeded by the Election of the helpless and determined sinner, the Man of Faith. The whole concept of evolutionary development has disappeared. The Old Adam of the flesh (blinded by the self-love, self-righteousness, and self-conceit pumped into him by the Secular Intelligence, the Wisdom of this World) must *mutate* into the New Adam of the spirit. Just as natural mutations are (often) the effects of extraterrestrial radiation, this supernatural mutation is an effect or aspect of the unearthly radiation of Grace —that is, it *is* Grace as it feels to us who receive it. (After making up this rather derisive simile I was astonished to find Auden, in something I hadn't read before, using it seriously: Agape is "Eros mutated by Grace.") The change of heart and its accompanying changes of behavior are now important only as a sign that we have *been* changed, elected—just as they were in Calvin; but the iron confidence of the theocrat (recreated for our age, in an unprecedented feat of the histrionic imagination, by Karl Barth) has scaled away, exposing its shaky armature of guilt and hope. The determinism of Stage I has returned, but transfigured by that Christian optimism which, in its avid acceptance of the worst evils of our world as necessarily inseparable from our fleshly existence, is more frightening than the most pessimistic of secular views. This already determined text of existence is neither presented, as in Stage I, nor categorized, as in Stage II, but *commented on.* Auden's work now consists of commentaries or glosses of every kind—dramatic, philosophical, critical. He becomes fond of writing criticisms or reviews which, under a vague show of criticizing a work some magazine has hopefully handed him, are secondary commentaries or glosses on those primary commentaries or glosses which are his creative works (so that readers of his reviews are continually exclaiming, *"Now* I see!") ; these primary and secondary commentaries are indistinguishable in dialectic and imagery—purple patches, heartfelt confessions, and magical feats of dialectical ingenuity reach their highest concentration in reviews of minor theologians.

In this stage Auden has not forsaken ethics in the least—how could so confirmed a moralist? But his morals are now, like the law in Luther or Niebuhr, merely a crutch to beat people into submission with, to force home to us the realization that there is none good but God, that no works can either save us or make us worth saving. The Old Auden he has been forced to forget entirely—just as, in Freud's myth, we *have* to wipe from our conscious memory all the experiences of our earliest childhood. (In his *Collected Poems* he makes extensive changes in the poems of Stage II, but either omits the poems of Stage I or leaves them unchanged—they are so genuinely and completely alien to him that he can do nothing with them. To prove that he has not kept the faintest understanding of or sympathy for his earliest work, he does worse than leave out *Paid on Both Sides*—he destroys it for good, by following Untermeyer's precedent of printing a few last surviving fragments as lyrics.) But the Secular Auden of Stage II is the New Auden's favorite target of attack. Herod—hitherto represented by everybody as an aboriginal ogre, Freud's Father of the Primal Horde—is presented in *For the Time Being* as the Humane, Secular, Liberal Auden of Stage II. This explains the fervid rudeness of the attack: Auden is attempting to get rid of a sloughed-off self by hacking it up and dropping the pieces into a bathtub full of lye. Why on earth should Auden choose to represent *Herod* as the typical Liberal? It would have been far more natural and far more plausible to pick Pontius Pilate (at that time the only regular subscriber to *The Nation* in all Palestine) ; but Auden could not risk the sympathy for Pilate which, increasingly injected into the Gospels as they developed—as anti-Semitic propaganda, incidentally—has been inherited by all of us. We are so *used* to rejecting Herod as a particularly bogey-ish Churchill that Auden can count on our going right on rejecting him when he is presented as Sir Stafford Cripps.

I I

BUT UNDER all the changing surface forms of Auden's development—often almost grotesquely at variance with one another—there is a constellation of a few persistent organizing forces, the examination of which is a key to the understanding of the changes themselves; particularly if we realize that in development the opposite of an attitude is often more immediately allied to it than any intermediate position—and that Auden's rationalizations of his changes, however irrational they may seem, should rarely be considered of any *causal* importance.

A complex of ideas, emotions, and unconscious attitudes about anxiety, guilt, and isolation—fused or not yet separated in a sort of sexual-authoritarian matrix —is the permanent causal core of Auden's ideology; it is structural and basic in his nature—compared to it most other things are skin or hair, the mere bloom of rouge. In Auden's work the elements of *anxiety, guilt, isolation, sexuality*, and *authority* make up a true Gestalt, a connected and meaningful whole; but the necessities of analysis force the analyst to sketch them one by one, as they appear in the successive stages of Auden's development.

In Stage I *guilt* is ubiquitous, since (a) from his Freudian point of view all levels are reduced to lower, genetically prior levels—"really" are "nothing but" these discreditable animal, savage, or infantile levels; since (b) from his dialectical-evolutionary, formally if vaguely Hegelian point of view, any success or good is temporary, already beginning to assume its permanent, discredited, and guilty status of failure or evil; since (c) if we look either through Freud's or Marx's eyes, our "reasons" for doing anything never by any chance coincide with the "real," less creditable reasons, so that our whole rational life is falsified by the guilty hypocrisy of our half-diseased, half-insane rationalization or ideology. ("Ideology is a process which of course is carried on with the consciousness of the so-called thinkers, but with a false consciousness. The real driving force which moves it remains unconscious, otherwise there would be no ideology." This careful and specific description of rationalization—*ideology* in Engels's terms—appeared in the *Anti-Dühring* in 1878.) Choice, will itself, Auden thinks of as a "necessary error" : whatever we do is wrong, inadequate, done for reasons we do not understand, so that we are never free of either guilt or *anxiety*. To a more or less rational anxiety are added sexual anxiety, that of repressed or forbidden sexual development; genetic anxiety, that of the creature which can neither grow nor evolve properly, whose most spectacular success is never anything more than a specialized and exaggerated impasse from which it is now too late to escape; moral anxiety —for in the early Auden the superego is as strong as it is confused, and he finds it horribly difficult but horribly imperative either to know what he should do or to find out how to do it; and hypochondriacal, neurotic anxiety, both psychic and somatic—in "this country of ours where nobody is well," even diseases normally considered organic are something that we *mean* (see Groddeck), so that our hypochondriacal anxiety is a guilty one as well.

In Stage I Auden is guiltily and partially rejecting, revolting against, *authority*. That part of us which does not revolt, judged either by Reason or by our own conscious standards, is despicable in its neurotic or diseased, bourgeois, corruptly passive guilt; but that part of us which revolts against the authority of the Father and the State is guilty by *their* standards, our own unconscious standards: so much so that it desperately seeks sanction in the mythical authority of that hastily invented fiction, our "real Ancestor," the Uncle. It is as if the gnawn and rockbound Prometheus had had to postulate a "real" Zeus and a "real" vulture under whose authority he "really" was. (And Prometheus, if he was not an orphan, probably did feel compelled to do something of the sort: we can remember in our own time how Little Father Nicholas was replaced by Little Fathers Lenin and Stalin, Holy Russia by the Fatherland.) Auden's early apotheosis of the (Wicked) Uncle is no more than a particularly innocent, Protestant, and Beatrix Potterish form of diabolism. It is no surprise to learn, in *Letters from Iceland* and other places, that Auden's parents were unusually good ones, very much venerated by the child: Auden moralizes interminably, cannot question or reject Authority except under the aegis of this pathetically invented opposing authority, because the superego (or whatever term we wish to use for the mechanism of conscience and authority) is exceptionally strong in him—as Kardiner says, "The superego is based on affection, not hatred; on delegated and not enforced authority." People have always been puzzled by the doom that hangs like a negative halo over the heads of the revolutionists of Auden's early works, who without exception commit suicide, die, or fail. But Auden *must* reward them only with failure or death, in order to relieve the guilt of his own revolt; those who defy Authority must come to bad ends, he knows, and he their creator has at least made them come to such ends, thus satisfying Authority at the same time he has revolted against it. This helps to explain, among other things, Auden's making his revolutionists as neurotic and diseased as the diseased and neurotic society they revolt against. But note his moral use of dadaist and surrealist elements as *symptoms;* the rather comic (and essentially Catholic) life cycle of the French surrealists— who die at advanced ages, prosperous, well adjusted, and *still surrealists*—is inconceivable to Auden, the product of a thoroughly moralistic and Protestant culture.

In Stage I guilt is particularly apparent in connection with *sexuality*, a sexuality repressed and condemned by both external and internal authority. This sexuality seems disease like so much else, revolt like so much else : the lover is presented as the leader of a secret cult, as the revolutionist, as the growing organism seduced into regression; but most of all as the sick neurotic—we are given so many lists of the fetishes of abnormal and difficult sexuality that we tend to believe a normal or easy sort not only rare but nonexistent. Love is condemned by the Immanent Will within the evolving animal as a fatal, fetal regression, as the great refusal of the creature; when we love women—who are always, in these cases, the primary vessels of sexual wrath—we are giving in to the Mother, stagnating, corruptly acquiescing to Author-

ity instead of persisting in the difficult revolution of
growth. Even when treated most favorably, love is
considered something to be transcended, to be replaced
by "independent delight"—it is an escape from which
Auden would like to escape. In the psychoanalytical
terms haunting Auden's head, it was nothing but oral,
anal, or genital stages of drives which, dammed up,
diverted, or finally breaking free in disguise, were
always subjective, predetermined states superficially
related to some objective pretext, rather than real responses to a person who is loved. Love is seen as a way
of hysterically blinding ourselves to our own essential, unchanging isolation—as a sort of Ignoble Lie.
(But Auden defends its excesses when other people
attack them, by retorting that naturally they seem
sick and distorted to a sick, distorted, and capitalist
world.) It would be hard to make a better summary of
what underlies much of Auden's development than
Kardiner's generalization of evidence gathered from
several cultures: "If the exercise of sexuality falls
under the influence of parental authority, all obedience constellations are reinforced, the parents' value
for good or evil becomes exaggerated, and guilt about
sexual activity leads to anticipation of punishment
and the fear of success." If this guilt is reinforced by
society in later life, as it may have been in Auden's
case, the whole process is considerably strengthened.

Auden has always insisted, with seemingly dis-
proportionate violence, upon the essential and inexorable *isolation* of the individual: one can find dozens of
different statements of the proposition. He usually

states flatly that it's *so*, and that's all there is to it; you must *be* alone and realize that you are alone, like it or not—any argument for unity is romantic or primitive wishful thinking. This attitude, in Stage I, is grounded both in his genetic view of the individual (who is separately frustrated and separately liquidated, without exception, even if his species triumphs) and in his Freudian view of ontogenetic development as an unaccountably faithful recapitulation of phylogenetic development. Some of his most beautiful poems express the terrifying and pathetic isolation of the growing organism, unwillingly alone from the moment it is thrust from the womb. He has been cut off from any real union with Authority by his revolt against it; and sexual relations, his next chance at Togetherness, are to him no more than a predetermined, repetitively senseless process of isolated growth —the object of love is a mere external pretext, not essentially differing from the class of abnormal fetishes of which it is the one normal member. The Family is gone. But if it, our culture's normal complex of Togetherness (Sex-Children-Authority), is broken up, both the feelings of isolation and the guilt feelings connected with sex are enormously intensified. This is particularly apparent in Hart Crane's case: his helpless rejection of the normal family, the normal sexual situation of union, isolated him both from his past and in his future—for he knew that he himself was never going to repeat this situation; and, in his present, what sexual ties he attempted had for him no trace of permanence, of recognition, of acceptance by and as Authority.

The hero of Stage I, the revolutionary cult leader—inadequately understood by his followers, entirely misunderstood by the rest of the world—is almost wholly isolated. The hero of *The Orators* resorts to political action of a fantastic sort, which necessarily fails; and he ends by "understanding" that a complete submission to Authority is the only method of re-forming Authority and saving himself : "God just loves us all, *but means to be obeyed* [my italics]." It is no accident that he winds up a couple of miles of cold air away from the nearest human being, about to commit suicide in an airplane; and it is no wonder that the creator of *The Orators*, finally understanding the use-lessness of his own political action in "that black year of which all the world heard"—1940 in this case—ends up *floating over 70,000 fathoms* in complete submission to that Authority Who means to be obeyed, the God of Kierkegaard and Barth. Laplace's Calculator might have predicted most of Auden's de-velopment from the last two pages of *The Orators*. (Kierkegaard's phrase about 70,000 fathoms attracts Auden so much that he adopts it as a disquieting slogan for our union with God—the only possible union, in-cidentally.)

In an approving summary of the existential point of view, Auden states that "the basic human problem is man's anxiety in time." In Stage II Auden's anx-iety finds expression in guilty activity rather than passive guilt—it is the period of his most active (and consequently least consciously guilty) anxiety. Our decision is always *the* decision, the great dividing watershed from which events fall to Evil or to Good; the crises of existence come as regularly and hyperbolically as elections. This political, liberal anxiety is rarely even temporarily soothed—since everything went, everything always goes against the Popular Front; the accompanying moral anxiety cannot be soothed, even temporarily—since the means to the Best end is never even Good, since acting with the best will in the world is still acting, since even the purest contemplation is always on the verge of signing its eternal, predestined pact with that "Hitlerian monster," the Will.

In Stage II guilt is first of all social, liberal, moral guilt—a guilt so general as to seem almost formal. It is *we* who are responsible, either by commission or—more generally—by omission, for everything from killing off the Tasmanians to burning the books at Alexandria. (*You didn't do it?* Then you should have stopped them from doing it. *You never heard of it?* Ignorant as well as evil, eh? *You weren't born?* You're guilty, I tell you—*guilty*.) Guilt is used to beat us into an easy but active submission, that of the voter, the signer of petitions, he who dies for freedom in the future the vote and the signature have prevented. Yet we are told that if we make up our minds, do anything, we are as guilty as before: for *all* will, *all* action, are evil. (From this universal secular condemnation it was easy for Auden to pass to Original Sin, the universal depravity of Calvinism.) Deep within the liberal—who feels, and usually correctly, that he *does* less than he ought—nothing calms more profoundly, alleviates more fundamentally, the anxiety always gnawing at the core of his goodheartedness, than the feeling of *group guilt*. What precarious individual acquittal can rival the *We are all guilty* that wipes out at one stroke any possible specific guilt of one's own? What proposition can express more fully and more tactfully one's own sensibility and honesty? (Look how guilty I feel over what most people wouldn't even be bothered by: most people think it's quite possible to will something or to do something without being *necessarily* guilty.) When, in early 1941, our liberal magazines were racking their brains over what to do, to think, or even to write about the war that was perhaps a crusade, and perhaps a struggle of rival imperialisms; the Russia that was perhaps Utopia, a trifle regimented, and perhaps the Companion of Hitler; the world that was, and no perhaps about it, a damnable puzzle; suddenly there was a great increase of articles about—the Negro in America. It would take a hard man to look unsympathetically at so touching and revealing a manifestation of our being.

Much of the guilt of Stage II is moral, the guilt the moralizer necessarily ascribes to his backward moralizees. But much of it is sexual. Love has come to be thought of as a guilty evasion, an escape—to excuse itself it must "implicate" itself in society, politics, the "real world." Love is a place we stop at when we should go on, a power or insight we bury selfishly and uselessly, instead of using in the social situation. It *should* be sublimated in Social Service. Eros is—at least potentially—a secular, humanitarian Agape which we have helplessly perverted. Love is a *problem:* one half of a struggle between love and duty, our moral and political duty to the world. In this contest between *public* and *private, objective* and *subjective,* Paris always dutifully awards his prize (that golden word, *Real*) to Minerva, but not without one burning backward glance. Love is "an island and therefore unreal"; both Auden and Hitler knew, in those days, that *There are no more islands.* (The *are,* in Auden's case, is not an existential but a normative judgment.) Auden's disapproval probably is grounded in society's disapproval; certainly his interminable moralizing is. If his attitudes and behavior had been accepted by society, he might have cared less about morality; as it is, he always has to be right, good, well-meaning—and he becomes a moral perfectionist of a variety distantly related to the more sensational varieties of the case histories.

In Stage II Auden feels the reluctant isolation of the liberal intellectual of the late-capitalist state—the terrible Popular Front aloneness of the Mediator who is neither fish nor fowl, but poor pink herring. He sits among the ashes of his own doubts, waiting, waiting— but nobody comes to persuade the Persuader; the only ties left to him are the pale vicarious ties of voting, of petition signing, of "the flat ephemeral pamphlet and the boring meeting." Staring enviously at the iron orthodoxy of the Communists his allies, at the beefy certainty of the Tories his opponents, at the folkish and bloody oneness of the Fascists his enemies, he insists, with wistful desperation, that his own isolation is inescapable for everyone in the world; that the machine has made everyone understand "the secret that was *always* [my italics] true / But known once only to the few," the secret that "Aloneness is man's real condition." He cries in a shaky voice, "I welcome the atomization of society"; and, in speaking of Kafka's heroes, states the Law of all modern life : "An industrial civilization makes *everyone* an exceptional reflective K." (O Churchill! O Stalin! You *very* exceptional K's!) What shall I say of this enchanting error, worthy of Peter Rabbit the day he first heard from his mother of the World of Mr. McGregor? This projection upon the universe of his own self and situation, as the necessary law of that universe, is usual in Auden . . . In Stage II his heroes are entirely alone : the false hero, the Extrinsically Successful One, wanders through the wilderness on the lonely quest that ends in an arbitrary and external success, completely misunderstood by the very public that applauds him; the real hero, the Intrinsically Successful One, potters around his garden at home, so completely alone that nobody in the world except the false hero even suspects that he is a success.

In Stage I Auden has rebelled, though guiltily, against a guilty Authority; he represents the new, potential Good rejecting the old and hardened Evil of an Authority which had itself come into power by revolting against, killing, and eating an earlier Authority (according to the Greek myths and according to Freud's myth in *Totem and Taboo*). In Stage II he tries to *reform* the Father, the State, Authority: everybody concerned has become much less guilty, and Auden's method of operation is now to persuade Authority into a recognition of its essential good-heartedness, into a reconciliation with himself and with the Reason which is over all things, gods and men alike. His relation to Authority is notably ambivalent —naturally so, since the relation is primarily that of Reform. A certain childishness (not too rare in young English intellectuals, who are sheltered and cherished in comparison with our own wild boys) becomes apparent in his attitudes—I remember a reviewer's talking of the "typical boyish charm" of the Auden poem of this period. Auden is managing to stay on surprisingly good terms with Authority by assuming the role of *enfant terrible* of the reformers—a very goodhearted and very childish one, the *enfant terrible* of the old father's long soft summer dreams. He becomes fond of saying that his favorite writers, those he would like most to *be*, are Lear, Carroll, and the author of *Peter Rabbit*—who themselves (as Auden wistfully realizes) reformed or rejected society in their ways, though not in any ways that kept them out of the nicest nurseries. (Of course much of the appeal of his statement, to Auden, lay in its shock value; but he could have dismayed his readers quite as heartily by telling them that his favorite writers were Tarski and Frege. His admiration was genuine and even predictable.)

In Stage II Auden nourishes a residual, partially perverse affection for any maladjustment to authority, for any complex or neurosis his development may have left lying around in him : after all, Authority itself, in the process of reform, has to get adjusted to poor ill-adjusted me. He feels an uneasy but thorough dislike for that "goddess of bossy underlings, Normality," and all the nursery schools and feeding formulas that follow in her train; he betrays an astonishing repugnance to such concomitants of Progress as antisepsis and central heating, prays *Preserve me from the Shape of Things to Be,* and invents as *his* educational slogan : "Let each child have that's in our care / As much neurosis as the child can bear." All this corresponds to the petulance with which Alice, an eminently reasonable child, greeted any divergence of Wonderland from one's own household's routine— which *is* Reason.

In Stage III Auden repudiates with fear and repulsion any attempt to revolt against Authority, to reform Authority, to question Authority, or to remain separate from Authority in any way. Such an attempt is an insane depravity that is the root of all sin. He knows that (as Kierkegaard puts it in his wonderful, if unintentional, eight-word summary of Calvinism) *the only thing which interests God is obedience.* This is lucky : it is all He gets. But Auden is no Calvin—no logician, either—and tactfully overlooks any direct hand of the Creator in the creature's guilt. The only responsibility that Auden, as a representative neurotic theologian, does not thankfully push

over onto God is the responsibility for his own guilty
depravity; *that* he is responsible for, he confesses—
with the abject, appealing leer of Peter Lorre in *M*—
but everything else in the universe God is responsible
for. This satisfies at one stroke Auden's anxiety—he is
assured that he can and should do nothing himself; his
need for guilt and his need to be reconciled to that
guilt; and his need of an inexorable and unconditioned
Authority.

When we have constructed God as the Wholly Other
than ourselves, the wholly evil; when we have decreed
that the image of God has been "wholly blotted out" in
man by the Fall, we naturally find the problem of
mediation between the Wholly Other and what it is
wholly other than, a logically insoluble problem. We
require—that is, we have made ourselves require—
a self-contradictory, paradoxical, absurd mediator.
Authority is now considered to be absolutely unconditioned, at once the Everything and the Not-Every-
thing: shall *we* attempt to depose or limit God by
demanding that He accord with our morality, our
reason, our anything? The demands of Authority are
equally unconditioned: but our own troubling actual
existence wholly disappears in our believing, vicarious
identification with Authority. Fortunate circumstances! since that existence is wholly evil: "In every
good work the just man sins." In every act we "do /
Evil as each creature does / In every definite decision / To improve; for even in / The germ-cell's primary division / Innocence is lost and Sin, / Already
given as a fact, / Once more issues as an act." If

Luther had only known about that germ cell's primary division! The advances of Science almost have enabled Auden to beat Luther and Calvin at their own game. But then they were handicapped by taking it so much more *seriously*. The later Auden is rarely serious: he is either solemn or ingeniously frivolous, like some massive and labyrinthine town clock from which a corked Topsy and a gilt Eva somersault to mark the hours of Time, but from which Uncle Tom himself, rattling the keys and surrounded by the flames of Judgment, emerges to herald the advent of Eternity.

The Buddha said that he taught nothing but suffering and the escape from suffering; Auden today could say that he teaches nothing but guilt, *which is* the escape from guilt. To be able to spend his time feeling guilty over the primary fission of the germ cell instead of over that primary fission of the atom which produced in a few minutes half a million casualties— what a God-sent mercy this ability is to Auden, what a final expression of the depths and necessities of his being! What escape from responsibility or from guilt can equal this responsibility, this guilt? And, after all, is not the death of these poor guilty creatures (damned as they were by their lack of any connection with God through that one Mediator, Christ) only one more relatively unimportant effect of the germ cell's division, that primary actualization of the *fact* of the first Fall—the Fall which has transformed every succeeding action of man into a guilty horror? How unimportant these inevitably trivial secular is-

sues must seem to us to whom God has brought it home
that there is only *one* issue : the obedience of the
guilty soul to God, the soul's salvation by the grace of
God.

Over and over Auden attacks every "good" act,
every attempt to "improve." He reiterates that "it is
not enough to bear witness [*i.e.*, to be a martyr] for
even protest is wrong." He writes, with that over-
weening humility which is the badge of all his saints,
the humility of Luther, Calvin, Kierkegaard, and
Barth :

> Convict our pride of its offense
> In all things, even penitence.

So far as his penitence, so far as all (theological)
things are concerned, it is hard to put up more than a
token resistance to his contention. When we look at the
world around us and within us, and then think of a
statement like Niebuhr's, that only rebellion against
God "is sin in the strictest sense of the word," how bitter it is not to be allowed to include that theology itself
within the category of *sin, in the strictest sense of the
word*. But I am applying ethical concepts to a realm in
which, as the most casual witness must have observed,
all ethics is suspended.

Auden first slipped into this dark realm of Faërie
(this "horrible nightmare," as the goaded Froude confessed) on the furtive excursions of the unbeliever who
needs some faked photographs of the Little People for
use as illustrations to a new edition of *Peter Pan*, but
who ends up as a cook's boy helping the gloomier

dwarfs boil toads and snails for the love feast that celebrates the consummation of their mysteries. Thus in *New Year Letter* many things are used as mere metaphors or conceits which a few months later are accepted as dogmatic and eternal truths. For instance, the status of the Devil (who has "no positive existence," but who nonetheless perpetually pushes us over into Good) is still exactly that of A. A. Milne's bears which eat you if you step on the cracks in the pavement—lovable hypostatized fictions of the pragmatic moralist. But I have no doubt that Milne, after a few years of avoiding cracks, sometimes woke screaming from a recurrent dream of being swallowed by a bear; and Auden of course lives in such a dream.

In Stage III Auden no longer feels so much anxiety about sexuality, after he has filed it away under Religion: even its guilt is drowned in the guilt of that universal depravity which has rolled its black flood over every human action. And Eros, considered as the not-yet-mutated Agape into which Agape is continually relapsing, has gained a new respectability: it is Grandmother, who was not everything she might have been, but who left us all the money for the Asylum. Sexuality is now no more than a relatively minor aspect of our religious life. Auden explains, in a summary of Kierkegaard, that for the individual once exposed to Christianity—whether or not he believes—there are only three possibilities: marriage, celibacy, or despair. Now all three of these possibilities are religious states, relations which involve both man and God: sexuality is swallowed up in salvation—or, at worst, in damnation. I'm not sure which of these possibilities Auden thinks of as his own state; probably he, as usual, considers all three "aspects of one Reality," and thus can credit himself with one-third of each. (This is an absurd but not impossible joke: Auden's favorite method of mediating between absolute irreconcilables is to declare them "merely aspects" of one reality, a "reality" that turns out to be as self-contradictory, paradoxical, and unsearchable as the ways of God.)

In Stage III Auden is completely alone, but the knowledge of his isolation is not a burden but a blessing: he knows that we have always been alone, will always be alone, except in our paradoxical, absurd union with the Wholly Other, God; and he knows that he is fortunate not to be blinded by illusions of any impossible union with the creatures rather than with their Creator. Our isolation is the complete aloneness of the man who stands for every minute of his life, in fear and trembling and abject dread, before his God. One could describe this isolation with authoritative immediacy by paraphrasing the many pages of Kierkegaard and Kafka from which Auden derives both the spirit and the letter of his treatment. Few of the ideas of Auden's last stage have the slightest novelty to a reader acquainted with Luther, Calvin, and Barth; even the expression of the ideas has no novelty to the reader familiar with Kierkegaard and Kafka. But this is a Godsend for everybody concerned, since the theological ideas which Auden does not adopt but invents are all too often on the level of those brown paper parcels, brought secretly to the War Department in times of national emergency, which turn out to be full of plans to destroy enemy submarines by tracking them down with seals.

A more radical anxiety has transformed the solutions of Stage II into *what we are anxious about* in Stage III: we are resignedly, humbly, interminably anxious about everything but God. What is not anxious *is* God, His Grace; though even that is agonizingly conscious, every instant, of those 70,000 fathoms over which it is precariously floating, trying desperately not even to wiggle its toes. What we are most anxious about is our anxiety itself: the greatest of all sins, Auden learns from Kafka, is impatience—and he decides that the hero "is, in fact, one who is not anxious." But it was inevitable that Auden should arrive at this point. His anxiety is fundamental; and the one thing that anxiety cannot do is to accept itself, to do nothing about itself—consequently it admires more than anything else in the world doing nothing, sitting still, waiting.

In Stages I and II *success* is important as the opposite of (hence, the goal of) the organism's core of anxiety, guilt, and isolation; in Auden's last stage success is naturally replaced by salvation, since Auden is running the Time-Machine in reverse, exhibiting the familiar development of Western man backwards. In Stage I success is something we are struggling for, developing into; it is unsatisfactory except as a goal—attained, it is seen as the failure away from which we struggle, back to which we regress. The Successful

One is the revolutionary cult leader who dies, the evolving qualitative leap that is in its turn superseded.

In Stage II success splits into extrinsic and intrinsic success. Extrinsic success is altogether externalized, something we earn by the external, arbitrary process of choosing, voting, making the lucky guess predestined to success. This extrinsic success is nothing more than the lucky charm, the Sacred Object of the fairytale quests—which you can have but never, alas! be. (Auden, spectacularly—and, to himself, guiltily—successful, realizes without any trouble that something is all wrong with this sort of extrinsic success, that not one thing is solved for him by it.) The Extrinsically Successful One is understood, forgivingly but rather contemptuously, to be a pathetic sham. Intrinsic success is entirely internalized, introjected: its humble, commonplace, and apparently wholly unsuccessful Successful One is all being and no doing. His success is, precisely, salvation without God, a secular salvation that seems necessarily and fatally incomplete without the divine ground from which it sprang. This intrinsic success is humble enough for Authority not to punish it except by a complete lack of recognition.

In Stage III success (always unconsciously feared and distrusted because of its element of revolt, independence, separateness) is seen to be impossible. Intrinsic success becomes religious salvation, Grace—and its passivity and determinism come to seem less arbitrary; extrinsic success is realized to be one of the more important varieties of sin, a variety particularly

characteristic of scientific, industrial, secular man. Influenced by Kafka's meditation on psychoanalysis,
Auden states that "half our troubles, both individual
neuroses and collective manias like nationalism, seem
to me to be caused largely by our poverty of symbols, so that not only do we fail to relate one experience to another but also we have to entrust our whole
emotional life to the few symbols we do have." (This
was written not by other people about Auden, but by
Auden about them.) Now it is true, in Auden's case,
that the great organizing symbols, the determiners of
his development, are few; but he is perfectly well able
to relate *any* experience to any other experience,
since the relation can be as superficial and paradoxical
—as absurd—as he pleases. It is this which makes it so
difficult for him to *learn* anything in the full sense of
the word : when we learn and assert A we cannot continue to assert not-A; but this Auden not only does,
but knows that he is required to do—not to do so, as he
states again and again, is a great sin, that sin by
which Adam fell : "He could only eat of the Tree of
Knowledge of Good and Evil by forgetting that its
existence was a fiction of the Evil One, that there is
only the Tree of Life." Nothing is good or bad but
thinking makes it so (*i.e.*, makes it *seem* so) : this is an
old song—there is a beautiful version of it in Herodo-
tus—but it is rare to find it utilized in just this way
by the religious. Statements important to Auden often
end with *there is only* ONE *Something-or-Other*, since
there is nothing he adores so extravagantly as

monism, nothing he fears so superstitiously as dualism; yet his rhetorical monism invariably flowers from an absolute dualism that he has stated only to transcend. The whole theological tradition Auden comes at the tail of is essentially a series of adaptations of the dualism of Paul; and as Auden—with the simplicity of genius—has understood, the only practical and effective way of transforming it into monism is to *state that it has already been transformed*. This Auden has done.

The stages of Auden's development can even be diagrammed. In Stage I Anxiety and Guilt are fused in an isolated sexual core, consciously repelling or cowering under (and unconsciously attracting or yearning up to) the Authority that hangs in menacing ambivalence just overhead. In Stage II an active Anxiety dominates this core; it has pushed Sexuality to the side as far as it can, and attempts rather unsuccessfully to mitigate its confessed Guilt and Isolation by *reforming* the Authority it pulls down to it in Auden's traditional Jacob-and-the-angel wrestling match. But in Stage III Anxiety, Guilt, and Isolation are themselves the *relations* of Authority to the core; they *are* Grace (its mirror image, as Auden puts it), the means by which Authority is manipulating the core into salvation. (Sexuality, mutated into Agape, is itself floating somewhere up near God.) The reader may complain about my last diagram: "But what is left to be the core?" That is the point I was making: there is nothing left. The one thing the Christian must realize is that he is "less than any of God's creatures," that he is swallowed up in Authority, the wholly determining Authority of God.

This was early plain to Auden: about New Year, 1940, he disapprovingly judged that the Calvinist tradition makes man "the passive instrument of daemonic powers"; but by the anniversary of this date, in *The Nation* of January 4, 1941, he is giving the theologian Niebuhr (who in Cromwell's time would undoubtedly have been named Death-on-Pride Niebuhr) a little neo-Calvinist lecture *à la* Kierkegaard: he is "not sure" that Niebuhr "is sufficiently *ashamed* [*my* italics]," mourns over Niebuhr's "orthodoxy," and ends by threateningly demanding that Niebuhr decide once and for all "whether he believes that the contemplative life is the highest and most exhausting of vocations, or not." Just so, in late 1939, months and months before, he had complained that the doctrines of the theologian MacMurray are distorted by his "determination to believe in the existence of God," and had suggested that those doctrines would lose little—and, obviously, gain a lot—if expressed as Auden expressed them: "Man is aware that his actions do not express his real nature. God is a term for what he imagines that nature to be. Thus man is always making God in his own image." (In a little over a year he is sure that God is the Wholly Other.) Those years were fun for Auden, but death for the theologians.

But I am being drawn into theology and the article

which will follow the present one: a discussion of the
effect on Auden's ideology of Freud, Marx, Paul,
Luther, Calvin, Kierkegaard, Kafka, Barth, and Niebuhr. *

I I I

AFTER OBSERVING in Auden this permanent anxiety,
guilt, and isolation, adhered to with unchanging firmness in every stage of his development, justified for
different reasons in every stage, we cannot fail to see
that these "reasons" are reinforcing rationalizations of
the related attitudes which, not even rationally considered—much less understood—have been for Auden
a core impervious to any change.

They form a core that Auden has scarcely attempted to change. He is fond of the statement *Freedom is the recognition of necessity*, but he has never
recognized what it means in his own case: that if he
understands certain of his own attitudes as *causally*
instead of logically necessary—insofar as they are
attitudes produced by and special to his own training
and culture—he can free himself from them. But this
Auden, like most people, is particularly unwilling to
understand. He is willing to devote all his energies and
talents to finding the most novel, ingenious, or absurd
rationalizations of the cluster of irrational attitudes he
has inherited from a former self; the cluster, the self,
he does not question, but instead projects upon the

* The article described here was never published. ED.

universe as part of the essential structure of that universe. If the attitudes are contradictory or logically absurd there, he saves them by taking Kierkegaard's position that everything really important is above logical necessity, is necessarily absurd. In the end he submits to the universe without a question; but it turns out that the universe is his own shadow on the wall beside his bed.

Let me make this plain with a quotation. On the first page of the *New York Times Book Review* of November 12, 1944, there appeared a review of the new edition of *Grimm's Tales*—a heartfelt and moral review which concluded with this sentence: "So let everyone read these stories till they know them backward and tell them to their children with embellishments—they are not sacred texts—and then, in a few years, the Society for the Scientific Diet, the Association of Positivist Parents, the League for the Promotion of Worthwhile Leisure, the Coöperative Camp for Prudent Progressives and all other bores and scoundrels can go jump in the lake."

Such a sentence shows that its writer has saved his own soul, but has lost the whole world—has forgotten even the nature of that world: for this was written, not in 1913, but within the months that held the mass executions in the German camps, the fire raids, Warsaw and Dresden and Manila; within the months that were preparing the bombs for Hiroshima and Nagasaki; within the last twelve months of the Second World War.

The logical absurdity of the advice does not matter,

though it could hardly be more apparent: people *have* been telling the tales to their children for many hundreds of years now (does Auden suppose that the S.S. men at Lublin and Birkenau had not been told the tales by their parents?); the secular world Auden detests has been produced by the *Märchen* he idealizes and misunderstands, along with a thousand other causes— so it could not be changed "in a few years" by one of the causes that have made it what it is. But the moral absurdity of the advice—I should say its moral imbecility—does matter. In the year 1944 these prudent, progressive, scientific, cooperative "bores and scoundrels" were the enemies with whom Auden found it necessary to struggle. Were *these* your enemies, reader? They were not mine.

Such mistaken extravagance in Auden is the blindness of salvation, a hysterical blindness to his actual enemies (by no means such safe enemies as the Prudent Progressives) and to the actual world. But it is hard for us to learn *anything*. When the people of the world of the future—if there are people in that world —say to us—if some of us are there, "What did you do in all those wars?" those of us left can give the old, the only answer, "I lived through them." But some of us will answer, "I was saved."

Robert Frost's

"Home Burial"

"H OME BURIAL" and "The Witch of Coös" seem
to me the best of all Frost's dramatic poems—
though "A Servant to Servants" is nearly as good. All
three are poems about women in extreme situations:
neurotic or (in "A Servant to Servants") psychotic
women. The circumstances of the first half of his
life made Frost feel for such women a sympathy
or empathy that amounted almost to identification. He
said that, "creature of literature that I am," he had
learned to "make a virtue of my suffering / From
nearly everything that goes on round me," and that
"Kit Marlowe taught me how to say my prayers: /
'Why, this is Hell, nor am I out of it.' " It is with such
women that he says this—this and more than this: the
Pauper Witch of Grafton's

> Up where the trees grow short, the mosses tall,
> I made him gather me wet snow berries
> On slippery rocks beside a waterfall.
> I made him do it for me in the dark.
> And he liked everything I made him do . . .

shows us, as few passages can, that for a while the
world was heaven too.

"Home Burial" is a fairly long but extraordinarily
concentrated poem; after you have known it long
enough you feel almost as the Evangelist did, that if
all the things that could be said about it were written
down, "I suppose that even the world itself could not
contain the books that should be written." I have
written down a few of these things; but, first of all,
here is "Home Burial" itself:

> He saw her from the bottom of the stairs
> Before she saw him. She was starting down,
> Looking back over her shoulder at some fear.
> She took a doubtful step and then undid it
> To raise herself and look again. He spoke
> Advancing toward her: "What is it you see
> From up there always—for I want to know."
> She turned and sank upon her skirts at that,
> And her face changed from terrified to dull.
> He said to gain time: "What is it you see,"
> Mounting until she cowered under him.
> "I will find out now—you must tell me, dear."
> She, in her place, refused him any help
> With the least stiffening of her neck and silence.
> She let him look, sure that he wouldn't see,
> Blind creature; and awhile he didn't see.
> But at last he murmured, "Oh," and again, "Oh."
>
> "What is it—what?" she said.
>
>   "Just that I see."
>
> "You don't," she challenged. "Tell me what it is."

"The wonder is I didn't see at once.
I never noticed it from here before.
I must be wonted to it—that's the reason.
The little graveyard where my people are!
So small the window frames the whole of it.
Not so much larger than a bedroom, is it?
There are three stones of slate and one of marble,
Broad-shouldered little slabs there in the sunlight
On the sidehill. We haven't to mind *those*.
But I understand: it is not the stones,
But the child's mound—"

        "Don't, don't, don't, don't," she cried.

She withdrew shrinking from beneath his arm
That rested on the banister, and slid downstairs;
And turned on him with such a daunting look,
He said twice over before he knew himself:
"Can't a man speak of his own child he's lost?"

"Not you! Oh, where's my hat? Oh, I don't need it!
I must get out of here. I must get air.
I don't know rightly whether any man can."

"Amy! Don't go to someone else this time.
Listen to me. I won't come down the stairs."
He sat and fixed his chin between his fists.
"There's something I should like to ask you, dear."

"You don't know how to ask it."

        "Help me, then."

Her fingers moved the latch for all reply.

"My words are nearly always an offence.
I don't know how to speak of anything
So as to please you. But I might be taught,
I should suppose. I can't say I see how.

A man must partly give up being a man
With women-folk. We could have some arrangement
By which I'd bind myself to keep hands off
Anything special you're a-mind to name.
Though I don't like such things 'twixt those that love.
Two that don't love can't live together without them.
But two that do can't live together with them."
She moved the latch a little. "Don't—don't go.
Don't carry it to someone else this time.
Tell me about it if it's something human.
Let me into your grief. I'm not so much
Unlike other folks as your standing there
Apart would make me out. Give me my chance.
I do think, though, you overdo it a little.
What was it brought you up to think it the thing
To take your mother-loss of a first child
So inconsolably—in the face of love.
You'd think his memory might be satisfied—"

"There you go sneering now!"

                              "I'm not, I'm not!
You make me angry. I'll come down to you.
God, what a woman! And it's come to this,
A man can't speak of his own child that's dead."

"You can't because you don't know how to speak.
If you had any feelings, you that dug
With your own hand—how could you?—his little grave;
I saw you from that very window there,
Making the gravel leap and leap in air,
Leap up, like that, like that, and land so lightly
And roll back down the mound beside the hole.
I thought, Who is that man? I didn't know you.
And I crept down the stairs and up the stairs

To look again, and still your spade kept lifting.
Then you came in. I heard your rumbling voice
Out in the kitchen, and I don't know why,
But I went near to see with my own eyes.
You could sit there with the stains on your shoes
Of the fresh earth from your own baby's grave
And talk about your everyday concerns.
You had stood the spade up against the wall
Outside there in the entry, for I saw it."

"I shall laugh the worst laugh I ever laughed.
I'm cursed. God, if I don't believe I'm cursed."

"I can repeat the very words you were saying.
'Three foggy mornings and one rainy day
Will rot the best birch fence a man can build.'
Think of it, talk like that at such a time!
What had how long it takes a birch to rot
To do with what was in the darkened parlor.
You *couldn't* care! The nearest friends can go
With anyone to death, comes so far short
They might as well not try to go at all.
No, from the time when one is sick to death,
One is alone, and he dies more alone.
Friends make pretense of following to the grave,
But before one is in it, their minds are turned
And making the best of their way back to life
And living people, and things they understand.
But the world's evil. I won't have grief so
If I can change it. Oh, I won't, I won't!"

"There, you have said it all and you feel better.
You won't go now. You're crying. Close the door.
The heart's gone out of it: why keep it up.
Amy! There's someone coming down the road!"

"*You*—oh, you think the talk is all. I must go—
Somewhere out of this house. How can I make you—"

"If—you—do!" She was opening the door wider.
"Where do you mean to go? First tell me that.
I'll follow and bring you back by force. I *will!*—"

The poem's first sentence, "He saw her from the bottom of the stairs / Before she saw him," implies what the poem very soon states: that, knowing herself seen, she would have acted differently—she has two sorts of behavior, behavior for him to observe and spontaneous immediate behavior. "She was starting down, / Looking back over her shoulder at some fear" says that it is *some fear,* and not a specific feared object, that she is looking back at; and, normally, we do not look back over our shoulder at what we leave, unless we feel for it something more than fear. "She took a doubtful step" emphasizes the queer attraction or fascination that the fear has for her; her departing step is not sure it should depart. "She took a doubtful step and then *undid* it": the surprising use of *undid* gives her withdrawal of the tentative step a surprising reality. The poem goes on: "To raise herself and look again." It is a little vertical ballet of indecision toward and away from a fearful but mesmerically attractive object, something hard to decide to leave and easy to decide to return to. "He spoke / Advancing toward her": having the old line end with "spoke," the new line begin with "advancing," makes the very structure of the lines express the way in which he looms up, gets bigger. (Five lines later Frost repeats the effect even more forcibly with : "He said to gain time : 'What is it you see,' / Mounting until she cowered under him.") Now when the man asks : "What is it you see / From up there always—for I want to know," the word "always" tells us that all this has gone on many times before, and that he has seen it— without speaking of it—a number of times before. The phrase "for I want to know" is a characteristic example of the heavy, willed demands that the man makes, and an even more characteristic example of the tautological, rhetorical announcements of his actions that he so often makes, as if he felt that the announcement somehow justified or excused the action.

The poem goes on : "She turned and sank upon her skirts at that. . . ." The stairs permit her to subside into a modest, compact, feminine bundle; there is a kind of smooth deftness about the phrase, as if it were some feminine saying : "When in straits, sink upon your skirts." The next line, "And her face changed from terrified to dull," is an economically elegant way of showing how the terror of surprise (perhaps with another fear underneath it) changes into the dull lack of response that is her regular mask for him. The poem continues : "He said to gain time"—to gain time in which to think of the next thing to say, to gain time in which to get close to her and gain the advantage of his physical nearness, his physical bulk. His next "What is it you see" is the first of his many repetitions; if one knew only this man one would say, "Man is the animal that repeats." In the poem's next phrase, "mounting until she cowered under him," the identity of the vowels in "mounting" and "cowered" physically connects the two, makes his mounting the plain immediate cause of her cowering. "I will find out now" is another of his rhetorical announcements of what he is going to do: "this time you're going to tell me, I'm going to make you." But this heavy-willed compulsion changes into sheer appeal, into reasonable beseeching, in his next phrase: "You must tell me, dear." The "dear" is affectionate intimacy, the "must" is the "must" of rational necessity; yet the underlying form of the sentence is that of compulsion. The poem goes on: "She, in her place, refused him any help. . . ." The separated phrase "in her place" describes and embodies, with economical brilliance, both her physical and spiritual lack of outgoingness, forthcomingness; she brims over none of her contours, remains sitting upon her skirts upon her stairstep, in feminine exclusion. "Refused him any help / With the least stiffening of her neck and silence": she doesn't say Yes, doesn't say No, doesn't say; her refusal of any answer is worse than almost any answer. "The least stiffening of her neck," in its concise reserve, its slight precision, is more nearly conclusive than any larger gesture of rejection. He, in extremities, usually repeats some proverbial or rhetorical generalization; at such moments she usually responds either with a particular, specific sentence or else with something more particular than any sentence: with some motion or gesture.

The next line, "She let him look, sure that he wouldn't see," reminds one of some mother bird so

certain that her nest is hidden that she doesn't even
flutter off, but sits there on it, risking what is no risk,
in complacent superiority. "Sure that he wouldn't
see, / Blind creature": the last phrase is quoted from
her mind, is her contemptuous summing up. "And
awhile he didn't see"; but at last when he sees, he
doesn't tell her what it is, doesn't silently understand,
but with heavy slow comprehension murmurs, "Oh,"
and then repeats, "Oh." It is another announcement of
what he is doing, a kind of dramatic rendition of his
understanding. (Sometimes when we are waiting for
someone, and have made some sound or motion we are
afraid will seem ridiculous to the observer we didn't
know was there, we rather ostentatiously look at our
watch, move our face and lips into a "What on earth
could have happened to make him so late?" as a way
of justifying our earlier action. The principle behind
our action is the principle behind many of this man's
actions.) With the undignified alacrity of someone
hurrying to reestablish a superiority that has been
questioned, the woman cries out like a child: "What is
it—what?" Her sentence is, so to speak, a rhetorical
question rather than a real one, since it takes it for
granted that a correct answer can't be made. His reply, "Just that I see," shows that his unaccustomed
insight has given him an unaccustomed composure;
she has had the advantage, for so long, of being the
only one who knows, that he for a moment prolongs
the advantage of being the only one who knows that
he knows. The immediately following " 'You don't,'
she challenged. 'Tell me what it is' " is the instant,

childishly assertive exclamation of someone whose human position depends entirely upon her knowing what some inferior being can never know; she cannot let another second go by without hearing the incorrect answer that will confirm her in her rightness and superiority.

The man goes on explaining, to himself, and to mankind, and to her too, in slow rumination about it and about it. In his "The wonder is I didn't see at once. / I never noticed it from here before. / I must be wonted to it—that's the reason," one notices how "wonder" and "once" prepare for "wonted," that provincial-, archaic-sounding word that sums up—as "used" never could—his reliance on a habit or accustomedness which at last sees nothing but itself, and hardly sees that; and when it does see something through itself, beyond itself, slowly marvels. In the next line, "The little graveyard where my people are!" we feel not only the triumph of the slow person at last comprehending, but also the tender, easy accustomedness of habit, of long use, of a kind of cozy social continuance—for him the graves are not the healed scars of old agonies, but are something as comfortable and accustomed as the photographs in the family album. "So small the window frames the whole of it," like the later "Broad-shouldered little slabs there in the sunlight / On the sidehill," not only has this easy comfortable acceptance, but also has the regular feel of a certain sort of Frost nature description: this is almost the only place in the poem where for a moment we feel that it is Frost talking first and the man talking second. But the man's "Not so much larger than a bedroom, is it?"—an observation that appeals to her for agreement—carries this comfortable acceptance to a point at which it becomes intolerable: the only link between the bedroom and the graveyard is the child conceived in their bedroom and buried in that graveyard. The sentence comfortably establishes a connection which she cannot bear to admit the existence of—she tries to keep the two things permanently separated in her mind. (What he says amounts to his saying about their bedroom: "Not so much smaller than the graveyard, is it?") "There are three stones of slate and one of marble, / Broad-shouldered little slabs there in the sunlight / On the side-hill" has a heavy tenderness and accustomedness about it, almost as if he were running his hand over the grain of the stone. The "little" graveyard and "little" slabs are examples of our regular way of making something acceptable or dear by means of a diminutive.

Next, to show her how well he understands, the man shows her how ill he understands. He says about his family's graves: "We haven't to mind *those*"; that is, we don't have to worry about, grieve over, my people: it is not your obligation to grieve for them at all, nor mine to give them more than their proper share of grief, the amount I long ago measured out and used up. But with the feeling, akin to a sad, modest, relieved, surprised pride, with which he regularly responds to his own understanding, he tells her that he does understand: what matters is not the old stones but the new mound, the displaced earth piled up above the grave which he had dug and in which their child is buried.

When he says this, it is as if he had touched, with a crude desecrating hand, the sacred, forbidden secret upon which her existence depends. With shuddering hysterical revulsion she cries: "Don't, don't, don't, don't." (If the reader will compare the effect of Frost's four *don't*'s with the effect of three or five, he will see once more how exactly accurate, perfectly effective, almost everything in the poem is.) The poem continues: "She withdrew shrinking from beneath his arm / That rested on the banister, and slid downstairs"; the word "slid" says, with vivid indecorousness, that anything goes in extremities, that you can't be bothered, then, by mere appearance or propriety; "slid" has the ludicrous force of actual fact, is the way things are instead of the way we agree they are. In the line "And turned on him with such a daunting look," the phrase "turned on him" makes her resemble a cornered animal turning on its pursuer; and "with such a daunting look" is the way he phrases it to himself, is quoted from his mind as "blind creature" was quoted from hers. The beautifully provincial, old-fashioned, folk-sounding "daunting" reminds one of the similar, slightly earlier "wonted," and seems to make immediate, as no other word could, the look that cows him. The next line, "He said twice over before he knew himself," tells us that repetition, saying something twice over, is something he regresses to under stress; unless he can consciously prevent himself from repeating, he repeats. What he says twice over (this is the third time already that he has repeated something) is a rhetorical question, a querulous, plaintive appeal to public opinion: "Can't a man speak of his own child he's lost?" He does not say specifically, particularly, with confidence in himself: "I've the right to speak of our dead child"; instead he cites the acknowledged fact that any member of the class *man* has the acknowledged right to mention, just to mention, that member of the class of his belongings, *his own child*—and he has been unjustly deprived of this right. "His own child he's lost" is a way of saying: "You act as if he were just yours, but he's just as much just mine; that's an established fact." "Can't a man speak of his own child he's lost" has a magnificently dissonant, abject, aggrieved querulousness about it, in all its sounds and all its rhythms; "Can't a man" prepares us for the even more triumphantly ugly dissonance (or should I say consonance?) of the last two words in her "I don't know rightly whether any man can."

Any rhetorical question demands, expects, the hearer's automatic agreement; there is nothing it expects less than a particular, specific denial. The man's "Can't a man speak . . ." means "Isn't any man allowed to speak . . . ," but her fatally specific answer, "Not you!" makes it mean, "A man cannot—is not able to—speak, if the man is you." Her "Oh, where's my hat?" is a speech accompanied by action, means: "I'm leaving. Where's the hat which social convention demands that a respectable woman put on,

to go out into the world?" The immediately following
"Oh, I don't need it!" means: in extremities, in cases
when we come down to what really matters, what
does social convention or respectability really matter?
Her "I must get out of here. I must get air" says that
you breathe understanding and suffocate without it,
and that in this house, for her, there is none. Then,
most extraordinarily, she gives a second specific answer to his rhetorical question, that had expected none:
"I don't know rightly whether any man can." The
line says: "Perhaps it is not the individual *you* that's
to blame, but man in general; perhaps a woman is
wrong to expect that any man can speak—really
speak—of his dead child."

His "Amy! Don't go to someone else this time" of
course tells us that another time she *has* gone to someone else; and it tells us the particular name of this most
particular woman, something that she and the poem
never tell us about the man. The man's "Listen to me.
I won't come down the stairs" tells us that earlier he
has come down the stairs, hasn't kept his distance. It
(along with "shrinking," "cowered," and many later
things in the poem) tells us that he has given her
reason to be physically afraid of him; his "I won't
come down the stairs" is a kind of euphemism for "I
won't hurt you, won't even get near you."

The poem's next sentence, "He sat and fixed his
chin between his fists"—period, end of line—with its
four short *i*'s, its "fixed" and "fists," fixes him in
baffled separateness; the sentence fits into the line as he
fits into the isolated perplexity of his existence. Once

more he makes a rhetorical announcement of what he
is about to do, before he does it: "There's something I
should like to ask you, dear." The sentence tiptoes in,
gentle, almost abjectly mollifying, and ends with a
reminding "dear"; it is an indirect rhetorical appeal
that expects for an answer at least a grudging: "Well,
go ahead and ask it, then." His sentence presupposes
the hearer's agreement with what it implies: "Anyone is at least allowed to *ask*, even if afterwards you
refuse him what he asks." The woman once more gives
a direct, crushing, *particular* answer: "You don't
know how to ask it." "Anyone may be allowed to ask,
but *you* are not because you are not able to ask"; we
don't even need to refuse an animal the right to ask
and be refused, since if we gave him the right he
couldn't exercise it. The man's "Help me, then," has
an absolute, almost abject helplessness, a controlled
childlike simplicity, that we pity and sympathize
with; yet we can't help remembering the other side of
the coin, the heavy, brutal, equally simple and helpless anger of his later *I'll come down to you.*

The next line, "Her fingers moved the latch for all
reply" (like the earlier "She . . . refused him any
help / With the least stiffening of her neck and silence"; like / "And turned on him with such a daunting look"; like the later "She moved the latch a little";
like the last "She was opening the door wider"), reminds us that the woman has a motion language more
immediate, direct, and particular than words—a language she resorts to in extremities, just as he, in
extremities, resorts to a language of repeated prover-

bial generalizations. "Home Burial" starts on the stairs but continues in the doorway, on the threshold between the old life inside and the new life outside.

The man now begins his long appeal with the slow, heavy, hopeless admission that "My words are nearly always an offence." This can mean, "Something is nearly always wrong with me and my words," but it also can mean—does mean, underneath —that she is to be blamed for nearly always finding offensive things that certainly are not meant to offend. "I don't know how to speak of anything / So as to please you" admits, sadly blames himself for, his baffled ignorance, but it also suggests that she is unreasonably, fantastically hard to please—if the phrase came a little later in his long speech he might pronounce it "so as to please *you*." (Whatever the speaker intends, there are no long peacemaking speeches in a quarrel; after a few sentences the speaker always has begun to blame the other again.) The man's aggrieved, blaming "But I might be taught, I should suppose" is followed by the helpless, very endearing admission: "I can't say I see how"; for the moment this removes the blame from her, and his honesty of concession makes us unwilling to blame him. He tries to summarize his dearly bought understanding in a generalization, almost a proverb: "A man must partly give up being a man / With women-folk." The sentence begins in the dignified regretful sunlight of the main floor, in "A man must partly give up being a man," and ends huddled in the basement below, in "With women-folk." He doesn't use the parallel, coordinate "with a woman," but the entirely different "with women-folk"; the sentence tries to be fair and objective, but it is as completely weighted a sentence as "A man must partly give up being a man with the kiddies," or "A man must partly give up being a man with Bandar-log." The sentence presupposes that the real right norm is a man being a man with men, and that some of this rightness and normality always must be sacrificed with that special case, that inferior anomalous category, "women-folk."

He goes on: "We could have some arrangement [it has a hopeful, indefinite, slightly helter-skelter sound] / By which I'd bind myself to keep hands off"—the phrases "bind myself" and "keep hands off" have the primitive, awkward materiality of someone taking an oath in a bad saga; we expect the sentence to end in some awkwardly impressive climax, but get the almost ludicrous anticlimax of "Anything special you're a-mind to name." And, too, the phrase makes whatever she names quite willful on her part, quite unpredictable by reasonable man. His sensitivity usually shows itself to be a willing, hopeful form of insensitivity, and he himself realizes this here, saying, "Though I don't like such things 'twixt those that love." Frost then makes him express his own feeling in a partially truthful but elephantine aphorism that lumbers through a queerly stressed line a foot too long ("Two that don't love can't live together without them") into a conclusion ("But two that do can't live together with them") that has some of the slow, heavy relish just in being proverbial that the man so often shows. (How hard it is to get through the monosyllables of the two lines!) His words don't convince her, and she replies to them without words: "She moved the latch a little." He repeats in grieved appeal: "Don't—don't go. / Don't carry it to someone else this time." (He is repeating an earlier sentence, with "Don't go" changed to "Don't carry it.") The next line, "Tell me about it if it's something human," is particularly interesting when it comes from him. When is something inside a human being not human, so that it can't be told? Isn't it when it is outside man's understanding, outside all man's categories and pigeonholes—when there is no proverb to say for it? It is, then, a waste or abyss impossible to understand or manage or share with another. His next appeal to her, "Let me into your grief," combines an underlying sexual metaphor with a child's "Let me in! let me in!" This man who is so much a member of the human community feels a helpless bewilderment at being shut out of the little group of two of which he was once an anomalous half; the woman has put in the place of this group a group of herself-and-the-dead-child, and he begs or threatens—reasons with her as best he can—in his attempt to get her to restore the first group, so that there will be a man-and-wife grieving over their dead child.

He goes on: "I'm not so much / Unlike other folks as your standing there / Apart would make me out." The "standing there / Apart" is an imitative, expressive form that makes her apart, shows her apart.

Really her apartness makes him out *like* other folks,
all those others who make pretense of following to the
grave, but who before one's back is turned have made
their way back to life; but he necessarily misunderstands her, since for him being like others is necessarily good, being unlike them necessarily bad. His
"Give me my chance"—he doesn't say *a* chance—reminds one of those masculine things fairness and
sportsmanship, and makes one think of the child's
demand for justice, equal shares, which follows his
original demand for exclusive possession, the lion's
share. "Give me my chance" means: "You, like everybody else, must admit that anybody deserves a
chance—so give me mine"; he deserves his chance not
by any particular qualities, personal merit, but just
by virtue of being a human being. His "I do think,
though, you overdo it a little" says that he is forced
against his will to criticize her for so much exceeding
(the phrase "a little" is understatement, politeness,
and caution) the norm of grief, for mourning more
than is usual or reasonable; the phrase "overdo it a
little" manages to reduce her grief to the level of a
petty social blunder. His next words, "What was it
brought you up to think it the thing / To take your
mother-loss of a first child / So inconsolably—in the
face of love," manage to crowd four or five kinds of
condemnation into a single sentence. "What was it
brought you up" says that it is not your essential
being but your accidental upbringing that has made
you do this—it reduces the woman to a helpless social
effect. "To think it the thing" is particularly insult-

ing because it makes her grief a mere matter of fash-
ion; it is as though he were saying, "What was it
brought you up to think it the thing to wear your
skirt that far above your knees?" The phrase "to take
your mother-loss of a first child" pigeonholes her loss,
makes it a regular, predictable category that demands
a regular, predictable amount of grief, and no more.
The phrase "So inconsolably—in the face of love"
condemns her for being so unreasonable as not to be
consoled by, for paying no attention to, that unargu-
ably good, absolutely general thing, love; the generalized *love* makes demands upon her that are inescapable, compared to those which would be made by
a more specific phrase like "in the face of my love for
you." The man's "You'd think his memory might be
satisfied" again condemns her for exceeding the reasonable social norm of grief; condemns her, jealously,
for mourning as if the dead child's demands for grief
were insatiable.

Her interruption, "There you go sneering now!"
implies that he has often before done what she calls
"sneering" at her and her excessive sensitivity; and,
conscious of how hard he has been trying to make
peace, and unconscious of how much his words have
gone over into attack, he contradicts her like a child, in
righteous anger: "I'm not, I'm not!" His "You make
me angry" is another of his rhetorical, tautological
announcements about himself, one that is intended
somehow to justify the breaking of his promise not to
come down to her; he immediately makes the simple
childish threat, "I'll come down to you"—he is re-

peating his promise, "I won't come down to you,"
with the "not" removed. "God, what a woman!" right-
eously and despairingly calls on God and public opinion (that voice of the people which is the voice of God)
to witness and marvel at what he is being forced to put
up with : the fantastic, the almost unbelievable wrongness and unreasonableness of this woman. "And it's
come to this," that regular piece of rhetorical recrimi-
nation in quarrels, introduces his *third* use of the
sentence "Can't a man speak of his own child he's
lost"; but this time the rhetorical question is changed
into the factual condemnation of "A man can't speak
of his own child that's dead." This time he doesn't end
the sentence with the more sentimental, decorous,
sympathy-demanding "that's lost," but ends with the
categorical "that's dead."

Earlier the woman has given two entirely different,
entirely specific and unexpected answers to this rhetorical question of his; this time she has a third specific
answer, which she makes with monosyllabic precision
and finality : "You can't because you don't know how
to speak." He has said that it is an awful thing not to
be permitted to speak of his own dead child; she replies
that it is not a question of permission but of ability,
that he is too ignorant and insensitive to be *able* to
speak of his child. Her sentence is one line long, and it
is only the second sentence of hers that has been that
long. He has talked at length during the first two-
thirds of the poem, she in three- or four-word phrases
or in motions without words; for the rest of the poem
she talks at length, as everything that has been shut

up inside her begins to pour out. She opens herself up, now—is far closer to him, striking at him with her words, than she has been sitting apart, in her place. His open attack has finally elicited from her, by contagion, her open anger, so that now he is something real and unbearable to attack, instead of being something less than human to be disregarded.

This first sentence has indicted him; now she brings in the specific evidence for the indictment. She says: "If you had any feelings, you that dug / With your own hand"—but after the three stabbing, indicting stresses of

$$\overset{/}{\text{your}}\ \overset{/}{\text{own}}\ \overset{/}{\text{hand}}$$

she breaks off the sentence, as if she found the end unbearable to go on to; interjects, her throat tightening, the incredulous rhetorical question, "how could you?"—and finishes with the fact that she tries to make more nearly endurable, more euphemistic, with the tender word "little" : "his little grave." The syntax of the sentence doesn't continue, but the fact of things continues; she says, "I saw you from that very window there."

$$\overset{/}{\text{That}}\ \overset{/}{\text{very}}\ \overset{/}{\text{window}}\ \overset{/}{\text{there}}$$

has the same stabbing stresses, the same emphasis on a specific, damning actuality, that

$$\overset{/}{\text{your}}\ \overset{/}{\text{own}}\ \overset{/}{\text{hand}}$$

had—and that, soon,

/ / /
my own eyes

and

/ / /   /
your own baby's grave

and other such phrases will have. She goes on: "Making the gravel leap and leap in air, / Leap up, like that, like that, and land so lightly / And roll back down the mound beside the hole." As the sentence imitates with such terrible life and accuracy the motion of the gravel, her throat tightens and aches in her hysterical repetition of "like that, like that": the sounds of "leap and leap in air, / Leap up, like that, like that, and land so lightly" are "le! le! le! li! li! la! li!" and re-create the sustained hysteria she felt as she first watched; inanimate things, the very stones, leap and leap in air, or when their motion subsides land "so lightly," while the animate being, her dead child, does not move, will never move. (The foxes have holes, and the birds of the air have nests; but the Son of man hath not where to lay his head.) Her words "leap and leap in air, / Leap up, like that, like that" keep the stones alive! alive! alive!—in the words "and land" they start to die away, but the following words "so lightly" make them alive again, for a last moment of unbearable contradiction, before they *"roll* back *down* the *mound* beside the *hole."* The repeated o's (the line says "oh! ow! ow! oh!") make almost crudely actual the abyss of death into which the

2 1 3

pieces of gravel and her child fall, not to rise again. The word "hole" (insisted on even more by the rhyme with "roll") gives to the grave the obscene actuality that watching the digging forced it to have for her.

She says: "I thought, Who is that man? I didn't know you." She sees the strange new meaning in his face (what, underneath, the face has meant all along) so powerfully that the face itself seems a stranger's. If her own husband can do something so impossibly alien to all her expectations, he has never really been anything but alien; all her repressed antagonistic knowledge about his insensitivity comes to the surface and masks what before had masked it. In the next sentence, "And I crept down the stairs and up the stairs / To look again," the word "crept" makes her a little mouselike thing crushed under the weight of her new knowledge. But the truly extraordinary word is the "and" that joins "down the stairs" to "up the stairs." What is so extraordinary is that she sees nothing extraordinary about it: the "and" joining the two coordinates hides from her, shows that she has repressed, the thoroughly illogical, contradictory nature of her action; it is like saying: "And I ran out of the fire and back into the fire," and seeing nothing strange about the sentence.

Her next words, "and still your spade kept lifting," give the man's tool a dead, mechanical life of its own; it keeps on and on, crudely, remorselessly, neither guided nor halted by spirit. She continues: "Then you came in. I heard your rumbling voice / Out in the kitchen"; the word "rumbling" gives this great blind creature an insensate weight and strength that are, somehow, hollow. Then she says that she did something as extraordinary as going back up the stairs, but she masks it, this time, with the phrase "and I don't know why." She doesn't know why, it's un-accountable, "But I went near to see with my own eyes." Her "I don't know why" shows her regular refusal to admit things like these; she manages by a confession of ignorance not to have to make the con-nections, consciously, that she has already made un-consciously.

She now says a sentence that is an extraordinarily conclusive condemnation of him : "You could sit there with the stains on your shoes / Of the fresh earth from your own baby's grave / And talk about your everyday concerns." The five hissing or spitting *s*'s in the strongly accented "sit," "stains," "shoes"; the whole turning upside down of the first line, with four trochaic feet followed by one poor iamb; the concen-tration of intense, damning stresses in

$$\overset{/}{\text{fresh}} \ \overset{/}{\text{earth}} \ \text{of} \ \overset{/}{\text{your}} \ \overset{/}{\text{own}} \ \overset{/}{\text{baby's}} \ \overset{/}{\text{grave}}$$

—all these things give an awful finality to the judge's summing up, so that in the last line, "And talk about your everyday concerns," the criminal's matter-of-fact obliviousness has the perversity of absolute in-sensitivity : Judas sits under the cross matching pennies with the soldiers. The poem has brought to life an unthought-of literal meaning of its title : this is home burial with a vengeance, burial *in* the home; the fresh dirt of the grave stains her husband's shoes and her kitchen floor, and the dirty spade with which he dug the grave stands there in the entry. As a final unnecessary piece of evidence, a last straw that comes long after the camel's back is broken, she states: "You had stood the spade up against the wall / Outside there in the entry, for I saw it." All her pieces of evidence have written underneath them, like Goya's drawing, that triumphant, traumatic, unarguable I SAW IT.

The man's next sentence is a kind of summing-up-in-little of his regular behavior, the ways in which (we have come to see) he *has* to respond. He has begged her to let him into her grief, to tell him about it if it's something human; now she lets him into not her grief but her revolted, hating condemnation of him; she does tell him about it and it isn't human, but a nightmare into which he is about to fall. He says: "I shall laugh the worst laugh I ever laughed. / I'm cursed. God, if I don't believe I'm cursed." The sounds have the gasping hollowness of somebody hit in the stomach and trying over and over to get his breath— of someone nauseated and beginning to vomit: the first stressed vowel sounds are "agh! uh! agh! uh! agh! uh!" He doesn't reply to her, argue with her, address her at all, but makes a kind of dramatic speech that will exhibit him in a role public opinion will surely sympathize with, just as he sympathizes with himself. As always, he repeats: "laugh," "laugh," and "laughed," "I'm cursed" and "I'm cursed" (the rhyme with "worst" gives almost the effect of another repetition);

as always, he announces beforehand what he is going to do, rhetorically appealing to mankind for justification and sympathy. His "I shall laugh the worst laugh I ever laughed" has the queer effect of seeming almost to be quoting some folk proverb. His "I'm cursed" manages to find a category of understanding in which to pigeonhole this nightmare, makes him a reasonable human being helpless against the inhuman powers of evil—the cursed one is not to blame. His "God, if I don't believe I'm cursed" is akin to his earlier "God, what a woman!"—both have something of the male's outraged, incredulous, despairing response to the unreasonableness and immorality of the female. He responds hardly at all to the exact situation; instead he demands sympathy for, sympathizes with himself for, the impossibly unlucky pigeonhole into which Fate has dropped him.

His wife then repeats the sentence that, for her, sums up everything: "I can repeat the very words you were saying. / 'Three foggy mornings and one rainy day / Will rot the best birch fence a man can build.' " We feel with a rueful smile that he has lived by proverbs and—now, for her—dies by them. He has handled his fresh grief by making it a part of man's regular routine, man's regular work; and by quoting man's regular wisdom, that explains, explains away, pigeonholes, anything. Nature tramples down man's work, the new fence rots, but man still is victorious, in the secure summing up of the proverb.

/ / /
The best birch fence

is, so far as its stresses are concerned, a firm, comfortable parody of all those stabbing stress systems of hers. In his statement, as usual, it is not *I* but *a man*. There is a resigned but complacent, almost relishing wit about this summing up of the transitoriness of human effort: to understand your defeat so firmly, so proverbially, is in a sense to triumph. He has seen his ordinary human ambition about that ordinary human thing, a child, frustrated by death; so there is a certain resignation and pathos about his saying what he says. The word "rot" makes the connection between the fence and the child, and it is the word "rot" that is unendurable to the woman, since it implies with obscene directness: how many foggy mornings and rainy days will it take to rot the best flesh-and-blood child a man can have? Just as, long ago at the beginning of the poem, the man brought the bedroom and the grave together, he brings the rotting child and the rotting fence together now. She says in incredulous, breathless outrage: "Think of it, talk like that at such a time!" (The repeated sounds, *th, t, t, th, t, t,* are thoroughly expressive.) But once more she has repressed the connection between the two things: she objects to the sentence not as what she knows it is, as rawly and tactlessly relevant, but as something absolutely irrelevant, saying: "What had how long it takes a birch to rot / To do with"—and then she puts in a euphemistic circumlocution, lowers her eyes and lowers the shades so as not to see—"what was in the darkened parlor."

But it is time to go back and think of just what it

was the woman saw, just how she saw it, to make her keep on repeating that first occasion of its sight. She saw it on a holy and awful day. The child's death and burial were a great and almost unendurable occasion, something that needed to be accompanied with prayer and abstention, with real grief and the ritual expression of grief. It was a holy or holi-day that could only be desecrated by "everyday concerns"; the husband's digging seemed to the wife a kind of brutally unfeeling, secular profanation of that holy day, her holy grief. Her description makes it plain that her husband dug strongly and well. And why should he not do so? Grief and grave digging, for him, are in separate compartments; the right amount of grief will never flow over into the next compartment. To him it is the workaday, matter-of-fact thing that necessarily comes first; grieving for the corpse is no excuse for not having plenty of food at the wake. If someone had said to him: "You dig mighty well for a man that's just lost his child," wouldn't he have replied: "Grief's no reason for doing a bad job"? (And yet, the muscles tell the truth; a sad enough man shovels badly.) When, the grave dug and the spade stood up in the entry, he went into the kitchen, he may very well have felt: "A good job," just as Yakov, in *Rothschild's Fiddle*, taps the coffin he has made for his wife and thinks: "A good job."

But unconsciously, his wife has far more compelling reasons to be appalled at this job her husband is doing. Let me make this plain. If we are told how a woman dreams of climbing the stairs, and of looking out through a window at a man digging a hole with a spade—digging powerfully, so that the gravel leaps and leaps into the air, only to roll back down into the hole; and still the man's spade keeps lifting and plunging down, lifting and plunging down, as she watches in fascinated horror, creeps down the stairs, creeps back up against her will, to keep on watching; and then, she doesn't know why, she has to go to see with her own eyes the fresh earth staining the man's shoes, has to see with her own eyes the man's tool stood up against the wall, in the entrance to the house—if we are told such a dream, is there any doubt what *sort* of dream it will seem to us? Such things have a sexual force, a sexual meaning, as much in our waking hours as in our dreams—as we know from how many turns of speech, religious rites, myths, tales, works of art. When the plowman digs his plow into the earth, Mother Earth, to make her bear, this does not have a sexual appropriateness only in the dreams of neurotic patients—it is something that we all understand, whether or not we admit that we understand. So the woman understood her husband's digging. If the spade, the tool that he stands up in the entry, stands for man's workaday world, his matter-of-fact objectivity and disregard of emotion, it also stands for his masculinity, his sexual power; on this holy day he brings back into the house of grief the soiling stains of fresh earth, of this digging that, to her, is more than digging.

That day of the funeral the grieving woman felt only misery and anguish, passive suffering; there was nobody to blame for it all except herself. And how often women do blame themselves for the abnormality or death of a baby! An old doctor says they keep blaming themselves; they should have done this, that, something; they forget all about their husbands; often they blame some doctor who, by not coming immediately, by doing or not doing something, was responsible for it all: the woman's feeling of guilt about other things is displaced onto the child's death. Now when this woman sees her husband digging the grave (doing what seems to her, consciously, an intolerably insensitive thing; unconsciously, an indecent thing) she *does* have someone to blame, someone upon whom to shift her own guilt: she is able to substitute for passive suffering and guilt an active loathing and condemnation—as she blames the man's greater guilt and wrongness her own lesser guilt can seem in comparison innocence and rightness. (The whole matrix of attitudes available to her, about woman as Madonna-and-child and man as brute beast, about sexuality as a defiling thing forced upon woman, helps her to make this shift.) The poem has made it easy for us to suspect a partial antagonism or uncongeniality, sexually, between the weak oversensitive woman and the strong insensitive man, with his sexual force so easily transformed into menace. (The poem always treats it in that form.) The woman's negative attitudes have been overwhelmingly strengthened, now; it is plain that since the child's death there has been no sort of sexual or emotional union between them.

To her, underneath, the child's death must have seemed a punishment. Of whom for what? Of them for what they have done—sexual things are always tinged with guilt; but now her complete grief, her separateness and sexual and emotional abstention, help to cancel out her own guilt—the man's matter-of-fact physical obliviousness, his desire to have everything what it was before, reinforce his own guilt and help to make it seem absolute. Yet, underneath, the woman's emotional and physiological needs remain unchanged, and are satisfied by this compulsory symptomatic action of hers—this creeping up the stairs, looking, looking, creeping down and then back up again, looking, looking; she stares with repudiating horror, with accepting fascination, at this obscenely symbolic sight. It is not the child's mound she stares at, but the scene of the crime, the site of this terrible symbolic act that links sexuality and death, the marriage bed and the grave. (Afterwards she had gone down into the kitchen to see the man flushed and healthy, breathing a little harder after physical exertion; her words "I heard your *rumbling* voice / Out in the kitchen" remind us of that first telling description of him on the stairs, "*Mounting* until she *cowered* under him." Her first response to the sight, "I thought: Who *is* that man? I didn't know you," makes him not her husband but a stranger, a guilty one, whom she is right to remain estranged from, must remain estranged from.) Her repeated symptomatic act has the consciousness of obsessional-compulsive symptoms, not the unconsciousness of hysterical blindness or paralysis: she is conscious of what she is doing, knows how it all began; and yet she cannot keep from doing it, does not really know why she does it, and is conscious only of a part of the meaning it has for her. She has isolated it, and refuses to see its connections, consciously, because the connections are so powerful unconsciously : so that she says, "And I crept down the stairs *and* up the stairs"; says, *"And I don't know why,* / But I went near to see with my own eyes"; says, "What had how long it takes a birch to rot / To do with what was in the darkened parlor?"

This repeated symptomatic action of hers satisfies several needs. It keeps reassuring her that she is right to keep herself fixed in separation and rejection. By continually revisiting this scene, by looking again and again at—so to speak—this indecent photograph of her husband's crime, she is making certain that she will never come to terms with the criminal who, in the photograph, is committing the crime. Yet, underneath, there is a part of her that takes guilty pleasure in the crime, that is in identifying complicity with the criminal. A symptom or symptomatic action is an expression not only of the defense against the forbidden wish, but also of the forbidden wish.

If the reader doubts that this symptomatic action of hers has a sexual root, he can demonstrate it to himself by imagining the situation different in one way. Suppose the wife had looked out of the window and seen her husband animatedly and matter-of-factly bargaining to buy a cemetery lot from one of the next day's funeral guests. She would have been

angered and revolted. But would she have crept back
to look again? have gone into the kitchen so as to see
the bargainer with her own eyes? have stared in fascination at the wallet from which he had taken the
money? Could she as easily have made a symptom
of it?

After she has finished telling the story of what she
had seen, of what he had done, she cries: "You
couldn't care!" The words say: "If you could behave
as you behaved, it proves that you didn't care and,
therefore, that you couldn't care; if you, my own
husband, the child's own father, were unable to care, it
proves that it must be impossible for anyone to care."
So she goes on, not about him but about everyone:
"The nearest friends can go / With anyone to death,
comes so far short / They might as well not try to go
at all." The sentence has some of the rueful, excessive
wit of Luther's "In every good act the just man sins";
man can do so little he might as well do nothing. Her
next sentence, "No, from the time when one is sick to
death, / One is alone, and he dies more alone," tolls
like a lonely bell for the human being who grieves for
death and, infected by what she grieves for, dies alone
in the pesthouse, deserted by the humanity that takes
good care not to be infected. When you truly feel
what death is, you must die: all her phrases about the
child's death and burial make them her own death and
burial.

She goes on: "Friends make pretense of following to
the grave, / But before one is in it, their minds are
turned"—her "make pretense" blames their, his, well-

meant hypocrisy; her "before one is in it" speaks of
the indecent haste with which he hurried to dig the
grave into which the baby was put, depriving her of
it—of the indecent haste with which he forgot death
and wanted to resume life. The phrases "their minds
are turned" and "making the best of their way back"
are (as so often with Frost) queerly effective adaptations of ordinary idioms, of "their backs are turned"
and "making the best of things"; these are the plain
roots, in the woman's mind, of her less direct and more
elaborate phrases. But when we have heard her whole
sentence: "Friends make pretense of following to the
grave, / But before one is in it, their minds are
turned / And making the best of their way back to
life / And living people, and things they understand," we reply: "As they must." She states as an
evil what we think at worst a necessary evil; she is
condemning people for not committing suicide, for not
going down into the grave with the corpse and dying
there. She condemns the way of the world, but it is
the way of any world that continues to be a world:
the world that does otherwise perishes. Her "But the
world's evil. I won't have grief so / If I can change it.
Oh, I won't, I won't!" admits what grief is to everybody else; is generally; and says that she will change
the universal into her own contradictory particular if
she can: the sentence has its own defeat inside it. What
this grieving woman says about grief is analogous to a
dying woman's saying about death: "I won't have
death so if I can change it. Oh, I won't, I won't!" Even
the man responds to the despairing helplessness in her

"Oh, I won't, I won't!" She is still trying to be faithful and unchanging in her grief, but already she has begun to be faithless, has begun to change. Saying "I never have colds any more," an hour or two before one has a cold, is one's first unconscious recognition that one has caught cold; similarly, she says that other people forget and change but that she never will, just when she has begun to change—just when, by telling her husband the cause of her complete separation, she has begun to destroy the completeness of the separation. Her "Oh, I won't, I won't!" sounds helplessly dissolving, running down; already contains within it the admission of what it denies. Her "I won't have grief so" reminds us that grief *is* so, is by its very nature a transition to something that isn't grief. She knows it too, so that she says that everybody else is that way, the world is that way, but they're wrong, they're evil; *someone* must be different; *someone* honorably and quixotically, at no matter what cost, must contradict the nature of grief, the nature of the world.

All this is inconceivable to the man: if everybody is that way, it must be right to be that way; it would be insanity to think of any other possibility. She has put grief, the dead child, apart on an altar, to be kept separate and essential as long as possible—forever, if possible. He has immediately filed away the child, grief, in the pigeonhole of man's wont, man's proverbial understanding: the weight is off his own separate shoulders, and the shoulders of all mankind bear the burden. In this disaster of her child's death, her husband's crime, her one consolation is that she is inconsolable, has (good sensitive woman) grieved for months as her husband (bad insensitive man) was not able to grieve even for hours. Ceasing to grieve would destroy this consolation, would destroy the only way of life she has managed to find.

And yet she has begun to destroy them. When she says at the end of the poem: "How can I make you—" understand, see, she shows in her baffled, longing despair that she *has* tried to make him understand; has tried to help him as he asked her to help him. Her "You *couldn't* care," all her lines about what friends and the world necessarily are, excuse him in a way, by making him a necessarily insensitive part of a necessarily insensitive world that she alone is sensitive in: she is the one person desperately and forlornly trying to be different from everyone else, as she tries to keep death and grief alive in the middle of a world intent on its own forgetful life. At these last moments she does not, as he thinks, "set him apart" as "so much / Unlike other folks"; if he could hear and respond to what she actually has said, there would be some hope for them. But he doesn't; instead of understanding her special situation, he dumps her into the pigeonhole of the crying woman—any crying woman—and then tries to *manage* her as one manages a child. She does try to let him into her grief, but he won't go; instead he tells her that now she's had her cry, that now he feels better, that the heart's gone out of it, that there's really no grief left for him to be let into.

The helpless tears into which her hard self-right-
eous separateness has dissolved show, underneath, a
willingness to accept understanding; she has de-
nounced him, made a clean breast of things, and now
is accessible to the understanding or empathy that he
is unable to give her. Women are oversensitive, exag-
gerate everything, tell all, weep, and then are all
right: this is the pigeonhole into which he drops her.
So rapid an understanding can almost be called a form
of stupidity, of not even trying really to understand.
The bewitched, uncanny, almost nauseated helplessness of what he has said a few lines before: "I shall
laugh the worst laugh I ever laughed. / I'm cursed.
God, if I don't believe I'm cursed," has already changed
into a feeling of mastery, of the strong man understanding and managing the weak hysterical woman.
He is the powerful one now. His "There, you have
said it all and you feel better. / You won't go now"
has all the grownup's condescension toward the child,
the grownup's ability to make the child do something
simply by stating that the child is about to do it. The
man's "You're crying. Close the door. / The heart's
gone out of it: why keep it up" shows this quite as
strikingly; he feels that he can manipulate her back
into the house and into his life, back out of the grief
that—he thinks or hopes—no longer has any heart in
it, so that she must pettily and exhaustingly "keep it
up."

But at this moment when the depths have been
opened for him; at this moment when the proper
management might get her back into the house, the

proper understanding get her back into his life; at this
moment that it is fair to call the most important
moment of his life, someone happens to come down the
road. Someone who will see her crying and hatless in
the doorway; someone who will go back to the village
and tell everything; someone who will shame them in
the eyes of the world. Public opinion, what people will
say, is more important to him than anything she will
do; he forgets everything else, and expostulates:
"Amy! There's someone coming down the road!" His
exclamation is full of the tense, hurried fear of social
impropriety, of public disgrace; nothing could show
more forcibly what he *is* able to understand, what he
does think of primary importance. Her earlier "Oh,
where's my hat? Oh, I don't need it!" prepares for, is
the exact opposite of, his "Amy! There's someone
coming down the road!"

She says with incredulous, absolute intensity and
particularity, "*You*—"

That italicized *you* is the worst, the most nearly
final thing that she can say about him, since it
merely points to what he is. She doesn't go on; goes
back and replies to his earlier sentences: "oh, you
think the talk is all." Her words have a despairing
limpness and sadness: there is no possibility of his
being made to think anything different, to see the
truth under the talk. She says: "I must go—" and her
words merely recognize a reality— "Somewhere out
of this house." Her final words are full of a longing,
despairing, regretful realization of a kind of final
impossibility: "How can I make you—" The word

that isn't said, that she stops short of saying, is as much there as anything in the poem. All her insistent anxious pride in her own separateness and sensitiveness and superiority is gone; she knows, now, that she is separate from him no matter what she wants. Her "How can I make you—" amounts almost to "If only I could make you—if only there were some way to make you—but there is no way."

He responds not to what she says but to what she does, to "She was opening the door wider." He threatens, as a child would threaten: "If—you—do!" He sounds like a giant child, or a child being a giant or an ogre. The "If—you—do!" uses as its principle of being the exaggerated slowness and heaviness, the *willedness* of his nature. (Much about him reminds me of Yeats's famous definition: "Rhetoric is the will trying to do the work of the imagination"; "Home Burial" might be called the story of a marriage between the will and the imagination.) The dashes Frost inserts between the words slow down the words to the point where the slowedness or heaviness itself, as pure force and menace, is what is communicated. Then the man says, trying desperately—feebly—to keep her within reach of that force or menace: "Where do you mean to go? First tell me that. / I'll follow and bring you back by force. I *will!*—" The last sentences of each of her previous speeches (her despairing emotional "Oh, I won't, I won't!" and her despairing spiritual "How can I make you—") are almost the exact opposite of the "I *will!*" with which he ends the poem. It is appropriate that "force," "I," and "*will*" are his last three words: his proverbial, town-meeting understanding has failed, just as his blankly imploring humility has failed; so that he has to resort to the only thing he has left, the will or force that seems almost like the mass or inertia of a physical body. We say that someone "throws his weight around," and in the end there is nothing left for him to do but throw his weight around. Appropriately, his last line is one more rhetorical announcement of what he is going to do: he will follow and bring her back by force; and, appropriately, he ends the poem with one more repetition—he repeats: "I *will!*"

Six Russian Short Novels

D OSTOEVSKY WROTE, "We all come out from under Gogol's *Overcoat.*" Here is *The Overcoat*
and five of the stories that came out from under it:
Turgenev's *A Lear of the Steppes*, Leskov's *Lady Macbeth of the Mtsensk District*, Tolstoy's *Master and
Man* and *The Death of Ivan Ilych*, and Chekhov's
Ward No. 6. Dostoevsky himself is missing: I meant
for *The Eternal Husband* to be the seventh story in the
group, but it (along with *Notes from Underground*
and *The Double*) has already been printed as an Anchor Book.

I

WHEN TURGENEV, reduced to despair over the recep-
tion of *Fathers and Sons*, gave expression to the
passive gloom that underlay anything else in his
nature, he wrote: "The terrible thing is that there is
nothing terrible, that the very substance of life itself
is petty, uninteresting—and insipid to beggary." How

like Gogol he sounds! In Gogol's most characteristic work, what is terrible or splendid has been removed from life, leaving a tremendous blank—and into this blank everything that is petty, uninteresting, and insipid has pushed its way, there to proliferate, to be magnified, to become charged with fantastic imaginative intensity. Gogol's exaggeration of the trivial details of life, the random, contingent irrelevance of existence, manages to give to the most grotesque or insignificant creature an infinite plausibility, an unimaginable and inexplicable significance. Gogol himself wrote: "Those who have dissected my literary abilities were not able to find out the essential features of my nature. Only Pushkin was able to do it. He always asserted that no other author had such a capacity for bringing out all the trivialities of life, of describing so well the vulgarity of the mediocre man and life." This capacity is not a realistic or naturalistic one; Gogol's stories are not slices of life but fairy tales—or, in the case of *The Overcoat*, parables—of things. "My imagination," as Gogol says, "gets hold of the fact, begins to develop it into most horrid apparitions, which torture me, deprive me of my sleep and waste my strength." Gogol withdraws from sexual objects their charge, and transfers it to food and sleep and money, all the ordinary vegetative processes of existence. There is something slightly uncanny about even so beautiful and touching a story as *Old-World Landowners*, since the blissful domestic happiness of this Ukrainian Baucis and Philemon is presented entirely in vegetable terms—one cannot help remember-

ing that this apotheosis of eating, this delectable day-
dream and its grim conclusion, were written by a man
who, not so many years later, starved himself to
death. Ordinarily Gogol is a very troubling writer:
"God, how sad our Russia is!" Pushkin exclaimed after
hearing Gogol read the first chapter of *Dead Souls*, and
there are few of his stories that do not conclude with
that famous sentence, "It is gloomy in this world,
gentlemen." And yet in Gogol man is an absurd creature who sometimes is complacent in, is absurdly
happy because of, his absurdity. Goethe said that at
bottom it is a man's mistakes and foibles, his absurdities, that make him lovable, and we feel this as we
read what is incomparably the sweetest of Gogol's
stories, *The Overcoat*. How pleasant it is to read this
sad story of poverty, misfortune, and death! how
interesting it all is, down to the last foolish, insignificant, uninteresting detail!

We terribly identify ourselves with Tolstoy's Ivan
Ilych, joyfully and tenderly identify ourselves
with Gogol's Akaky Akakyevitch; Akaky Akakyevitch stands for the possible success in everybody's
failure, just as Ivan Ilych stands for the necessary
failure in everybody's success. *The Overcoat* seems to
us reality itself—who can keep from feeling the propriety, rightness, requiredness of everything in it?—
yet if we summarize it in a few sentences we realize
that it is a fairy tale about that dear simpleton the
third son, a parable about the Gospels' sparrows or children or poor in spirit. Once upon a time there was a
poor clerk that everybody made fun of, but he was

happy just the same. But then his overcoat wore out, and he didn't know what to do; but he worked and schemed and went without until finally he managed to get a wonderful new one. He was so happy! But the very first night he wore the overcoat someone stole it. He did everything to get it back, he even went to a general to get him to help; the general wouldn't help though, but gave him a terrible scolding—and what with getting so cold and being so upset, the clerk died. Then the clerk's ghost came back and began to steal people's overcoats, until finally one night he stole the general's; and the general was sorry he had been so cruel to the clerk, and never treated anyone that way again.

"Ivan Ilych's life had been most simple and most ordinary and therefore most terrible," Tolstoy writes, in one of the most frightening sentences in literature. Akaky Akakyevitch's life had been even simpler and even more ordinary and therefore—and therefore what? "Remember:" Gogol once wrote, "when the world is at its pettiest and life has become emptier than ever; when everything is covered with egoism and coldness and no one believes in miracles— it is precisely at such a time that the miracle of miracles can take place." *The Overcoat* is this miracle of miracles. Tolstoy makes us feel that since Ivan Ilych's powerful and successful bureaucratic existence is not reasonable, is not the truth, it is false, absurd, and terrible; Gogol makes us feel that the humble vanities, pleasures, and absurdities of Akaky Akakyevitch's meekly insignificant bureaucratic existence are, in spite of everything, a religious good. "He loved his work. . . . Certain letters were favorites of his, and when he came to them he was delighted; he chuckled to himself and moved his lips, so that it seemed as though every letter his pen was forming could be read in his face. . . . Whatever Akaky Akakyevitch looked at, he saw nothing anywhere but his clear, evenly written lines, and only perhaps when a horse's head suddenly appeared from nowhere just on his shoulder, and its nostrils blew a perfect gale upon his cheek, did he notice that he was not in the middle of his writing, but rather in the middle of the street. On reaching home, he would sit down at once to the table, hurriedly sup his soup and eat a piece of beef with an onion; he did not notice the taste at all, but ate it all up together with the flies and anything else that Providence chanced to send him. When he felt that his stomach was beginning to be full, he would rise up from the table, get out a bottle of ink and set to copying the papers he had brought home with him. When he had none to do, he would make a copy expressly for his own pleasure. . . . After working to his heart's content, he would go to bed, smiling at the thought of the next day and wondering what God would send him to copy."

The blissful possibility of "what God would send him to copy" is joined by its phrasing to the abject actuality of "flies and anything else that Providence chanced to send him." When a man's professional existence has swallowed up his human reality Sartre calls his life "unauthentic"; *The Death of Ivan Ilych*,

that most existential of stories, condemns such a life
more bitterly and more conclusively than any other
work of art has ever condemned it. Akaky Akakyevitch's life is so thoroughly unauthentic that "they
used to declare that he must have been born a copying
clerk in uniform all complete and with a bald patch on
his head." In Petrovitch, too, the man is swallowed up
in the tailor; his making of the overcoat, his final
delivery of the overcoat, represent a positive triumph
of unauthenticity. Yet this, like Akaky Akakyevitch's life-in-love-with-copying, is made to seem to
us funny, dear, and humbly authentic—what is man
not to be a clerk or a tailor? It is not until Akaky
Akakyevitch has fallen in love with the idea of the
overcoat, until his "whole existence had in a sense
become fuller, as though he had married, as though
some other person were present with him, as though he
were no longer alone, but an agreeable companion had
consented to walk the path of life hand in hand with
him," that for the first time in his life "when he was
copying a document, he very nearly made a mistake,
so that he almost cried out 'Ow' aloud and crossed
himself." But underneath the absurd, enchanted existence of the good child, the loving clerk, the man who
married his overcoat, there had always been the life of
the plain human being who must "sweat out his human lot" like the rest of us: "Only when the jokes
were too unbearable, when they jolted his arm and
prevented him from going on with his work, he would
bring out: 'Leave me alone! Why do you insult me?'
and there was something strange in the words and in

the voice in which they were uttered." The young man who has mocked him with the rest pities him and never forgets him, so that from then on "in those heartrending words he heard others: 'I am your brother.' "

Gogol tells us: "It must be remembered that Akaky Akakyevitch for the most part expressed himself by prepositions, adverbs, and particles which have absolutely no significance whatsoever. If the subject was a very difficult one, it was his habit indeed to leave his sentences quite unfinished." Akaky Akakyevitch's avenging ghost, even, says *er* and leaves its sentences unfinished. Akaky Akakyevitch is himself a kind of human particle which has absolutely no significance whatsoever and which has, also, whatever significance a human being can have: he is a kind of least common denominator of all humanity. So Gogol dismisses him: "A creature had vanished and departed whose cause no one had championed, who was dear to no one, of interest to no one, who never even attracted the attention of the student of natural history, though the latter does not disdain to fix a common fly upon a pin and look at him under the microscope—a creature who bore patiently the jeers of the office and for no particular reason went to his grave, though even he at the very end of his life was visited by a gleam of brightness in the form of an overcoat that for one instant brought color into his poor life—a creature on whom calamity broke as insufferably as it breaks upon the heads of the mighty ones of this world . . . !" Thus the man Akaky Akakyevitch ends; but there is a ghostly echo of him, that trails away in mid-air like an unfinished sentence—leaving the story to end with the wrong ghost, a ghost that is not a ghost, almost as if we were hearing for a last time one of those ambiguous pronouncements that keep recurring in Gogol: "We cannot say. About this nothing more is known."

I I

TOLSTOY SAID that Leskov had "an excess of talent." Reading one of his strong, wild, sprawling stories, so close in language and content to the folk themselves, so Russian as to disregard any ordinary European considerations of form and objectivity, you feel that the story is both helped and hurt by an excess of individuality. *Lady Macbeth of the Mtsensk District* is different. It is one of Leskov's first stories, and has few or none of the idiosyncrasies that make most of his work immediately recognizable. When you first read it you feel: "This is the masterpiece of some great Russian writer I don't know," and you are more impressed with the general power and rightness that join it to other great works than by the particular qualities that differentiate it from these. The story— surely one of the best stories ever written—is genuinely tragic: everything in it happens necessarily, out of the real nature of the story's situation and characters, and its events are followed to their necessary end. Leskov's treatment is at once full and laconic; his attitude toward his characters is both extraordinarily dispassionate and extraordinarily human—it is a peculiarly just story. It is interesting that one of the best treatments of romantic love in all literature should be so matter-of-fact and plainly truthful: you are carried away, but there is never anything that can be called an attempt to carry you away.

Dostoevsky, with spiteful penetration, called Tolstoy the last and greatest of the landowning writers—writers who, however much they knew, admired, or sympathized with the classes below them, were still aristocrats looking at them from the outside, from above. (Thus Chekhov, the grandson of a serf, was able to say about Tolstoy's idealization of peasants: "I have peasant blood in my veins, and you won't astonish me with peasant virtues.") Leskov knew such classes on their own level, from inside. The world of *Lady Macbeth* is nearest to the world of Ostrovsky's *The Storm*, that old-fashioned, entirely Russian world of the merchant class and its dependents, for whom the nobility and the intellectuals, Western things, barely exist. Leskov's Katerina Izmaylov is a kind of dark sister of Katerina Kabanova, the heroine of *The Storm*; bored, childless captives of arranged marriages, imprisoned in the big dark merchant houses, they look longingly for someone to love and be loved by. But Ostrovsky, very differently from Leskov, emphasizes the crushing oppressiveness of the whole system, the dreary, senseless tyranny of the old who rule—so that Katerina Kabanova, in spite of the directness and emotional force of her nature, her willingness to run away with her weak lover, at last can only drown herself. There is a lyric innocence and pathos in the defeat to which she helplessly consents; our feeling for her is very different from our feeling for Leskov's Katerina, who for the walls to fall needs only to hold out her finger and push. From the beginning we feel an uncanny identity with her and with the pleasure principle that magically, as if in a dream or wish-fantasy, sees any obstacle disappear from its path; Katerina's direct sexuality and sensuality, her passionate adoration of a base object, have their own innocence and rightness. Leskov makes the rug under the apple tree, where Katerina lies with Sergey, a second Garden of Eden:

" 'Look, Sergey! Ah my darling! What a paradise, what a paradise!' Katerina cried, looking up through the thick branches of the blossoming apple tree into the clear, blue sky where the full moon shone serenely.

"She lay on her back under the tree and the moonlight, streaming through the leaves and blossoms, drifted across her face and body forming bizarre spots. The air was still; only a light, warm breeze slightly stirred the sleepy leaves, scattering the faint fragrance of blossoming herbs and leaves. Every breath she drew filled her with languor, laziness, and dark voluptuous desires. . . .

"A lovely night! Stillness, light, scented air, and beneficent life-giving warmth. Far away, beyond the ravine, on the other side of the garden, someone began singing loudly; in the bird-cherry thicket near the fence a nightingale trilled once and then burst into song; a sleepy quail in a cage set on a long pole uttered a few shrill calls, and a fat horse sighed languorously behind the stable wall, while a pack of excited dogs ran noiselessly across the common behind the garden fence and disappeared into the hideous black shadows of the ancient, almost dilapidated, salt warehouses.

"Katerina raised herself on an elbow and looked at the tall garden grass. It seemed to her that the grass was playing games with the moonbeams which broke into flickers of light as they fell on the flowers and the leaves of the trees; everything was gilded with capricious, bright spots of light that twinkled and trembled like fireflies; it was as if the grass under the trees had been scooped up in a net of moonbeams and moved from side to side.

" 'Oh, how lovely it is, darling,' Katerina cried, looking about her.

"Sergey looked without enthusiasm."

Katerina is ready "to go to prison or the cross" for the cunning, efficient Sergey, who matter-of-factly manipulates the emotions he evokes and does not feel, and whom Leskov describes with disinterested accuracy; now Katerina says, "I want to be kissed so that the blossoms of the apple tree fall to the ground. Like this, like this." And Leskov goes on: "The old clerk, asleep in the barn, heard in the stillness of the night through his slumber whispers and low laughter, as if naughty children plotted tricks to play on decrepit old age, and then, loud, gay laughter, as if the water nixies from the lake were tickling someone. But it was only Katerina gamboling in the moonlight, rolling on the soft rug, making love to her husband's young clerk. The leafy apple tree shed fresh, white blossoms on them until at last no further blossoms fell. The short white night was passing away; the moon hid itself behind the steep roof of the high barns, and as it grew dimmer and dimmer gazed slantingly down on the earth. From the roof of the kitchen came the piercing sounds of a cats' duet, followed by angry spittings and splutterings, after which two or three of the animals, losing their foothold, rolled noisily down some planks that were propped up against the roof."

The marvelous objectivity (interrupting and contradicting as it does the paradise, the world of the naughty children, the world of the water nixies) of "But it was only Katerina gamboling in the moonlight, rolling on the soft rug, making love to her husband's young clerk" is followed, when "at last no further blossoms fell," by the animal caricature of the "cats' duet," which introduces immediately afterwards the second dream-visitation of the huge cat— "such a lovely tabby, large and fat, and with whiskers like a quit rent bailiff's"—who thrusts "his blunt snout against her firm breasts," and finally "started purring and mewing close to her ear, and thrust its muzzle forward, and said distinctly: 'What sort of cat do you think I am? It's very smart of you, Katerina dear, to take me for a cat at all. Actually I'm Boris Timofeyevich, a highly esteemed merchant of this town and your father-in-law. Only one thing is wrong with me: my bowels have burst because of the fine treatment my dear daughter-in-law gave me.' "

These dreams not only help to give its wonderfully firm, characteristic coloring to the whole love affair, but also prepare for Katerina's last vision: "Suddenly out of one of the breakers rolled the blue head of her father-in-law, Boris Timofeyevich, and out of another came her husband, and he clasped the drooping head of Fedya." The detailed factuality of the murder of the husband (Leskov's "Katerina stooped down, pressed Sergey's hands, which were around her husband's throat, with her own and put her ear to his breast. After five quiet minutes she got up and said: 'That'll do. You can leave him now' " is as calm as his description of how Katerina takes "a copper slop basin and a soaped bast sponge" and, "carefully examining all the floor boards," washes away everything, even "two tiny bloodstains the size of a cherry") is terrible to us, but our sympathetic identification with Katerina remains unchanged. It is not until the young heir is introduced, with his "light squirrel-fur coat," his illness, his gentle "Auntie," that we cannot bear for her to do what the insatiable Sergey manages to make her do; we watch with frightened revulsion, shudder away from the so appropriately sexual method of the murder ("Katerina with one movement covered the face of the sufferer with a large down pillow and lay on it herself with her firm, resilient bosom"), and are overjoyed to have the murder so extraordinarily interrupted, since Katerina's discovery, punishment, and suffering permit us to return to the sympathetic identification with her that we have felt from the start of the story. It is right that she should suffer, right that she should be steadfast and beautiful in her love and suffering; divorced at last from the petty, efficient Sergey, she transmutes his cruelly mocking "Don't forget, my darling, how we used to pass the long autumn nights together making love and hurrying off your family to eternal peace without the help of a priest or deacon" into a sentence that is the quintessence of bleak and longing remembrance: "How we used to make love together in the long autumn nights, and hurry people out of this world." As we read the last phrases of the story, no word of which we would change—"but Katerina broke from another wave, emerging almost to the waist, and threw herself on Sonetka like a strong pike on a soft little perch, and neither appeared again"—we realize that there is nothing in the whole story that we would want changed: it seems to us the exactly sufficient truth.

I I I

A Lear of the Steppes is one of the best and most unusual short novels that I know. Even a faithful and imaginative reader of the rest of Turgenev would not be able to guess that Turgenev—or, really, any writer—could do just this; as close as it is to *A Sportsman's Sketches*, it is more tragic and active, and has an organized inclusiveness, a working-out-to-the-limit, that the sketches do not wish to have. When the narrator (a younger version of the Turgenev of the sketches) begins by telling us that he "used to know a

King Lear," we consent merely out of politeness;
when we have finished the story of Martyn Petrovich
Harlov and his daughters Anna and Yevlampia, we
realize with astonishment that we have known a Lear
—and have known, both in precisely grotesque detail
and in delicately suggested generality, the Russia
that made the man and his story possible. *A Lear of
the Steppes'* humor and grandeur; its unerring rightness of scale; its calm comprehensiveness of social and
moral understanding; its incisive completeness of presentation, of actors, action, and setting; its naturalness
and conviction; its classical dispassionateness and objectivity—all this makes the piteous and terrible
story something we neither weep at nor protest over,
but accept as the fitting truth. The surface of the
story (what with all its odd or amusing, provincial,
characteristic details, all its eighteenth-century survivals) is so continual a pleasure that we find it easy
to bear the pain of what lies underneath. It is as if the
most imaginative anthropological expedition ever organized had lived in Russia for a generation, and had
returned not with a report but with a tragedy. And
how marvelously natural, how much a production of
nature itself, the tragedy seems! (It reminds us that in
A Sportman's Sketches the nobleman's knowledge of
the serfs he observes on his hunting trips somewhat
corresponds to the naturalist's knowledge of the animals he observes; and, people or animals, plants or
weather, it is always a natural process that is being
described.) Harlov may be like Lear, but he is also
very like a bear, as Turgenev tells us in convincing

detail; Anna's voice is "very pleasant, resonant and plaintive—like the note of some birds of prey"; and Yevlampia has "something wild and almost fierce in the glance of her huge eyes. 'A free bird, wild Cossack breed,' so Martyn Petrovich used to say of her." We see them act, we hear them call, but we are no more permitted to enter their minds than we should be permitted to enter the bear's or hawk's mind; like almost all of Turgenev's best work, this is the narrative of an observer, not a real participant—and of an observer who reproduces action, speech, all the small external expressions or betrayals of thought or emotion, instead of going directly into another's soul and telling us what he finds there.

Turgenev's worst work (from *Enough* and *Poems in Prose* to the most directly emotional passages of the novels) expresses his own nature with astonishing frankness; his best work, in comparison, is reticent and objective, with Turgenev himself a passive or impassive mirror at the side of things. Turgenev tells us: "In my childhood I had a finch which the cat once held in her paws for a while; the finch was rescued and nursed, but it never recovered." By what Turgenev's worst work says and by what his best work does not permit itself to say, we are reminded that the cat had once held Turgenev in her paws, and that he had never recovered. Turgenev's weak men helpless in the clutch of—as Chekhov called them—"lionesses, burning, avid, insatiable"; ideally inspired by—as Chekhov called them—"not Russian girls but some sort of Pythian prophetesses, full of extravagant pretensions": how much of all this is personal, the direct emotional expression of the life and wishes of a man who, from earliest childhood, had been made to feel himself superfluous or existing on sufferance! Yet Anna and Yevlampia are as objective as they are haunting, the sketches are impersonal as few master-pieces are. Turgenev once wrote to a young man: "If the study of human physiognomy, of the lives of others, interests you *more* than the statement of your feelings and thoughts; if it is, for example, *pleasanter* for you to describe truthfully the outward appear-ance not of a man but of a simple object rather than to express fervently and glowingly what you feel upon seeing this object or man, then it means that you're an objective writer and you can start writing a story." In *A Sportsman's Sketches* and *A Lear of the Steppes* Turgenev is such a writer.

Yet I suppose that for every reader who knows *A Lear of the Steppes* there are a hundred readers who know *Fathers and Sons* or some other novel of Turgenev's; the *Lear* is lost among the long and short stories scattered throughout the collected works, and it is natural to assume that the best of a writer's novels is more important than a story. As one critic remarks: "For ten years, from 1867 to 1877, Turgenev was to publish no major work, though many minor works of great beauty—*A Lear of the Steppes* (1870), *The Torrents of Spring* (1871), *Punin and Baburin* (1874), *Living Relics* (1874), along with several lesser works—were to come from his pen." The "major works" which came at the beginning and the end of these ten years were *Smoke* (half an astonishingly spiteful journalistic attack on everything Russian, and half what the reader of Turgenev will think of as one of the regular love affairs) and *Virgin Soil* (a carefully worked out, thoroughly unconvincing political novel considered a failure by its readers, its critics, and even by Turgenev himself). Are not Turgenev's "minor works of great beauty"—the short stories that form *A Sportsman's Sketches*, a longer story like *A Lear of the Steppes*—Turgenev's major works, and the novels his minor ones?

Turgenev once wrote to Goncharov (in 1859, after he had published *Rudin* and *A Nest of Gentlefolk*) one of those letters in which a writer discusses his own limitations. What Turgenev wrote must have seemed to him somewhat exaggerated, so that he could hope to be contradicted both by Goncharov and by the future. He says: "Whoever is in need of a novel in the epic sense, that person will not need me; I would as soon think of creating a novel as of walking on my head; no matter what I write, my work will always take the form of a series of sketches." But isn't Turgenev almost literally correct in what he says? In his novels Turgenev, as Mirsky says, "voluntarily submitted to the obligation of writing works of social significance," of civic responsibility, that would be accepted by enlightened public opinion as ideologically and morally representative. If Turgenev's novels seem dated, today, in a way in which *Lear* and the sketches do not, part of the reason is that Turgenev deliberately made them up to date, deliberately included in them what enlightened opinion considered the most important issues of the day, and had these formally and lengthily debated by characters who were themselves, so far as ideas and ideals are concerned, typical. Nor do their obligatory love affairs make them any less typical or any less dated—the coloring that Turgenev gives these is always somewhat conventional and Victorian. Sentences like those in which Turgenev describes Elena's love for Insarov ("The silence of bliss, the silence of a tranquil harbor, of a goal attained, that heavenly silence which imparts even to death itself both meaning and beauty, filled her whole being with its divine flood. She wished for nothing because she possessed everything") would fit into almost any novel of his, almost any Victorian novel of a certain sort; they would seem grotesquely out of place in *A Sportsman's Sketches* or *Lear*. Tolstoy spoke cruelly but truthfully when he said about the novels: "It always surprises me that Turgenev with his mental powers and poetic sensibility should even in his methods not be able to refrain from banality." The virtues of *Fathers and Sons* and *A Nest of Gentlefolk* are obvious—but so, alas, are *Fathers and Sons* and *A Nest of Gentlefolk*. We are troubled by their slightly conventional regularity; the techniques of Turgenev's novels are always a little too much in the open—their plots, frail as they are, always show a little too much. It is possible to say that Turgenev's novels are "representative only of his class, the idealistically educated middle gentry"; the sketches are representative of a wider, more old-fashioned, very

Russian world—of an existence which Turgenev himself, writing in the seventies, called "country life, that squirearchal, slow, expansive, and petty life, the very memory of which has already been forgotten by the present generation, with its usual round of tutors and teachers." This life found its ideal observer in Turgenev; in *Lear* and in that extraordinary masterpiece, *A Sportsman's Sketches,* he has reproduced it with a truth, a delicacy, and an individuality that are unique. There are greater writers than Turgenev, better books than *A Sportsman's Sketches,* as long as we are not reading it; but for as long as we read, it is beyond comparison.

I V

BOTH *Master and Man* and *The Death of Ivan Ilych* are stories of conversion; in each a successful man comes to see his life as a false or irrelevant thing that is replaced, in death, by something new that he sees as reality. But in *Master and Man* Brekhunof's conversion is so quickly and completely accomplished, with so few details, so little preparation or explanation, that no matter how many times you read the story you still cannot remember exactly how it was done. Up until the time that he sees that the man Nikita is freezing, nothing but business exists for the master Brekhunof. Suddenly everything is inverted or turned inside out, so that the man's life, the continuation of his own life in the man's, is all that exists for the master; he has not understood before, but *"Now I*

know," he says with fierce emphasis and finality.
The moral of the story is close to the moral of *How
Much Land Does a Man Need?*—but there the moral
is merely implied by the events of the story; here the
main character is directly converted to the realization
of the moral, and announces it to the reader. The
doctrinal conclusion of *Master and Man*—some of its
sentences will seem very familiar to the reader of
Tolstoy's religious works—is not actual in the way
that everything else in the story is; the reader may
consent to it as a matter of faith, but he is not made to
feel it as a matter of fact. All this is particularly
noticeable because of what makes *Master and Man*, in
spite of this fault, so astonishing a work of art: the
plain, overwhelming, matter-of-fact reality of everything else in it. As you encounter each new link in
this chain of actions you feel like blurting out, "*Now
I know*"; for many pages the immediately satisfying, engrossing actuality of the story is unbroken, so
that after a while you come to take for granted the
feeling: "Why, this is happening, really happening." And the causal and rhythmical organization of
the events is equally compelling: the reader's experience of what has already happened, his uneasy expectation of what is about to happen, seem a physical
state, something too incontestable for criticism. (The
feeling of simply being engrossed in the reality of a
series of actions is something that we associate with the
best of Hemingway's stories; yet in comparison with
the texture of *Master and Man*, how mannered and
special-case, how essentially rhetorical—even though

beautifully rhetorical—the texture of such stories is!) We have known the four principal characters of Tolstoy's story—master and man, horse and storm—so completely that the conclusion to which they are made to come is almost irrelevant. We are sorry to have Tolstoy, so to speak, add them up incorrectly, but we do not really care: nothing that Tolstoy says can contradict the reality he has created.

Brekhunof is converted in a few hours. It takes many months of illness and agony—takes, finally, the continued presence of death itself—to bring Ivan Ilych to the point of conversion; and Tolstoy's long, detailed, terrible account of how Ivan Ilych is brought low is preceded by his logical, exactly organized, terrible summary of Ivan Ilych's life up to that point, the successful life that "ran its course as he believed life should do: easily, pleasantly, and decorously." The essential elements of *The Death of Ivan Ilych* are derived from Tolstoy's *Confession*, but Tolstoy has rearranged or transformed them so that their effect is very different. One reads Tolstoy's *Confession* with intense interest, reasons about it, connects it with one's own life, and walks away unhurt; it relates something terrible, but it is not terrible. *The Death of Ivan Ilych* is terrible: Tolstoy has created something that is half implacable factual demonstration and half torture. We argue against it, we point out its exaggerations and falsities, we thank God that our life is as different as it is from Ivan Ilych's, our death as different as it will be from Ivan Ilych's; but nothing helps. Is any story more terrible? Certainly no account of disease and

death is: reading *The Death of Ivan Ilych*, for anyone who has been badly ill, badly in pain, is like
being deported to a country one has lived in for a long
time and hoped to forget the existence of. The story is
a snake left in our path, our only path, and it has the
snake's quivering tongue, the snake's gleaming and
mechanical coils. The story itself is like Ivan Ilych's
"old, familiar, dull, gnawing pain, stubborn and serious"; like the death Ivan Ilych cannot look away
from: "*It* would come and stand before him and look
at him, and he would be petrified and the light would
die out of his eyes, and he would again begin asking
himself whether *It* alone was true. . . . And what
was worst of all was that *It* drew his attention to itself
not in order to make him take some action but only
that he should look at *It*, look *It* straight in the face:
look at *It* and without doing anything, suffer inex-
pressibly."

Let me quote to the reader, from Tolstoy's *Confession*, some of the sections that Tolstoy reproduced, rearranged, or transformed in *The Death of Ivan Ilych*.
Childhood was good, Tolstoy tells us, but society
made the child into a man by encouraging in him
"ambition, lust of power, selfishness, voluptuousness,
pride, anger, revenge—all that was respected. By
abandoning myself to these passions I became like a
grown person, and I felt that people were satisfied with
me. . . . I began to write through vanity, avarice,
and pride. In my writings I did the same as in life. In
order to have glory and money, for which I wrote, I
had to conceal what was good and speak what was bad.

And so I did. . . . For this I was paid, and I had excellent food, quarters, women, society; I had fame. . . .

"During my stay in Paris, the sight of a capital punishment showed me the frailty of my superstition of progress. When I saw the head severed from the body, and both falling separately with a thud into a box, I understood, not with my reason, but with my whole being, that no theories of the reasonableness of everything existing and of progress could justify that deed, and that if all men on earth, beginning with the creation, had some theory which made this necessary—I knew that it was not necessary, that it was bad. . . . Another occasion which made me conscious of the insufficiency for life of the superstition of progress was the death of my brother. An intelligent, good, serious man, he grew sick when he was young, suffered for more than a year, and died an agonizing death, without comprehending what he had lived for, and still less why he should die. No theories could give any answers either to me or to him, during his slow and painful death. . . .

"I got married. The new conditions of my happy family life completely drew me away from all search for the general meaning of life. All my life during that time was centered in my family, my wife, my children and, therefore, in cares for the increase of the means of existence. . . . I continued to write. . . . In my writings I advocated, what to me was the only truth, that it was necessary to live in such a way as to derive the greatest comfort for oneself and one's family. . . .

"Thus I proceeded to live, but five years ago something very strange began to happen with me: I was overcome by minutes at first of perplexity and then of an arrest of life, as though I did not know how to live or what to do, and I lost myself and was dejected. But that passed, and I continued to live as before. Then those minutes of perplexity were repeated oftener and oftener, and always in one and the same form. These arrests of life found their expression in ever the same question: 'Why? Well, and then?'

". . . There happened what happens with any person who falls ill with a mortal internal disease. At first there appear insignificant symptoms of indisposition, to which the patient pays no attention; then these symptoms are repeated more and more frequently and blend into one temporally indivisible suffering. The suffering keeps growing, and before the patient has had time to look around, he becomes conscious that what he took for an indisposition is the most significant thing in the world to him—is death.

"The same happened to me. . . . I could breathe, eat, drink, and sleep, and could not help breathing, eating, drinking, and sleeping; but there was no life, because there were no desires the gratification of which I might find reasonable. . . . There was nothing to wish for. . . . The truth was that life was meaningless. It was just as though I had been living and walking along, and had come to an abyss, where I saw clearly that there was nothing ahead but perdition. And it was impossible to stop and go back, and impossible to shut my eyes, in order that I might not see that there was nothing ahead but suffering and imminent death—complete annihilation.

"What happened to me was that I, a healthy, happy man, felt that I could not go on living—an insurmountable force drew me on to find release from life. I cannot say that I *wanted* to kill myself. The force which drew me away from life was stronger, fuller, more general than wishing. It was a force like the former striving after life, but in an inverse sense. I tended with all my strength away from life. . . . I had to use cunning against myself, in order that I might not take my life. This mental condition expressed itself to me in this form: my life is a stupid, mean trick played on me by somebody. . . . Sooner or later there would come diseases and death (they had come already) to my dear ones and to me, and there would be nothing left but stench and worms. . . . I cannot help seeing day and night, which run and lead me up to death. I see that alone, because that alone is the truth. Everything else is a lie. . . .

" 'My family—' I said to myself, 'but my family, my wife and children, they are also human beings. They are in precisely the same condition that I am in: they must either live in the lie or see the terrible truth. . . . Since I love them, I cannot conceal the truth from them—every step in cognition leads them up to this truth. And the truth is death.' "

Socrates and Solomon, Schopenhauer and Buddha—all, says Tolstoy, have agreed to this truth. It is a truth that is inescapable for those who neglect "man's chief, primary, and undoubted duty: *In the sweat of thy face shalt thou eat bread.*" Meaninglessness, falseness, and death are the final truth for the selfish, parasitic classes whose lives are intent only upon their own happiness—for Ivan Ilych; but they are not the final truth for the humble majority of mankind, who since the beginning of time have "mined the iron, taught how to cut down the forest, domesticated cows and horses, taught how to sow, how to live together," and served without thought of happiness—for Gerasim. A false life is dreadful, but "Death—real, serious, all-absorbing death—is, thank God, not dreadful"; the atom of life, dying, is absorbed into the world's continuing life.

In his *Confession* Tolstoy shows a man coming to these conclusions by the force of his own more or less free, more or less arbitrary thought and life; the reader accepts or rejects the conclusions as a matter of logic or feeling—he has a choice. But *The Death of Ivan Ilych* shows a man forced to these conclusions by disease and death, by a long inescapable process described in the most terrible factual detail, so that the reader has no choice—just as he, as a reader, has been forced to identify his own life with Ivan Ilych's, so he, as a reader, is forced to accept Ivan Ilych's conclusions about his life. In Tolstoy's *Confession* he uses the process by which disease leads to death as a metaphor for the process of thought and feeling that led him to his despairing obsession with death. (The person he loved and respected most, his brother Nikolai, had died in just this way; anyone who reads Maude's biography of Tolstoy will notice that some of the most troubling and intimate details of Ivan Ilych's dying are taken from Nikolai's.) But in *The Death of Ivan Ilych* the metaphor is made reality—and everything else is derived from this reality.

The story begins with the official announcement of Ivan Ilych's death, and with the official rites by which society disposes of Ivan Ilych's corpse and, also, of the reality of Ivan Ilych's death; we see these through the eyes of an official and social acquaintance of Ivan Ilych's, the eyes of another Ivan Ilych. This is, we think, the end of Ivan Ilych, and everything connected with the end is false. Nor is the conventional, hypocritical falseness of the funeral touching to us, as it normally would be, since Tolstoy has eliminated almost all of the selfless feelings the survivors normally would have: even to the person presumably closest to him, his wife, the death of Ivan Ilych is a matter of selfishness, inconvenience, and greed. The impatient acquaintance's interview with the wife is an almost farcically conclusive demonstration of this, what with the pension, the possibility of an additional grant of money, the prices of the cemetery lots, the pouffe, the wife's "For the last three days he screamed incessantly. It was unendurable. I cannot understand how I bore it."

Turgenev once said about Tolstoy: "He never believed in people's sincerity. Every spiritual movement seemed to him false, and with his extraordinarily penetrating eyes he used to pierce those on whom his suspicion fell." No other writer is so great a master of negative analysis, can so surely reduce anything to its component atoms of falsity. History, as the saying goes, is an agreed-upon falsehood or convention (*War and Peace* is, among other things, a demonstration of this); in *The Death of Ivan Ilych* society itself is this agreed-upon, conventional lie. Ivan Ilych preferred to anything else in the arbitrary, agreed-upon convention of his existence his favorite game of cards; now, with savage precision, the acquaintance is made to sulk when it looks as if Ivan Ilych's funeral will keep him from this game of cards —to rejoice when, in the last sentence of the introduction, he gets his game in after all. This first section demonstrates to us the conclusive falsity of Ivan Ilych's death; it is not until we come to the end of the story that we realize that this first section was not a conclusion but a mere appendix or afterword about the disposal of Ivan Ilych's corpse—the real death of Ivan Ilych was different. But now after this—so to speak— overture in the key of falsehood, it seems natural for the story to continue in this key with its account of Ivan Ilych's life. But here Tolstoy changes his methods : what has been the direct narration of a series of particular events, as seen through one person's eyes, now becomes a highly organized, logical, omniscient summary of the typical events, the classes of happenings, that compose Ivan Ilych's life, and of the ruling principles that underlie these. (After he has accustomed us to this style of presentation in the central portion of the story, Tolstoy is able to change over with tremendous effect to the detailed immediacy of the last long account of Ivan Ilych's sickness and death.)

The story's analysis of the conventional falseness of Ivan Ilych's life is far more effective than Tolstoy's similar analysis of his own life in his *Confession*. To treat Tolstoy's contradictory and extraordinary life as a typically and conventionally evil one seems the rhetorical exaggeration of an evangelist. But Ivan Ilych's life *is* typical, the tendencies of his life are thoroughly consistent: he has managed to make himself into an entirely proper, entirely efficient, entirely false and conventional part of the machinery of society. (Tolstoy's dislike of any complicated system, of any form of government, and of any of the upper levels of society, along with his particular dislike of judges and doctors, finds extraordinarily effective expression in the story.) Ivan Ilych has managed so successfully to turn a human being into an aristocratic, bureaucratic machine part that the operation of the machine has taken the place of ordinary human reality for him: his profession, his little dinners, his card games are the easy, pleasant, decorous machine existence that the machine part requires instead of life. His marriage alone, from the time of his wife's first pregnancy, manages to bring a raw live squalor into this successful machine existence of his. (Tolstoy said that to endure the first pregnancy of his own wife was "to have the troubles of an eating-house, baby-powders, and jam-making, along with grumblings, and devoid of all that can brighten family life. . . . All this is not merely wrong but dreadful when compared with what I desire. I don't know what I would not do for the sake of our happiness; but she can debase and defile our relation so as to make it seem as though I begrudged her a horse or a peach.") But by "taking a definite line" about his marriage Ivan Ilych as far as possible makes it a part of the machinery or disregards it; just so his wife "takes a definite line" about his disease and death, so that she can make it a part of her own machine existence or disregard it. And just as Ivan Ilych has always managed to regard any human reality as mere raw material for the machinery of his profession, so his doctors regard Ivan Ilych's disease and death as the mere raw material of *their* profession, and answer his despairing human plea with his own: "Prisoner, if you will not keep to the questions put to you, I shall be obliged to have you removed from the court."

Tolstoy once said about an illness of his own: "It was as if a wheel had seized me and were beginning to drag me into the machine"; when Ivan Ilych stumbles, a wheel seizes him and begins to drag him out of the machine of society into the machine of death. This machine of disease and death (it reminds one of the machine in *The Penal Colony*, and yet is a thousand times more terrible, just as the process by which it destroys its victim is a thousand times more complicated) before long teaches Ivan Ilych, in flesh-and-blood letters, that he is no machine part but a human being. But it is precisely this that the machinery of society will not admit: "the awful, terrible act of his dying was, he could see, reduced by those about him to the level of a casual, unpleasant, and almost indecorous incident (as if someone entered a drawing-room diffusing an unpleasant odor) and this was done by that very decorum which he had served all his life long. No one even wished to grasp his position. Only Gerasim recognized it and pitied him. He even said straight out: 'We shall all of us die, so why should I grudge a little trouble?' " The only human reality Ivan Ilych can reach to, from out of the machinery, is Gerasim, who represents not the conventional falseness of society but the truth of peasant life, as he serves and pities the man he alone admits is dying. (At the very end of his life Ivan Ilych also manages to reach out to a human reality in the form of childhood, of his own son—who represents the human being Ivan Ilych once was, before he was converted into the machine part Ivan Ilych.) Gerasim sitting all night with the legs of Ivan Ilych on his shoulders—of that Ivan Ilych who wants to cry like a child and be comforted like a child—is the humble, indecorous human reality, the terrible but touching truth; and it is not until Ivan Ilych can accept this as the truth and somehow good, and can reject his former easy, pleasant, decorous life as "not the right thing" but a conventional, mechanical falsehood, that he can get through the black sack into the light, and can feel pity not only for his son and Gerasim but even for his wife and the other machine parts.

Ivan Ilych's life has been a conventional falsehood; *The Death of Ivan Ilych* is the story of how he is tortured into the truth. No matter how alien they

may have seemed to him to begin with, in the end the
reader can dissociate himself neither from the falsehood, the torture, nor the truth: he *is* Ivan Ilych.
After so much falseness, such terrible tortures, the
reader is very willing to accept the end of the story,
even the *It is finished* that Tolstoy took from the account of another death. But the end is truly imagined
in terms of the story itself, not in terms of Tolstoy's
religious doctrines: the light on the other side of the
black sack, the life that comes out of death, all correspond to the human life that has finally emerged from
the machinery of falsehood and death.

v

WE PARTICULARLY associate with Tolstoy the kind of
story which shows that under the differing or contradictory surfaces of human experience, if you look
hard enough, there is always the same underlying
reality; under happiness or sorrow, decorous success or
indecorous failure—as Tolstoy puts it in *What I Believe*—"death, death, death awaits you every second.
Your life passes in the presence of death. If you labor
personally for your own future, you yourself know
that the one thing awaiting you is—death. And that
death ruins all you work for. Consequently, life for
oneself can have no meaning. If there is a rational life
it must be found elsewhere." You must change your
life by substituting for your varying attitudes toward the varying surfaces of experience a uniform
and rational attitude toward the uniform substratum

beneath all experience. This uniform and rational attitude, for Tolstoy, is one of nonresistance, of having nothing to do with direction or government of any kind, of converting evil into good by always turning the other cheek.

In *Ward No. 6* Chekhov detailedly and forcibly contradicts this Tolstoyan analysis of experience. Not only does *Ward No. 6* show experience—the pure immediacy of pleasure or pain, good or evil—as something ultimate, it regards the attempt to substitute for this a uniform attitude toward a uniform reality as a rationalization or subterfuge that permits a passive nature to justify its own passivity. Andrei Yefimitch Ragin, the hero of *Ward No. 6*, is a doctor in charge of a hospital in a "dirty, sleepy little town two hundred versts from the nearest railway." The town is a purgatory for a sensitive and intelligent man; the hospital itself is a hell of ignorance, stupidity, and evil. The patients die of the callous mismanagement of the doctors and nurses, the lunatics imprisoned in the sixth ward are regularly beaten by their jailer. Andrei Yefimitch knows this, but there is nothing he can do about it—that is, there is nothing that his nature will permit him to do: "to command, to prohibit, to insist he had never learned. It seemed almost that he had sworn an oath never to raise his voice or to use the imperative mood." Since he cannot satisfy by any action the active moral demands the hospital makes on him, Andrei Yefimitch substitutes for action an elaborate rationalization, a whole philosophical system, that makes any action not only useless but absurd. Soon he extends this systematic rationalization to his

own practice as a doctor: since the thousands of patients can at best be given only a kind of token treatment, he before long makes his practice a kind of token practice. He knows how overwhelmingly medicine has improved during his lifetime, knows that "such an abomination as Ward No. 6 is possible [in Chekhov's repeated symbolic phrase] only in a town situated two hundred versts from the nearest railway. . . . 'But in the end?' asks Andrei Yefimitch, opening his eyes. 'What is the difference? In spite of antiseptics and Koch and Pasteur, the essence of the matter has no way changed. Disease and death still exist. Lunatics are amused with dances and theatricals, but they are still kept prisoners. . . . In other words, all these things are vanity and folly, and between the best hospital in Vienna and the hospital here there is in reality no difference at all. . . . And, indeed, why hinder people from dying, if death is the normal and lawful end of us all? Why should suffering be mitigated? In the first place, we are told that suffering leads men to perfection; and in the second, it is plain that if men were really able to alleviate their sufferings with pills and potions, they would abandon that religion and philosophy in which until now they had found not only consolation, but even happiness.' "
And so, "defeated by such arguments," Andrei Yefimitch substitutes for action, for practice, the passive theoretical routine of his life: he methodically reads, methodically drinks vodka, and to his friend Mikhail Averyanitch, the postmaster, methodically blames the present and praises the future, the future in which he would have been an honest man. As, far into the

night, Andrei Yefimitch sits reading, "time, it seems, stands still and perishes, and nothing exists but a book and a green lamp-shade."

So life might have gone on indefinitely for the doctor. But one day, after having been called in to treat a patient suffering from delusions of persecution, he "prescribed cold compresses for his head, ordered him to take drops of bay rum, and went away saying that he would come no more, as it was not right to prevent people going out of their minds." Soon the patient is confined in that Ward No. 6 which, so to speak, it was not right to prevent the existence of. But Ivan Dmitritch is not only a lunatic, but also the most sensitive and intelligent person in the town. When Andrei Yefimitch at last discovers this, he substitutes for the established routine of his life the more attractive routine of daily philosophical arguments with his patient. He does nothing for him, but demonstrates that it is not possible to do anything for him, and that he would be no better off if it were possible to do anything for him; as he says, "The rest and tranquillity of a man are not outside but within him. . . . Try to understand life—in this is true beatitude." The captive Ivan Dmitritch indignantly and ingeniously disproves the doctor's arguments, and the doctor listens with emotion. Looking into the ward, the other doctor, the assistant, and the jailer see how "Ivan Dmitritch with a nightcap on his head and Doctor Andrei Yefimitch sat side by side on the bed. The lunatic shuddered, made strange faces, and convulsively clutched his dressing-gown; and the doctor sat motionless, inclining his head, and his face was red and helpless and

sad." Soon everyone is convinced that Andrei Yefimitch himself is insane. He is forced to accept mental
examinations and insults; to retire from the hospital;
to take, with Mikhail Averyanitch, an intolerably
long and expensive trip "for his health." In Warsaw
he lies on the sofa with his face to the wall, unwilling
to leave the hotel room; at home, in cheap lodgings,
badly in debt, he continues to lie on the sofa with his
face to the wall; he no longer reads his books but only
catalogues them—"the more monotonous and trifling
the occupation the more it calmed his mind." He tells
Mikhail Averyanitch: "My complaint lies merely in
this, that in twenty years I have found in this town
only one intelligent man, and he was a lunatic. I
suffer from no disease whatever; my misfortune is
that I have fallen into a magic circle from which there
is no escape." He does not understand that he fell into
the real magic circle twenty years before. He says:
"It is all the same to me—I am ready for anything";
he is willing "to go into the pit." To one who has felt
the metaphysical or existential anguish underlying
all life, Andrei Yefimitch is certain, there is no difference between the sort of meaningless evil people call
good and pleasant and the sort they call bad and unpleasant.

Then Andrei Yefimitch is tricked into the pit, into
Ward No. 6 itself. There, in the nightcap and dressing
gown of the lunatic, unable to philosophize any
longer, unable even to prevent his hands from trembling, he finds that nothing is the same to him, that he
is not ready for anything: when the cold livid moon
rises above the wall of the prison, Andrei Yefimitch

looks at it and, terrified, thinks: *So this is real life.*
"Everything was terrible: the moon, the prison, the
spikes in the fence, and the blaze in the distant bone-
mill. Andrei Yefimitch turned away from the window, and saw before him a man with glittering stars
and orders upon his breast. The man smiled and
winked cunningly. And this, too, seemed terrible."
The tortured Andrei Yefimitch pulls at the bars with
all his strength, demands that the jailer let him out
into the yard; the lunatics shout their own demands;
and the jailer strikes him "with his clenched fist full in
the face. It seemed to Andrei Yefimitch that a great
salt wave had suddenly dashed upon his head and
flung him upon his bed; in his mouth was a taste of
salt, and the blood seemed to burst from his gums.
. . . But at this moment Nikita struck him again and
again in the back. . . . It seemed as if someone had
taken a sickle, thrust it into his chest and turned it
around. In his agony he bit his pillow and ground his
teeth, and suddenly into his head amid the chaos
flashed the intolerable thought that such misery had
been borne year after year by these helpless men
who now lay in the moonlight like black shadows
around him. In twenty years he had never known of
it, and never wanted to know. He did not know, he had
no idea of their wretchedness, therefore he was not
guilty; but conscience, as rude and unaccommodating
as Nikita's fists, sent an icy thrill through him from
head to foot."

What neither reason nor imagination could teach
Andrei Yefimitch experience has at last brought home

to him, so that he understands that Ward No. 6 is able
to torture him now, just as for twenty years it has
tortured the others, simply because he has allowed it
to go on existing. He sees that the moral demands of
everyday life are inescapable, just as our experience
of everyday life is ultimate. But there is nothing
Andrei Yefimitch can do about it: life is not given to
us twice. Nor is death any better. What the lunatic
Ivan Dmitritch has growled comes true: "What is
most bitter, most abominable of all, is that this life
ends not with rewards for suffering, not with apo-
theoses as in operas, but in death; men come and drag
the corpse by its arms and legs into the cellar." The
apoplectic stroke from which Andrei Yefimitch dies is
"something loathsome like rotting sour cabbage or bad
eggs"; if for a moment there rushes through the mind
of the dying man "a herd of antelopes, extraordinarily beautiful and graceful, of which he had been
reading the day before," this piece of meaningless
apotheosis is replaced by a last piece of everyday
existence, by a woman stretching out to the postmaster Mikhail Averyanitch "a hand holding a regis-
tered letter." Then everything disappears: they
carry Andrei Yefimitch away, bury him the next
day, and only Mikhail Averyanitch and the cook
Daryushka come to his funeral.

Ward No. 6 was written in 1892; it is to a great
extent the result of Chekhov's journey, in 1890, to
the island of Sakhalin, a penal colony off the coast of
Siberia. The governor of the island, as Magarshack
writes in his biography of Chekhov, "was a humane

but ineffectual man who refused to confirm any punishment by the birch or cat. His subordinates, however, paid little attention to his orders and the prison
governors accepted birching as a regular practice,
while the warders made money by blackmailing the
richer convicts, who were birched every time they
refused to pay up." The prisons and the convict settle-
ments, both of which Chekhov studied carefully, were
a nightmare of cruelty and stupidity. Chekhov "had
known long before he set foot on Sakhalin of the
atrocities committed there in the name of justice, but
the three months on the island showed him that there
was all the difference in the world between knowing a
thing objectively and feeling it subjectively. Sakhalin
had taught him the difference between an emotional experience and an intellectual attitude." If
Sakhalin did this, then it was responsible for *Ward No.
6*, since these differences are exactly what *Ward No. 6*
is designed to teach. And Sakhalin, by disproving the
Tolstoyan doctrines that had had so much effect on
Chekhov during the late 1880's, was responsible for
making *Ward No. 6* as specifically anti-Tolstoyan as
it is. "Before my journey to Sakhalin," Chekhov
wrote, "*The Kreutzer Sonata* was an event in my life,
but now it just seems silly and ridiculous to me."
Tolstoy's whole philosophy of nonresistance to evil
(it underlies Andrei Yefimitch's philosophizing and
passivity, though Chekhov was careful to disguise the
fact) seemed absurd when brought face to face with
Sakhalin; the convicts and their families were unable
to make the least resistance to the evils of their life, but

as a result they had simply come to take these for granted, just as Andrei Yefimitch and the inmates of the hospital take its evils for granted. "It is not a question of being 'for' or 'against' anything," Chekhov wrote; "what matters is that for one reason or another Tolstoy no longer exists for me, that he is no longer in my heart, and that he went out of it, saying, 'I leave thy dwelling empty. . . .' People who are sick of a fever do not want to eat, but they want something, and they express their vague desire by saying, 'I'd like something nice, something sour.' I, too, want something sour."

Is *Ward No. 6* this something sour? There is a terrible plainness about the dreary and troubling story; and yet there is something sour and bitter and specific about it, so far as morality is concerned. His life makes its ordinary demands upon Andrei Yefimitch, and Andrei Yefimitch does not even attempt to satisfy them: consequently he lives as badly as he does and dies as badly as he does. We pity him, but we blame him; the story's *You must behave differently* is plain and ordinary, but inescapable. After reading *Ward No. 6* I once happened to read Goethe's "How can a man come to know himself? Never through contemplation, but only through action. Try to do your duty, and you will know what you amount to. But what is your duty? The demand of each day." The matter-of-fact, old-fashioned words are incarnate in *Ward No. 6.*

The English in England

To most of us Kipling means India. Kipling's masterpiece, *Kim*, is an Indian story; so are the *Jungle Books*; so are the stories that made Kipling, in his thirties, the best-known writer in the world. It was this Indian Kipling whom Henry James called "the most complete man of genius (as distinct from fine intelligence) that I have ever known." Yet many, even most, of Kipling's best stories are stories of the English in England; the stories of Kipling's old age or late middle age—work that shows the easy and decisive mastery that was the result of a lifetime of imaginative realization—are with a few exceptions stories about England.

Here are fourteen such stories. Ten or eleven of them, perhaps, are among the best stories Kipling ever wrote, and the others have a particular interest of one kind or another. *Baa Baa, Black Sheep* is the one purely autobiographical story of a reticent and private-spirited author (his story of the future, *As Easy as A.B.C.*, makes "invasion of privacy" the sin upon which his new society is based) ; and since *Baa Baa, Black Sheep* is the only early story in this volume, it gives the reader a chance to compare some good and some excellent examples of his later style with an example of the live and effective, but relatively crude, style of the earlier stories. *The Vortex* is one of the funnier examples of a compulsive form, Kipling's practical-joke story; the reader may feel, as I do, that he enjoys Kipling's farce for its charm and landscape, and is indifferent to its point. As for *"In the Interests of the Brethren,"* it is pure charm—who would have supposed that you could make, of the meeting of an imaginary Masonic lodge, one of the most winning of sketches? I imagine that, except for *The Magic Flute*, it is the most attractive work of art Masonry has produced.

But at this point the reader may feel like remarking, "Autobiography, compulsive practical jokes, Masonry—do the subjects of the stories keep on like this?" Well, yes. But let me sum up the subjects in a sentence, and you can judge for yourself. In these fourteen stories a drugged, lovesick, and consumptive pharmacist, on an icy winter night, writes part of *The Eve of St. Agnes;* an elderly cook tells an elderly countrywoman, her friend, the story of how she took upon herself her lover's cancer; an urban intellectual, after inheriting a place in the country, gradually falls in love with country and county ways; a man visits the house of a blind woman, a house haunted by children; the boys of a Latin class translate an ode of Horace's and apply it to their everyday affairs; two countrymen eat their midday meal beside a flooded brook, and discuss a providential murder the brook has committed; a child from India undergoes five years of bullying and torture in a lower-middle-class English household; the railway station and crossroads of an English village are immobilized by four cartons of bees; a rich and nervous American and his wife are converted to the tranquil country ways of their English forebears; some motorists of varied distinction, fined and insulted in a village road trap, avenge themselves by a geometrical progression of practical jokes that leaves the village the laughingstock of several continents; a shell-shocked artilleryman encounters at the front a little group of admirers of Jane Austen; a middle-aged woman, while burning the effects of a dead R.F.C. pilot, her employer's nephew, finds a wounded German pilot in the underbrush and watches him die there; a man gives up, out of ordinary human feeling, his long-prepared revenge upon a petty and despicable scholar.

Revenge, love, disease and death, the supernatural, extreme situations, practical jokes, country ways, literature: these are some of the things that keep recurring in the stories. Yet the list of subjects seems to me, as I imagine it seems to the reader, a surprisingly varied and unusual one. Kipling is one of the most effectively realistic of writers—his stories are dazzling in their verisimilitude, their extraordinarily broad and detailed knowledge of special ways of speech and life, of a hundred varieties of local color; yet they are never mere slices of life, and are even more notable for their imagination than for their realism. If the reality principle has pruned and clipped them into plausibility, it is the pleasure principle out of which they first rankly and satisfyingly flowered. Kipling is far closer to Gogol than to a normal realist or naturalist: in Kipling the pressure of the imagination has forced facts over into the supernatural, into personally satisfying jokes or revenges, into personally compulsive fantasies or neuroses. Then too, like Gogol, Kipling is one of the great stylists of his language, one of those writers who can make a list more interesting than an ordinary writer's murder. For instance: "Everything his eyes opened upon was his very own to keep for ever. The carved four-post Chippendale bed, obviously worth hundreds; the wavy walnut William and Mary chairs—he had seen worse ones labelled twenty guineas apiece; the oval medallion mirror; the delicate eighteenth-century wire fireguard; the heavy brocaded curtains were his—all his. So, too, a great garden full of birds that faced him when he shaved; a mulberry tree, a sun-dial, and a dull, steel-colored brook that murmured level with the edge of a lawn a hundred yards away. Peculiarly and privately his own was the smell of sausages and coffee that he sniffed at the head of the wide square landing, all set round with mysterious doors and Bartolozzi prints. He spent two hours after breakfast in exploring his new possessions. His heart leaped up at such things as sewing-machines, a rubber-tired bath-chair in a tiled passage, a malachite-headed Malacca cane, boxes and boxes of unopened stationery, seal-rings, bunches of keys, and at the bottom of a steel-net reticule a little leather purse with seven pounds ten shillings in gold and eleven shillings in silver."

All the things of the list—beginning and ending with that great thing, money—are alive, and either move us specifically or hold out to us the general possibility of motion. The man who can fill two sentences with those semicolons, and then not use another in the paragraph; who can begin two sentences *So, too, a great garden* . . . and *Peculiarly and privately his own* . . . and give every other sentence a perfectly ordinary beginning; who can invent the passagework that, from a *rubber-tired bath-chair in a tiled passage,* makes its way, through an elderly invalid's possessions, into the culminating *little leather purse with seven pounds ten shillings in gold and eleven shillings in silver*—the man who can do this, and still not have a word obvious or a rhythm obtrusive, really knows how to write. As Chekhov said, and as everybody remembers, you must never hang a pistol on the wall in the first act unless someone is going to shoot himself with it in the last; here the dull, steel-colored brook murmurs level with the edge of a lawn a hundred yards away only because, twenty pages later, that brook is to flood the whole story.

Yet the story from which I am quoting, *"My Son's Wife,"* is a live thing with one leg missing. If Kipling had read it and not written it, he could not have helped seeing that the country is created in beautiful detail, favorable and unfavorable, but that the city intellectuals are set up and knocked down with blankly abstract, pharisaical irony; they are just Bandar-log, after all, and the few details Kipling is willing to waste on them are not observed but invented. We more or less gather that Midmore spent his London hours lying on pillows with women, at teatime, but we neither see the women nor feel the pillows. When we finish the story we are as sure that the country Midmore read Surtees (down to that last haunting sentence: "When at length they rose to go to bed it struck each man as he followed his neighbour upstairs, that the man before him walked very crookedly") as that the idiot wailed, " 'Fraid o' the water! 'Fraid o' the water!" But what did the unconverted Midmore read in London? The Webbs? Wells? Frazer? We respond: "Since you say so," to Midmore's previous condition of servitude, but it is about as real to us as is the earlier career of one of those people in Mark Twain who used to be pirates but have taken to making testimonial speeches for temperance societies, now. Yet, ordinarily, no writer of fiction is better at making literature alive to us as social fact. Literature, in Kipling's stories, is something that makes behavior, is as much an effective part of life as religion or politics. We see this in exaggerated form in *The Janeites:* part of the reader's pleasure in the story—as in so many of Kipling's stories—is that it couldn't possibly really have happened so, and yet it is happening before our eyes. But Kipling's treatment of literature and education in *Regulus* seems exactly truthful in both essence and detail—*is* there a better treatment of a class in fiction?

If Kipling had written: "What do they know of

England who only England know?" a few years
earlier than he did, his readers might have replied:
"What does he know of England who has spent most
of his life in India and Vermont?" But in 1896, after
the public difficulties with his wife's brother that led
him to remark: "There are only two places in the
world where I want to live—Bombay and Brattleboro.
And I can't live at either," Kipling and his American
wife went to live in the English countryside, in a
house so hauntingly unpleasant to them that Kipling
wrote a kind of psychiatric ghost story about it (*The
House Surgeon*); they did not find "Bateman's," the
Sussex house where they spent the rest of their lives,
until 1902. *An Habitation Enforced* is, I think, a
fantasy about the way it would have been if the
Kiplings had returned to a house and country at once
magically their own: the American millionaire and
his wife are blank sticks on which a wish is hung.
And, too, there is the same family romance behind the
story that is behind *Kim* and the *Jungle Books;* it is
not until they leave their ostensible ones that the
Americans discover their true home and family. (*Baa
Baa, Black Sheep* and the chapter on the same subject
in *Something of Myself* show us why Kipling, the
most devoted of sons, had his lifelong compulsive belief in this fantasy.) *Friendly Brook* and *The Wish
House* are two of the stories that demonstrate the
microscopic, loving knowledge of Sussex and its inhabitants that Kipling eventually came to have. A
farm laborer whom Kipling knew particularly well
said to someone, after Kipling's death, that the old fool

did nothing but ask you questions; stories like these
are the result of many asked and many unasked questions. The primary pleasure of a story like *Friendly
Brook* is the atmosphere ("so choked with fog that one
could scarcely see a cow's length across a field")
through which it comes to us; grim, plain, warped
through work and workaday speech, the happenings
have the harshly satisfactory reality that they have
in one of Frost's country stories: " 'Dada' he says, an'
'Mumma' he says, with his great rollin' head-piece all
hurdled up in that iron collar. *He* won't live long—his
backbone's rotten, like. . . . No! 'Twadn't no stroke.
It stifled the old lady in the throat here. First she
couldn't shape her words no shape; then she clucked,
like, an' lastly she couldn't more than suck down spoon-
meat an' hold her peace. Jim took her to Doctor Harding, an' Harding he bundled her off to Brighton Hospital on a ticket, but they couldn't make no stay to
her afflictions there; and she was bundled off to Lun-
non, an' they lit a great old lamp inside her, and Jim
told me they couldn't make out nothing in no sort
there; and, along o' one thing an' another, an' all their
spyin's and pryin's, she come back a hem sight worse
than when she started. Jim said he'd have no more
hospitalizin', so he give her a slate, which she tied to
her waist-string, and what she was minded to say she
writ on it." The happenings of *The Wish House* are
given something of the same atmosphere and the same
reality, but the happenings themselves are the strange
mixture of love, disease, and the supernatural that had
an almost obsessive attraction for Kipling. The love

affairs of most stories, compared to those of Kipling's later stories, seem attractive preoccupations of the young; in his the poor and ugly and sick and middle-aged are overwhelmed by something drab, raw, but ultimate.

There are few stories that seem, first of all and last of all, beautiful; *"They"* is one. It is almost as if the story's extraordinary beauty of picturing, and of the style which pictures, came out of Kipling's desire to have the story a memorial to his own dead daughter. It is a memorial in three tapestries, an early-summer, a late-summer, and an autumn day; the days themselves are hardly more beautiful than the story's movement through the days, the gradual change from loving ignorance into knowledge, the change from the first glimpses of the children, out of the corner of the eye, into the last "little brushing kiss" that "fell in the centre of my palm—as a gift on which the fingers were, once, expected to close: as the all-faithful half-reproachful signal of a waiting child not used to neglect even when grown-ups were busiest—a fragment of the mute code devised very long ago. Then I knew." The treatment of the children is so delicately and hauntingly convincing that it is no wonder *Burnt Norton* should have been influenced by it; yet the tallies with which the blind woman runs her farms, the colored Egg of the soul which the blind woman sees, the blind woman's last piteous, "Oh, you *must* bear or lose. There is no other way"—all this and much more than this are as convincing.

It is interesting to compare the naturally beautiful

"They" with the harshly and uncannily colorful *"Wireless,"* a story that leaves a sort of stained-glass deposit in the memory. It is seen and felt and heard as few stories are: if genius is the ability to perceive (and to make us perceive) likenesses never before seen, in concise hallucinatory form, then *"Wireless"* is a work of genius. It is certainly a work of astonishing originality, of the most extraordinary professional skill. Here, for instance, is Kipling's description of a drugstore on a cold night: "Across the street blank shutters flung back the gaslight in cold smears; the dried pavement seemed to rough up in goose-flesh under the scouring of the savage wind, and we could hear, long ere he passed, the policeman flapping his arms to keep himself warm. Within, the flavours of cardamoms and chloric-ether disputed those of the pastilles and a score of drugs and perfume and soap scents. Our electric lights, set low down in the windows before the tun-bellied Rosamond jars, flung inward three monstrous daubs of red, blue, and green, that broke into kaleidoscopic lights on the faceted knobs of the drug-drawers, the cut-glass scent flagons, and the bulbs of the sparklet bottles. They flushed the white-tiled floor in gorgeous patches; splashed along the nickel-silver counter-rails, and turned the polished mahogany counter-panels to the likeness of intricate grained marbles——slabs of porphyry and malachite. Mr. Shaynor unlocked a drawer, and ere he began to write, took out a meagre bundle of letters. From my place by the stove, I could see the scalloped edges of the paper with a flaring monogram in the corner and

could even smell the reek of chypre. At each page he turned toward the toilet-water lady of the advertisement and devoured her with over-luminous eyes. He had drawn the Austrian blanket over his shoulders, and among those warring lights he looked more than ever the incarnation of a drugged moth—a tiger-moth as I thought." One feels after reading this : well, no one ever again will have to describe a drugstore; many of Kipling's descriptive sentences have this feeling of finality.

As he got older, Kipling found it necessary to write more and more elaborately farcical practical-joke stories—stories of revenge, often; the confirmed reader will immediately think of pieces like *"Brugglesmith," My Sunday at Home, The Puzzler, The Vortex, The Village That Voted the Earth Was Flat, The Bonds of Discipline, Steam Tactics, "Their Lawful Occasions," Aunt Ellen, The Miracle of St. Jubanus, Beauty Spots.* I myself can read these stories with pleasure. (But if Kipling had written instructions on how to make a bed with hospital corners, or how to can gooseberries, I could read them with pleasure : as one of his characters exclaims, "It was the tone, man, the tone!") Most of these farces are stories for the confirmed reader only, since they have been written by the writer for the writer : in them, often, the writer tells us how he laughs so hard that he cannot speak or see or stand up, and how that luckiest of all winds, the dawn wind, comes and whispers to him that the next day everything is going to be even better. *The Village That Voted the Earth Was Flat* quite overcomes these humble, compulsive beginnings: a little of it is a little too good to be true, but what a knowing ingenuity of invention it has, how extraordinarily it is imagined! When the true flat-earthers strike up their hymn,

> Hear ther truth our tongues are telling,
> Spread ther light from shore to shore,
> God hath given man a dwelling
> Flat and flat for evermore.
>
> When ther Primal Dark retreated,
> When ther deeps were undesigned,
> He with rule and level meted
> Habitation for mankind!

you feel like muttering with the envious music-hall impresario: "Curse Nature, she gets ahead of you every time," till you remember that it is Kipling himself, here, who is both Nature and Art.

I had always supposed that Kipling wrote *Mary Postgate* a few months after his son was killed in the First World War, and it had seemed to me an awful but in some sense normal thing. When you learn that the story was written several months before his son's death, you are troubled just as you are when you learn that Mahler's *Kindertotenlieder* was written before and not after the death of his child. This truthfully cruel, human-all-too-human wish-fantasy is as satisfying to one part of our nature as it is terrible to another. What happens is implausible but intensely actual: the German pilot isn't really there, of course, except in our desire, but his psychological reality is absolute, down to the last groan of the head that "moved ceaselessly from side to side . . . as pale as a baby's, and so closely cropped that she could see the disgusting pinky skin beneath"; we are forced to believe in him just as Freud was forced to believe in his first patients' fantasies of seduction. *Dayspring Mishandled*, one of the most morally appealing of Kipling's stories, is very human in the opposite sense of the word. When, dying under the expectant scrutiny of his knowing and faithless wife, the knighted and successful Castorley, in puzzled misery, in all the agony of disease and doubt, begs for the reassurance of the man who for twenty years has worked out the ruin he can accomplish with a word, and who now interrupts unsteadily: "I can confirm every word you've said. You've nothing to worry about. It's *your* find—*your* credit—*your* glory and—all the rest of it"—when he gets to this point, Kipling has made his way to something past revenge, past any human division: the sentences are as beautiful in their inclusiveness as the last sentence of the story is beautiful in its precise exclusion: "As, on the appointed words, the coffin crawled sideways through the noiselessly-closing door-flaps, I saw Lady Castorley's eyes turn towards Gleeag."

If you compare one of the best of Kipling's early stories (*Without Benefit of Clergy*, say) with some of the best of his late stories, you realize that the late stories are specialized in their moral and human attitudes—in their subject matter, even—in a way in which the early story is not. The early story's subject is a general subject that will repay any amount of general skill or general talent: you can imagine a greater writer's rewriting *Without Benefit of Clergy* and making a much better story out of it. But this is precisely what you cannot imagine with Kipling's later stories: Chekhov and Tolstoy and Turgenev together couldn't improve *"They"* or *"Wireless,"* since in each a highly specialized subject has received an exactly appropriate, extraordinarily skilled and talented treatment. These later stories of Kipling's don't compete, really, with *Gusev* and *The Death of Ivan Ilych* and *A Sportsman's Sketches,* but have set up a kingdom of their own, a little off to the side of things, in which they are incomparable: their reader feels, "You can write better stories than Kipling's, but not better Kipling stories." This kingdom of theirs is a strange, disquieting, but quite wonderful place, as if some of the Douanier Rousseau's subjects had been repainted by Degas. If we cannot make the very greatest claims for the stories, it would be absurd not to make great ones: as long as readers enjoy style and skill, originality and imagination—in a word, genius—they will take delight in Kipling's stories.

Fifty Years

of American Poetry

I N 1910 American poetry was a bare sight. We
were not, like Canada or New Zealand, a province
without a national poetry of its own. There had been
good American poets—but how few, and already how
far in the past! Whitman and Dickinson, the two
greatest and most decidedly American, seemed to owe
both their greatness and their Americanness to their
own entire originality and eccentricity. Three other
genuinely American poets, Melville, Emerson, and
Thoreau, had written good poems, most of them less
notably un-English than Whitman's and Dickinson's.
But the American poets who were admired most during the nineteenth century, who seemed most plainly
the center of American poetry, and who fitted into the
regular tradition of English poetry as plainly as Whitman and Dickinson did not, were Longfellow, Lowell,
Whittier, and Bryant. There had been a gap of thirty
or forty years, from the seventies until 1910, during
which almost no good American poetry had been written. If in 1912 someone had predicted that during the

next fifty years American poetry would be the best and most influential in the English language, and that the next generation of poets would be American classics, men who would establish once and for all the style and tone of American poetry, his prediction would have seemed fantastic. Yet all this is literally true of the generation of American poets that included Frost, Stevens, Eliot, Pound, Williams, Marianne Moore, Ransom. When we read the poems of these poets and of the Irishman Yeats, we realize that the whole center of gravity of poetry in English had shifted west of England.

It is worth our while, then, to look hard at the American poetry of the last fifty years. I'll try not to theorize about movements and tendencies but to stick to the poets and their poems; as Goethe says, "Theories are as a rule impulsive reactions of an over-hasty understanding which would like to have done with phenomena and therefore substitutes for them images, concepts, or often even just words." I have written out for you the opinions of a devoted reader of this poetry; often I have summarized or quoted from what I have already written about a poet.*

When you read Edwin Arlington Robinson's poems, you are conscious of a mind looking seriously at a world with people in it and expressing itself primarily in terms of these human beings it has observed and created. Robinson's steady human sympathy is accompanied by a steady hatred of the inhuman world that people have made for themselves, the world

---

* From his essay "The Collected Poems of Wallace Stevens" (pp. 55–73), for example. ED.

of business and greed and hypocritical morality; he felt for the America of the end of the century the same gloomy despair that Henry Adams and Mark Twain felt, asking it:

> Are you to pay for what you have
> With all you are?

You see his qualities at their rare best in "Mr. Flood's Party," at their ordinary best in "Eros Turannos," "George Crabbe," "The Clerks." He is far better when he is reserved and prosaic than when he is poetic; his poetic rhetoric is embarrassingly threadbare and commonplace, as when he writes about his own lost belief:

> I can hear it only as a bar
> Of lost, imperial music, played when fair
> And angel fingers wove, and unaware,
> Dead leaves to garlands where no roses are.

Such rhetoric is accompanied, characteristically, by an emptily antithetical, quibbling, riddling paradoxicalness. Robinson wrote a great deal of poetry and only a few good poems; and yet there is a somber distinction and honesty about him—he is a poet you respect.

If Edgar Lee Masters's *Spoon River Anthology* seems to us, today, more a part of literary history than of living poetry, still it is a surprisingly live part, a "Main Street" through whose mud the old buggies and the new horseless carriages are still pushing. It tells the historical truth of the late nineteenth- and early twentieth-century towns of the Middle West—the struggle of greed and puritanicalness and provinciality with innocent radicalism and idealism and culture—directly in terms of the people who embodied them; it is a kind of "Ironies of Circumstance" told by an honest muckraker. Its whole is more effective than any of its parts; and the poems' prosaic effects are always better than their poetic effects, since Masters's rhetoric, his whole idea of what a poetic effect is, is commonplace—he is either sincerely prosaic or ingenuously poetic. His work has less distinction than Robinson's; and yet his style and tone are his own, the poems plainly come out of the life they describe. He writes:

> The earth keeps some vibration going
> There in your heart, and that is you.

Such a vibration is still going in some of the poems.

Carl Sandburg's poems, generally, are improvisations whose wording is approximate; they do not have the exactness, the guaranteeing sharpness and strangeness of a real style. Sandburg is a colorful, appealing, and very American writer, so that you long for his little vignettes or big folk editorials, with their easy sentimentality and easy idealism, to be made into finished works of art; but he sings songs more stylishly than he writes them, says his poems better than they are written—it is marvelous to hear him say "The People, Yes," but it is not marvelous to read it as a poem. Probably he is at his best in slight pieces like "Grass" or "Losers," or in such folkish inventions as:

> tell me why a hearse horse snickers
> hauling a lawyer's bones.

The oddest and most imaginative of these poets is Vachel Lindsay. He has the innocent, desperate eccentricity of the artist in a world with no room for, no patience with, artists; you could die for what you believed, Lindsay said, and no one would notice or care, but if you had the nerve to go broke time after time, they would notice. Nowadays when a poet with one privately printed book can have his next three years taken care of by a Guggenheim fellowship, a *Kenyon Review* fellowship, and the Prix de Rome, it is hard to remember what chances the poet took in that small-town world, how precariously hand to mouth his existence was. And yet in one way the old days were better; Lindsay after a while, by luck and skill, got far more readers than any poet could get today. His rhetoric with its wild, queer charm (half vaudeville and half grammar-school pageant, dreamed by a provincial Blake) and his almost childlike imagination produced a good many poems that we make allowances for and complacently enjoy; but at his best—in "Bryan, Bryan, Bryan, Bryan," in "A Negro Sermon : Simon Legree," and in "Daniel"—the poems are truly imagined and written; they have a rightness all their own. In "Bryan, Bryan, Bryan, Bryan," for instance, you find a real aesthetic distance, an unexpected objectivity and historical truth that go along with the consciously exaggerated and audacious phrases. What other writer, in the smiling expectation of his reader's smile, has ever called his sweetheart and himself "fairy Democrats"? The rest of literature, the rest of the world were for Lindsay a kind of second-hand shop from which he could get, cheap, the properties of his poems; but he had more sheer imagination, sheer objective command than most of his contemporaries, so that several of his poems are perfected as almost none of theirs are.

Robert Frost, along with Stevens and Eliot, seems to me the greatest of the American poets of this century. Frost's virtues are extraordinary. No other living poet has written so well about the actions of ordinary men; his wonderful dramatic monologues or dramatic scenes come out of a knowledge of people that few poets have had, and they are written in a verse that uses, sometimes with absolute mastery, the rhythms of actual speech. It is hard to overestimate the effect of this exact, spaced-out, prosaic movement, whose objects have the tremendous strength—you find it in Hardy's best poems—of things merely put down and left to speak for themselves. (Though Frost has little of Hardy's self-effacement, his matter-of-fact humility; Frost's tenderness, sadness, and humor are adulterated with vanity and a hard complacency.) Frost's seriousness and honesty; the bare sorrow with which, sometimes, things are accepted as they are, neither exaggerated nor explained away; the many, many poems in which there are real people with their real speech and real thought and real emotions—all this, in conjunction with so much subtlety and exactness, such classical understatement and restraint, makes the reader feel that he is not in a book but a world, and a world that has in common with his own some of the things that are most important in both. I don't need to praise anything so justly famous as Frost's observation of and empathy with everything in Nature from a hornet to a hillside; and he has observed his own nature, one person's random or consequential chains of thoughts and feelings and perceptions, quite as well. The least crevice of the good poems is saturated with imagination, an imagination that expresses itself in the continual wit and humor and particularity of what is said, and in the hand-hewn or hand-polished texture of its saying. And when you remember that Frost has written "The Witch of Coös," "Home Burial," "A Servant to Servants," "Directive," "Neither Out Far Nor In Deep," "Provide, Provide," "Acquainted with the Night," "After Apple-Picking," "Mending Wall," "The Most of It," "An Old Man's Winter Night," "To Earthward," "Stopping by Woods on a Snowy Evening," "Spring Pools," "The Lovely Shall Be Choosers," "Design," "Desert Places"—these and "The Fear," "The Pauper Witch of Grafton," "The Gift Outright," "The Need of Being Versed in Country Things," and a dozen or two dozen more as good— when you remember this you are astonished, almost as you are with Yeats and Rilke, that one man could have written so *many* good poems.

How little Frost's poems seem performances, no matter how brilliant or magical, how little things made primarily of words, and how much things made out of lives and the world that the lives inhabit! In Frost's poems men are not only the glory and jest and riddle of the world but also the habit of the world, its strange ordinariness, its ordinary strangeness, and they too trudge down the ruts along which the planets move in their courses. Frost is that rare thing, a complete or representative poet, and not one of the brilliant partial poets who do justice, far more than justice, to a portion of reality, and leave the rest of things forlorn. When you know Frost's poems, you know surprisingly well what the world seemed to one man. The grimness and awfulness and untouchable sadness of things, both in the world and in the self, have justice done to them in the poems—the limits which existence approaches and falls back from have seldom been stated with such bare composure—but no more justice than is done to the tenderness and love and delight; and everything in between is represented somewhere too, some things willingly and often and other things only as much— in Marianne Moore's delicate phrase—"as one's natural reticence will allow." To have the distance from the most awful and most nearly unbearable parts of the poems to the most tender, subtle, and loving parts, a distance so great; to have this whole range of being treated with so much humor and sadness and composure, with such plain truth; to see that a man can still include, connect, and make humanly understandable or un-understandable so *much*—this is one of the freshest and oldest of joys, a joy strong enough to make us say, with the Greek poet, that many things in this world are wonderful, but of all these the most wonderful is man.

Athens was called the education of Hellas; from 1912 till 1922 Ezra Pound could have been called the education of poetry. (I once read all the issues of *Poetry* printed during those years, and what stood out most was one poet, Yeats, and one critic, Pound.) His advice to poets could be summed up in a sentence: Write like speech—and *read French poetry!* He had needed his own advice; his earliest work was a sort of anthology of romantic sources—Browning, early Yeats, the *fin-de-siècle* poets, Villon and the troubadours (in translations or adaptations that remind one of Swinburne's and Rossetti's), Heine. His own variety of modernist poetry, though influenced by Laforgue and Corbière, was partly a return to the fresh beginnings of romantic practices, from their diluted and perfunctory ends; partly an extension to their limits of some of the most characteristic obsessions of romanticism, for instance, its passion for "pure" poetry, for putting everything in terms of sensation and emotion, with logic and generalizations excluded; and partly an adaptation of the exotic procedures of Chinese poetry, those silks that swathe a homely heart. Much of Pound's earlier poetry was a sort of bohemian *vers de société;* Pound's best work before *The Cantos,* with the exception of some parts of *Mauberly,* consists of adaptations of Chinese and Latin poetry. The best poems in *Cathay* are marvelous in their crystalline clearness, in the way their words stand out in delicate lucid pure being; Pound's style at its best is always a part of—in Pound's words—"the radiant world where one thought cuts through another with clean edge, a world of moving energies. . . . the glass under water, the form that seems a form seen in a mirror." This style comes to us, mostly, in beautiful fragments or adaptations; it is surprising that a poet of Pound's extraordinary talents should have written so few good poems all his own.

Most of Pound's life has been spent on *The Cantos*. Many writers have felt, like Pound: Why not invent an art form that will permit me to put all my life, all my thoughts and feelings about the universe, directly into a work of art? But the trouble is, when they've invented it, it isn't an art form. *The Cantos* are a "form" that permits Pound, much of the time, not even to try to write poetry; but since he is a poet, a wonderful one, he sometimes still writes it. *The Cantos* are less a "poem containing history" than a heap containing poetry, history, recollections, free associations, obsessions. Form, as Kenneth Burke says, is a satisfied expectation; in much of *The Cantos* it is only our expectation of disorder, of an idiosyncratic hodgepodge, that is satisfied. Some of the lines have an easy elegance, a matter-of-fact reality; the bare look and motion of the words, sometimes, is a delight. A great deal of *The Cantos* is interesting in the way an original soul's indiscriminate notes on books and people, countries and centuries, are interesting; all these fragmentary citations and allusions remind you that if you had read exactly the books Pound has read, known exactly the people Pound has known, and felt about them exactly as Pound has felt, you could understand *The Cantos* pretty well. Gertrude Stein was most unjust to Pound when she called that ecumenical alluder a village explainer: he can hardly *tell* you anything (unless you know it already), much less explain it. He makes notes on the margin of the universe; to tell how just or unjust a note is, you must know that portion of the text yourself. Some of the poetry is clearly beautiful, some of the history live: Pound can pick out, make up, a sentence or action that resurrects a man or a time. Many of Pound's recollections are as engaging as he is; his warmth, delight, disinterestedness, honest indignation help to make up for his extraordinary misuse of extraordinary powers, for everything that makes *The Cantos* a *reductio ad absurdum* of genius. His obsessions, at their worst, are a moral and intellectual disaster and make us ashamed for him:

> Democracies electing their sewage
> till there is no clear thought about holiness
> a dung flow from 1913
> and, in this, their kikery functioned, Marx, Freud
>   and the American beaneries
> Filth under filth. . . .

What is worst in Pound and what is worst in the age have conspired to ruin *The Cantos* and have not succeeded. I cannot imagine any future that will think the whole of it a good poem, a finished work of art; but, then as now, scholars will process it, anthologies present a few of its beauties, readers dig through all that blue clay for more than a few diamonds.

At the bottom of Wallace Stevens's poetry there is wonder and delight, the child's or animal's or savage's —man's—joy in his own existence, and thankfulness for it. He is the poet of well-being: "One might have thought of sight, but who could think / Of what it

sees, for all the ill it sees?" This sigh of awe, of wondering pleasure, is underneath all these poems that
show us the "celestial possible," everything that has
not yet been transformed into the infernal impossibilities of our everyday earth. Stevens is full of the
natural or Aristotelian virtues; he is, in the terms of
Hopkins's poem, all windhover and no Jesuit. There is
about him, under the translucent glazes, a Dutch solidity and weight; he sits surrounded by all the good
things of this earth, with rosy cheeks and fresh clear
blue eyes, eyes not going out to you but shining in
their place, like fixed stars. If he were an animal he
would be, without a doubt, that rational, magnanimous, voluminous animal, the elephant.

His best poems are the poetry of a man fully
human—of someone sympathetic, disinterested, both
brightly and deeply intelligent; the poems see, feel,
and think with equal success; they treat with mastery
that part of existence which allows of mastery, and
experience the rest of it with awe or sadness or delight.
Minds of this quality of genius, of this breadth and
delicacy of understanding, are a link between us and
the past, since they are, for us, the past made living;
and they are our surest link with the future, since
they are the part of us which the future will know.
Many of the poems look grayly out at

> . . . the immense detritus of a world
> That is completely waste, that moves from waste
> To waste, out of the hopeless waste of the past
> Into a hopeful waste to come.

306

But more of the poems see the unspoilable delights, the inexhaustible interests of existence.

Stevens did what no other American poet has ever done, what few poets have ever done: wrote some of his best and newest and strangest poems during the last year or two of a very long life. These are poems from the other side of existence, the poems of someone who sees things in steady accustomedness, as we do not, and who sees their accustomedness, and them, as about to perish. Many of the poems' qualities come naturally from age, so that they are appropriately and legitimately different from other people's poems, from Stevens's own younger poems. The poems are calmly exact, grandly plain, as though they themselves had suggested to Stevens his "Be orator but with an accurate tongue / And without eloquence"; and they seem strangely general and representative, so that we could say of them, of Stevens, what Stevens himself says "To an Old Philosopher in Rome":

> . . . each of us
> Behold himself in you, and hears his voice
> In yours, master and commiserable man. . . .

How much of our existence is in that "master and commiserable man"! Poems like these, in their plainness and human rightness, remind me most of a work of art superficially very different, Verdi's *Falstaff*. Both are the products of men at once very old and beyond the dominion of age; such men seem to have entered into (or are able to create for us) a new existence, a world in which everything is enlarged and yet no more than itself, transfigured and yet beyond the need of transfiguration.

Stevens has an extraordinarily original imagination, one that has created for us, so to speak, many new tastes and colors and sounds, many real, half-real, and nonexistent beings. He has spoken, always, with the authority of someone who thinks of himself as a source of interest, of many interests. He has never felt it necessary to appeal to us, make a hit with us, nor does he try to sweep us away, to overawe us; he has written as if poems were certain to find, or make, their true readers. Throughout half this century of the common man, this age in which each is like his sibling, Stevens has celebrated the hero, the capacious, magnanimous, excelling man; has believed, with obstinacy and good humor, in all the heights which draw us toward them, make us like them, simply by existing. In an age when almost everybody sold man and the world short, he never did, but acted as if joy *were* "a word of our own," as if nothing excellent were alien to us.

William Carlos Williams is as magically observant and mimetic as a good novelist. He reproduces the details of what he sees with surprising freshness, clarity, and economy; and he sees just as extraordinarily, sometimes, the forms of this earth, the spirit moving behind the letters. His quick transparent lines have a nervous and contracted strength, move as jerkily and intently as a bird. Sometimes they have a marvelous delicacy and gentleness, a tact of pure showing; how well he calls into existence our pre-

carious, confused, partial looking out at the world—
our being-here-looking, just looking! And if he is
often pure presentation, he is often pure exclamation,
and delights in yanking something into life with a
galvanic imperative or interjection. All this proceeds
from the whole bent of his nature: he prefers a clear,
active, intense confusion to any "wise passiveness," to
any calm and clouded two-sidedness.

He has a boyish delight and trust in Things: there
is always on his lips the familiar, pragmatic, American "These are the facts"—for he is the most pragmatic of writers and so American that the adjective
itself seems inadequate; one exclaims in despair and
delight: He is the America of poets. His imagist-objec-
tivist background and bias have helped his poems by
their emphasis on truthfulness, exactness, concrete
presentation; but they have harmed the poems by
their underemphasis on organization, logic, narrative,
generalization. The materials of Williams's unsuccessful poems have as much reality as the brick one
stumbles over on the sidewalk; but how little has been
done to them!—the poem is pieces or, worse still, a
piece. But sometimes just enough, exactly as little as is
necessary, has been done; and in these poems the
Nature of the edge of the American city—the weeds,
clouds, and children of vacant lots—and its reflection
in the minds of its inhabitants exist for good.

Anyone would apply to Williams such adjectives
as outspoken, warmhearted, generous, fresh, sympathetic, enthusiastic, spontaneous, impulsive, emotional,
observant, curious, rash, courageous, undignified, un-

affected, humanitarian, experimental, empirical, liberal, secular, democratic. One is rather embarrassed at the necessity of calling him original; it is like saying that a Cheshire cat smiles. He is even less logical than the average poet—he is an intellectual in neither the good nor the bad sense of the word—but loves abstractions for their own sake and makes accomplished, characteristic, inveterate use of them, exactly as if they were sensations or emotions. Both generalizations and particulars are handled with freshness and humor and imagination, with a delicacy and fantasy that are especially charming in so vigorous, realistic, and colloquial a writer. He is full of homely shrewdness and common sense, of sharply intelligent comments dancing cheek-to-cheek with prejudices and random eccentricity; he is someone who, sometimes, does see what things are like, and he is able to say what he sees more often than most poets, since his methods permit (indeed encourage) him to say anything at all without worrying: *Can* one say such things in poetry? in this particular poem?

Williams's poetry is more remarkable for its empathy, its muscular and emotional identification with its subjects, than any modern poetry except Rilke's. His knowledge of plants and animals, our brothers and sisters in the world, is surprising for its range and intensity; and he sets them down in the midst of the real weather of the world, so that the reader is full of an innocent lyric pleasure just in being out in the open, in feeling the wind tickling his skin. At first people were introduced into the poems mainly as overheard or overlooked landscape; they spread. Williams has the knowledge of people one expects, and often does not get, from doctors; a knowledge one does not expect, and very seldom gets, from contemporary poets. Williams's attitude toward his people is particularly admirable; he has neither that condescending, impatient, pharisaical dismissal of the illiterate mass of mankind, nor that manufactured, mooing awe for an equally manufactured Little or Common Man, that disfigures so much contemporary writing.

Williams's ability to rest (or at least to thrash happily about) in contradictions, doubts, and general guesswork, without ever climbing aboard any of the monumental certainties that go perpetually by, per- petually on time—this ability may seem the opposite of Whitman's gift for boarding every certainty and riding off into every infinite, but the spirit behind them is the same. Williams's range (it is roughly *Paterson*, that microcosm which he has half discov- ered, half invented) is narrower than Whitman's, and yet there too one is reminded of Whitman: Williams has much of the freeness of an earlier America, though it is a freedom haunted about by desperation and sorrow. The little motto one could invent for him— "In the suburbs, there one feels free"—is particularly ambiguous when one considers that those suburbs of his are overshadowed by, are a part of, the terrible industrial landscape of northeastern New Jersey. But the ambiguity is one that Williams himself not only understands but insists upon: if his poems are full of what is clear, delicate, and beautiful, they are also full of what is coarse, ugly, and horrible. There is no optimistic blindness in Williams, though there is a fresh gaiety, a stubborn or invincible joyousness: in his best poems, and in the first and best parts of *Paterson*, the humor and sadness and raw absurdity of things, and the things themselves, exist in startling reality.

In John Crowe Ransom's best poems every part is subordinated to the whole, and the whole is accomplished with astonishing exactness and thoroughness. Their economy, precision, and restraint give the poems, sometimes, an original yet impersonal perfection; and Ransom's feel for the exact convention of a particular poem, the exact demands of a particular situation, has resulted in poems different from each other and everything else, as unified, individualized, and unchangeable as nursery rhymes. In Ransom the contradictions of existence are clear, exactly contradictory, not fused in arbitrary over-all emotion; one admires the clear, sharp, Mozartian lightness of texture of the best poems. And sometimes their phrasing is magical—light as air, soft as dew, the real old-fashioned enchantment. The poems satisfy our nostalgia for the past, yet themselves have none. They are the reports (written by one of the most elegant and individual war correspondents who ever existed) of our world's old war between power and love, between those who efficiently and practically know and those who are "content to feel / What others understand." And these reports of battles are, somehow, bewitching: disenchantment and enchantment are so beautifully and inextricably mingled in them that we accept everything with sad pleasure, and smile at the poems' foreknowing, foredefeated, half-acceptant pain. For in the country of the poems wisdom is a poor butterfly dreaming that it is Chuang-tzu, and not an optimistic bird of prey; and the greatest single subject of the romantics, pure potentiality, is treated with a classical grace and composure.

Most writers become overrhetorical when they are insisting on more emotion than they actually feel; Ransom is perpetually insisting, by his detached, mock-pedantic, wittily complicated tone, that he is not feeling much at all, not half so much as he really should be feeling—and this rhetoric becomes overmannered, too protective, only when there is not much emotion for him to pretend not to be feeling, and he keeps on out of habit. Ransom has the personal seriousness that treats the world as it seems to him, not the solemnity that treats the really important things, the world as everybody knows it is. His poems are full of an affection that cannot help itself for an innocence that cannot help itself—for the stupid travelers lost in the maze of the world, for the clever travelers lost in the maze of the world. The poems are not a public argument but personal knowledge, personal feeling; and their virtues are the "merely" private virtues—their characters rarely vote, rarely even kill one another, but often fall in love.

Ransom's poems profess their limitations so candidly, almost as a principle of style, that it is hardly necessary to say they are not poems of the largest scope or the greatest intensity. But they are some of the most original poems ever written, just as Ransom is one of the best, most original, and most sympathetic poets alive; it is easy to see that his poetry will always be cared for, since he has written poems that are perfectly realized and occasionally almost perfect—poems that the hypothetical generations of the future will be reading page by page with Wyatt, Campion, Marvell, and Mother Goose.

And then there is Eliot. During the last thirty or forty years Eliot has been so much the most famous and influential of American poets that it seems almost absurd to write about him, especially when everybody else already has: when all of you can read me your own articles about Eliot, would it have really been worth while to write you mine? Yet actually the attitude of an age toward its Lord Byron—in this case, a sort of combination of Lord Byron and Dr. Johnson—is always surprisingly different from the attitude of the future. Won't the future say to us in helpless astonishment: "But did you actually believe that all those things about objective correlatives, classicism, the tradition, applied to *his* poetry? Surely you must have seen that he was one of the most subjective and daemonic poets who ever lived, the victim and helpless beneficiary of his own inexorable compulsions, obsessions? From a psychoanalytical point of view he was far and away the most interesting poet of your century. But for you, of course, after the first few years, his poetry existed undersea, thousands of feet below that deluge of exegesis, explication, source listing, scholarship, and criticism that overwhelmed it. And yet how bravely and personally it survived, its eyes neither coral nor mother-of-pearl but plainly human, full of human anguish! Think of the magical rightness of 'Prufrock,' one of the most engaging and haunting and completely accomplished poems that ever existed. Or take the continuation of it, that mesmeric subjective correlative *The Waste Land*, which Eliot would have written about the Garden of Eden, but which your age thought its own realistic photograph. And if none of the poets of your age—except perhaps for your greatest, Yeats—could write a really good play, still, how genuinely personal, what a subjective therapeutic success *Murder in the Cathedral* and *The Family Reunion* are! And if none of the poets of your age could write a long poem that compares with the best of their short poems, still, how wonderful the *Four Quartets* are: a long poem by a good poet that (as neither *The Cantos* nor *The Bridge* nor *Paterson* does) brings an intelligent man's own world view into an organized and thoughtful whole. If the reasons you gave were often the wrong reasons, the poet and the poems you loved were the right poet and the right poems; so far as Eliot is concerned, your age can be satisfied with itself."

Marianne Moore has as careful and acute an eye as anybody alive, and almost as good a tongue. The reader relishes in her poems a fineness and strangeness and firmness of discrimination that he is not accustomed to. Her poems are notable for their wit and particularity and observation; a knowledge of "prosaic" words that reminds one of "Comus"; a texture that will withstand any amount of rereading; a restraint and delicacy that make many more powerful poems seem obvious. Their forms have the lacy, mathematical extravagance of snowflakes, seem as arbitrary as the prohibitions in fairy tales; difficulty is the chief technical principle of her poetry, almost. What intelligence vibrates in the sounds, the rhythms, the pauses, in all the minute particulars that make up the body of the poem! The tone of her poems, often, is enough to give the reader great pleasure, since it is a tone of imagination and precision and intelligence, of irony and forbearance, of unusual moral penetration—is plainly the voice of a person of good taste and good sense and good will, of a genuinely human being. It is the voice, too, of a natural, excessive, and magnificent eccentric. In some of her poems she has discovered both a new sort of subject (a queer many-headed one) and a new sort of connection and structure for it, so that she has widened the scope of poetry; if poetry, like other organisms, wants to convert into itself everything that is, she has helped it to. She has shown us that the world is more poetic than we thought.

She has great limitations—her work is one long triumph of them. How often she has written about Things (hers are aesthetic-moral, not commercial-utilitarian—they persist and reassure); or Plants (how can anything bad happen to a plant?); or Animals with holes, a heavy defensive armament, or a massive and herbivorous placidity superior to either the dangers or temptations of aggression! Because so much of our own world is evil, she has transformed the Animal Kingdom, that amoral realm, into a realm of good; her consolatory, fabulous bestiary is more accurate than, but is almost as arranged as, any medieval one. The poems say, sometimes, to the beasts: "You reassure me and people don't, except when they are like you—but really they are always like you"; and it is wonderful to have it said so, and for a moment to forget, behind the animals of a darkening landscape, their dark companions.

Some of her poems have the manners or manner of ladies who learned a little before birth not to mention money, who neither point nor touch, and who scrupulously abstain from the mixed, live vulgarity of life. "You sit still if, whenever you move, something jingles," Pound quotes an officer of the old school as saying. There is the same aristocratic abstention behind the restraint, the sitting still as long as it can, of this poetry. "The passion for setting people right is in itself an afflictive disease. / Distaste that takes no credit to itself is best," she says in an early poem: and says, broadly and fretfully for her, "We are sick of the earth, / sick of the pig-sty, wild geese and wild men." One feels like quoting against her her own "As if a death-mask could replace / Life's faulty excellence," and blurting that life masks have their disadvantages too. We are uncomfortable—or else too comfortable—in a world in which feeling, affection, charity are so entirely divorced from sexuality and power, the bonds of the flesh. In the world of her poems there are many thoughts, things, animals, sentiments, moral insights; but money and passion and power, the brute fact that *works*, whether or not correctly, whether or not precisely—the whole Medusa face of the world : these are gone.

A good deal of Marianne Moore's poetry is specifically (and changingly) about armor, weapons, protection, places to hide; and she is not only conscious that this is so, but after a while writes poems about the fact that it is so. As she says, "armor seems extra," but it isn't; and when she writes about "another armored animal," about another "thing made graceful by adversities, conversities," she does so with the sigh of someone who has come home. Sometimes she writes about armor and wears it, the most delicately chased, live-seeming scale armor anybody ever put together : armor hammered out of fern seed, woven from the silk of invisible cloaks—for it is almost, though not quite, as invisible as it pretends to be, and is when most nearly invisible most nearly protecting. And yet in the long run she has learned to put no trust in armor and says, "Pig-fur won't do, I'll wrap / myself in salamander-skin like Prester John," the "inextinguishable salamander" who "revealed / a formula safer than / an armorer's : the power of relinquishing / what one would keep," and whose "shield was his humility." And "What Are Years" begins : "All are naked, none are safe," and speaks of overcoming our circumstances by accepting them; just as "Nevertheless" talks not about armor, not about weapons, but about what is behind or above them both:

> The weak overcomes its
> menace, the strong over-
> comes itself. What is there
> like fortitude? What sap
> went through that little thread
> to make the cherry red!

Just so the poet overcomes herself, when she says at last: "What is more precise than precision? Illusion." There is so much of a life concentrated into, objectified on, the poet's hard, tender, serious pages, there is such wit and truth and moral imagination inhabiting this small space, that we are surprised at possibility, and marvel all over again at the conditions of human making and being. What Marianne Moore's best poetry does, I can say best in her own words: it "comes into and steadies the soul," so that the reader feels himself "a life prisoner, but reconciled."

E. E. Cummings persisted so boldly and stubbornly, for a whole career, in his own extraordinary individuality, that it is hard for his readers to believe that he is gone. No one else has ever made avant-garde, experimental poems so attractive both to the general and the special reader; since the early twenties, Cummings has been more widely imitated and more easily appreciated than any other modernist poet. His fairy godmother, after giving him several armfuls of sensibility, individuality, and rhetorical skill, finished by saying: "And best of all, everyone will forgive you everything, my son." Just as he persisted in the interests with which he began—his disposition was unchanging—so he persisted in the development of the style with which he began, and worked out the most extraordinary variations, inversions, and extrapolations of the romantic rhetoric of his earliest poems. His rhetoric was as skillful, approached as nearly to the limit of every last possibility, as the acts of the circus performers or burlesque comedians he felt an admiring kinship for. Many a writer has spent his life putting his favorite words in all the places they belong; but how many, like Cummings, have spent their lives putting their favorite words in all the places they don't belong, thus discovering many effects that no one had even realized were possible? As Cummings said, "Every man is wonderful / and a formula"; often this is true of Cummings himself, so that you get tired of the hundredth application of the formula—but often it is from that very formula, worked out into a fantastic new one, that Cummings has derived an effect of wonderful originality.

Language is a world of signs, and of prescribed relations between the signs, that stand for the things in the natural world and *their* relations. But there are all sorts of impossible, unprescribed relations between words that seem to stand for something, have quasi-denotations, vague or contradictory but exciting meanings. And since we feel that words and their prescribed relations don't fully or satisfactorily describe the world, that there is a disorder or meta-order in the world to which ordered words are inadequate, we sympathize with the contradictory or impossible order of words, and try to feel what it must stand for. The round-square may be impossible, but we believe in it because it is impossible. Cummings is a very great expert in all these, so to speak, illegal syntactical devices : his misuse of parts of speech, his use of negative prefixes, his word coining, his systematic relation of words that grammar and syntax don't permit us to relate—all this makes him a magical bootlegger or moonshiner of language, one who intoxicates us on a clear liquor no government has legalized with its stamp.

The accomplished body of Conrad Aiken's work— which has been at once respected and neglected—is something you read with consistent pleasure, but without the astonished joy that you feel for the finest poetry, which is always extraordinary. It is peculiarly hard to say what is lacking in Aiken's work, since he has written poems that come as close to being good poems, without ever quite being so, as any I know. Isaac Babel said about style : "A phrase is born into the world good and bad at the same time. The secret lies in a slight, almost invisible twist. The lever should rest in your hand, getting warm, and you can turn it once, not twice." Aiken has kept his hand on the lever all his life, and he has turned it over and over and over. He is a kind of Midas : everything that he touches turns to verse; so that reading his poems is like listening to Delius—one is experiencing an unending undifferentiating wash of lovely sounds—or like watching an only moderately interesting, because almost entirely predictable, kaleidoscope. Aiken's diluted world is a world where everything blurs into everything else, where the accomplished, elegiac, nostalgic verse turns everything into itself, as the diffused Salon photography of the first years of this century turned everything into Salon photographs.

Another respected but somewhat neglected poet is Allen Tate. But the best of his harshly formed, powerful poems are far more individual, unusual, than even the best of Aiken's. Perhaps they are read less than they are admired because of their lack of charm, of human appeal and human sympathy, and because of their tone of somewhat forbidding authority; but the neglect of poems as good as "Mother and Son," "The Cross," and "The Mediterranean" will surely be temporary.

Robinson Jeffers has taken an interesting and unusual part of the world and has described it, narrated some overpowering events that have occurred in it, with great—but crude and approximate—power. He celebrates the survival of the fittest, the war of all against all, but his heart goes out to animals rather than to human beings, to minerals rather than to animals, since he despises the bonds and qualifications of existence. Because of all this, his poems do not have the exactness and concision of the best poetry; his style and temperament, his whole world-view, are to a surprising extent a matter of simple exaggeration. The motto of his work is "More! more!"—but as Tolstoy says, "A wee bit omitted, overemphasized, or exaggerated in poetry, and there is no contagion"; and Frost, bearing him out, says magnificently: "A very little of anything goes a long way in a work of art." Archibald MacLeish first employed his delicate lyric gift upon more easily and immediately attractive versions of poems like Eliot's, Pound's, and Apollinaire's; the smoothly individual style that he developed makes such a poem as "And You, Andrew Marvell" beautiful in just the way that a Georgia O'Keeffe painting is beautiful. In his later work he began to make overpowering general demands upon this limited and specific talent. The directly impressive rhetoric of a play like *J. B.* is akin to the rhetoric of the most cultivated and effective television programs: the play, like so much of MacLeish's later work, is the "public speech" of an authoritative public figure who is controlling the responses of a mass audience. MacLeish's work suffers, characteristically, from something akin to the "metaphysical pathos": it is almost more conscious of the impressiveness of what it says than of what it says.

Hart Crane's *The Bridge* does not succeed as a unified work of art, partly because some of its poems are bad or mediocre, and partly because Crane took for his subject an ambiguous failure and tried to treat it as a mystical triumph: it is as if Fitzgerald had tried to make an ecstatic patriotic success out of Gatsby's world by showing, with real rhetorical magnificence, how the Brooklyn Bridge joins West Egg to the American continent. Actually Crane had some of Fitzgerald's understanding of, feeling for, the worst changes in the

United States, but instead of making these into a controlling image—as Fitzgerald did in his valley of ashes, his deserted mansion with its scrawled obscenity on the front steps—Crane tried to transcend them by means of the contradictory "positive" image of the bridge. And yet how wonderful parts of *The Bridge* are! "Van Winkle" is one of the clearest and freshest and most truly American poems ever written; "The Dance," "Harbor Dawn," "The Tunnel," and "To Brooklyn Bridge," if they are in part rhetorical failures, are in part magical successes. Crane's poetry is hurt most by rhetoric and sentimentality—his automatic ecstatic mysticism, often of a Whitmanesque kind, is a form of sentimentality—and yet it is helped sometimes by the rhetorical risks Crane takes: if sometimes we are bogged down in lines full of "corymbulous," "hypogeum," "plangent," "irrefragably," "glozening," "tellurian," "conclamant," sometimes we are caught up in the soaring rapture of something unprecedented, absolutely individual. Remember the beautifully imaginative, haunting sympathy of "Black Tambourine"; the composed magic of "Repose of Rivers"; the serious exact interest, the organized concision, of "National Winter Garden"; the mesmeric rhetoric of "Voyages II," one of the most beautiful of all those poems in which love, death, and sleep "are fused for an instant in one floating flower." All these poems have the clear freshness (both young in itself and, somehow, in the America from which it came) of Crane at his inspired, astonishing, and attractive best.

Elizabeth Bishop's *Poems* seems to me one of the best books an American poet has written, one that the future will read almost as it will read Stevens and Moore and Ransom. Her poems are quiet, truthful, sad, funny, most marvelously individual poems; they have a sound, a feel, a whole moral and physical atmosphere, different from anything else I know. They are honest, modest, minutely observant, masterly; even their most complicated or troubled or imaginative effects seem, always, personal and natural, and as unmistakable as the first few notes of a Mahler song, the first few patches of a Vuillard interior. Her best poems—poems like "The Man-Moth," "The Fish," "The Weed," "Roosters," "The Prodigal Son," "Faustina, or Rock Roses," "The Armadillo"—remind one of Vuillard or even, sometimes, of Vermeer. The poet and the poems have their limitations; all exist on a small scale, and some of the later poems, especially, are too detailedly and objectively descriptive. But the more you read her poems, the better and fresher, the more nearly perfect they seem; at least half of them are completely realized works of art.

Robert Penn Warren's narrative and dramatic gifts seem to me greater than his lyric gifts, though he has written lyrics as memorable as "Original Sin" and "Pursuit"; he is at his best in one of the only good long poems of our century, *Brother to Dragons*. It is a terrible but sometimes very touching poem, one of extraordinary immediacy, strength, and scope. The poem's traumatic subject is Original Sin, but there is no Saviour left to save anybody in the poem; the consoling veil of religion and art and philosophy is gone, leaving us raw nature, raw morality, and the saving grace, the shaky grace, of custom. Cruel sometimes, crude sometimes, obsessed sometimes, *Brother to Dragons* has its touches of tender inconsequence, of forbearance and magnanimity. Some of Warren's wrenching historical understanding, his rhetoric, and his moralizing are hard for us to accept; but there is a wonderful amount of life in the poem—of human beings who, in the end, are free both of Warren's rhetoric and moralizing and of our own.

Theodore Roethke's poems began under glass (his greenhouse poems give you the live feel of a special world) and moved underground, underwater, out into the growing universe of roots and slugs, of all the "lewd, tiny, careless lives that scuttled under stones." One is struck by what the world of his poems is full of or entirely lacking in; plants and animals, soil and weather, sex, ontogeny, and the unconscious swarm over the reader, but he looks in vain for hydrogen bombs, world wars, Christianity, money, ordinary social observations, his everyday moral doubts. Many poets are sometimes childish; Roethke, uniquely, is sometimes babyish, though he is a powerful Donatello baby who has love affairs, and whose marshlike unconscious is continually celebrating its marriage with the whole wet dark underside of things. He is a thoroughly individual but surprisingly varied poet: if we were to read aloud four or five of his best poems ("Dolor," "My Papa's Waltz," "Frau Bauman, Frau Schmidt, and Frau Schwartze," "I Knew a

Woman," and "Meditations of an Old Woman" or one of the poems from *Praise to the End!*), we should see to our astonishment that each is in a decidedly different style; instead of conquering and living in one country, Roethke has led expeditions into several and has won notable victories in each. His best large poems are not, perhaps, as thoroughly satisfying as the best small ones. Certainly the long poems in *Praise to the End!* are partially or superficially successful, but do they mean enough? Are not the parts (except where these are derived from a formula, so that they can be duplicated or replaced too easily) better than the whole? Don't such poems tend to have impressive "positive" endings of a certain rhetorical insincerity? "Meditations of an Old Woman" is a more directly meaningful adaptation of this *Praise to the End!* type of long poem; it is interestingly influenced by the *Four Quartets*, just as some of Roethke's later poems are overpoweringly influenced by Yeats. Roethke is a forceful, delicate, and original poet whose poetry is still changing.

As these accounts must have reminded you, good American poets are surprisingly individual and independent; they have little of the member-of-the-Academy, official-man-of-letters feel that English or continental poets often have. When American poets join literary political parties, doctrinaire groups with immutable principles, whose poems themselves are manifestoes, the poets are ruined by it. We see this in the beatniks, with their official theory that you write a poem by putting down anything that happens to come into your head; this iron spontaneity of theirs makes it impossible for even a talented beatnik to write a good poem except by accident, since it eliminates the selection, exclusion, and concentration that are an essential part of writing a poem. Besides, their poems are as direct as true works of art are indirect: ironically, these conscious social manifestoes of theirs, these bohemian public speeches, make it impossible for the artist's unconscious to operate as it normally does in the process of producing a work of art.

This doctrinaire directness is as noticeable in the beatniks' opposites, the followers of Yvor Winters. These poets have—if I may invent a parable—met an enchanter who has said to them: "You have all met an enchanter who has transformed you into obscure romantic animals, but you can become clear and classical and human again if you will only swallow these rules." The poets swallow them, and from that moment they are all Henry Wadsworth Longfellow, a wax one; from that moment they wander, grave weighing shades, through a landscape each leaf of which rhymes, and scans, and says softly: "And the moral of *that* is . . ."

Does the Muse come to men with a ruler, a pair of compasses, and a metronome? Is it all right to say anything, no matter how commonplace and pompous and cliché, as long as you're sober, and say what the point is, and see that it scans? The worst thing about such planned poems as these is that they are so unnaturally silly: this is a learned imbecility, a foolishness of the schools; and ordinary common sense, ordinary human nature, will dismiss it with Johnson's "Clear your mind of cant," or with his "Sir, a man might write such stuff forever, if he would *abandon* his mind to it."

There is another, larger group of poets who, so to speak, come out of Richard Wilbur's overcoat. The work of these academic, tea-party, creative-writing-class poets rather tamely satisfies the rules or standards of technique implicit in what they consider the "best modern practice," so that they are very close to one another, very craftsman-like, never take chances, and produce (extraordinarily) a pretty or correctly beautiful poem and (ordinarily) magazine verse. Their poems are without personal force—come out of poems, not out of life; are, at bottom, social behavior calculated to satisfy a small social group of academic readers, editors, and foundation executives.

Earlier in this century there was a tradition of feminine verse—roughly, an Elizabeth Barrett Browning tradition—which produced many frankly romantic and poetic poems, most of them about love or nature. Elinor Wylie was the most crystalline and superficially metaphysical of these writers, and Edna St. Vincent Millay the most powerful and most popular. (One thinks with awe and longing of this real and extraordinary popularity of hers : if only there were *some* poet—Frost, Stevens, Eliot—whom people still read in canoes!) Millay seems to me at her best in a comparatively quiet and unpretentious poem like "The Return"; two later poets in this tradition, Léonie Adams and Louise Bogan, have produced (in poems like "The Figure Head" and "Henceforth, from the Mind") poems more delicately beautiful than any of Millay's or Wylie's. I have already written about two poets in a very different tradition, Marianne Moore and Elizabeth Bishop, who seem to me the best woman poets since Emily Dickinson; an extraordinarily live, powerful, and original poet, Eleanor Taylor, is a fitting companion of theirs; and I am sorry to have no space in which to write about such individual poets as Adrienne Rich and Katherine Hoskins.

I should like, if I had room, to write about such interesting and intelligent poets as John Berryman, Howard Nemerov, and Delmore Schwartz; such charming, individual, or forceful poets as W. D. Snodgrass, James Wright, Theodore Weiss, James Dickey, and Louis Simpson; and such respected poets as Mark Van Doren, Horace Gregory, Yvor Winters, Stanley Kunitz, Babette Deutsch, Richard Eberhart, Muriel Rukeyser, Louis Untermeyer, and John Peale Bishop. Instead let me finish by writing about Karl Shapiro, Richard Wilbur, and Robert Lowell.

Karl Shapiro's poems are fresh and young and rash and live; their hard clear outlines, their flat bold colors create a world like that of a knowing and skillful neoprimitive painting, without any of the confusion or profundity of atmosphere, of aerial perspective, but with notable visual and satiric force. The poet early perfected a style, derived from Auden but decidedly individual, which he has not developed in later life but has temporarily replaced with the clear Rilke-like rhetoric of his Adam and Eve poems, the frankly Whitmanesque convolutions of his latest work. His best poems—poems like "The Leg," "Waitress," "Scyros," "Going to School," "Cadillac"—have a real precision, a memorable exactness of realization, yet they plainly come out of life's raw hubbub, out of the disgraceful foundations, the exciting and disgraceful surfaces of existence. Both in verse and in prose Shapiro loves, partly out of indignation and partly out of sheer mischievousness, to tell the naked truths or half-truths or quarter-truths that will make anybody's hair stand on end; he is always crying: "But he hasn't any clothes on!" about an emperor who is half the time surprisingly well dressed.

Petronius spoke of the "studied felicity" of Horace's poetry, and I can never read one of Richard Wilbur's books without thinking of this phrase. His impersonal, exactly accomplished, faintly sententious skill produces poems that, ordinarily, compose themselves into a little too regular a beauty—there is no eminent beauty without a certain strangeness in the proportion; and yet "A Baroque Wall-Fountain in the Villa Sciarra" is one of the most marvelously beautiful, one of the most nearly perfect poems any American has written, and poems like "A Black November Turkey" and "A Hole in the Floor" are the little differentiated, complete-in-themselves universes that true works of art are. Wilbur's lyric calling-to-life of the things of this world—the things, rather than the processes or the people—specializes in both true and false happy endings, not by choice but by necessity;

he obsessively sees, and shows, the bright underside of every dark thing. What he says about his childhood is true of his maturity:

> In my kind world the dead were out of range
> And I could not forgive the sad or strange
> In beast or man.

This compulsion limits his poems; and yet it is this compulsion, and not merely his greater talent and skill, that differentiates him so favorably from the controlled, accomplished, correct poets who are common nowadays.

More than any other poet Robert Lowell is the poet of shock: his effects vary from crudity to magnificence, but they are always surprising and always his own—his style manages to make even quotations and historical facts a personal possession. His variant of Tolstoy's motto, "Make it strange," is "Make it grotesque"—largely grotesque, grandly incongruous. The vivid incongruity he gives the things or facts he uses is so decided that it amounts to a kind of wit; in his poetry fact is a live stumbling block that we fall over and feel to the bone. But it is life that he makes into poems instead of, as in Wilbur, the things of life. In Wilbur the man who produces the poems is somehow impersonal and anonymous, the composed conventional figure of The Poet; we know well, almost too well, the man who produces Lowell's poems. The awful depths, the plain absurdities of his own actual existence in the prosperous, developed, disastrous world he and we inhabit are there in the poems. Most poets, most good poets even, no longer have the heart to write about what is most terrible in the world of the present: the bombs waiting beside the rockets, the hundreds of millions staring into the temporary shelter of their television sets, the decline of the West that seems less a decline than the fall preceding an explosion. Perhaps because his own existence seems to him in some sense as terrible as the public world—his private world hangs over him as the public world hangs over others—he does not forsake the headlined world for the refuge of one's private joys and decencies, the shaky garden of the heart; instead, as in his wonderful poem about Boston Common, he sees all these as the lost paradise of the childish past, the past that knew so much but still didn't *know*. In *Life Studies* the pathos of the local color of the past—of the lives and deaths of his father and mother and grandfather and uncle, crammed full of their own varied and placid absurdity—is the background that sets off the desperate knife-edged absurdity of the jailed conscientious objector among gangsters and Jehovah's Witnesses, the private citizen returning to his baby, older now, from the mental hospital. He sees things as being part of history; if you say about his poor detailedly eccentric, trust-fund Lowells, "But they *weren't*," he can answer, "They are now."

Lowell has always had an astonishing ambition, a willingness to learn what past poetry was and to compete with it on its own terms. In many of his early poems his subjects have been rather monotonously wrenched into shape, organized under a terrific unvarying pressure; in the later poems they have been allowed, in comparison, to go on leading their own lives. (He bullied his early work, but his own vulnerable humanity has been forced in on him.) The particulars of all the poems keep to an extraordinary degree their stubborn toughness, their senseless originality and contingency; but the subject matter and peculiar circumstances of Lowell's best work—for instance, "Falling Asleep over the Aeneid," "For the Union Dead," "Mother Marie Therese," "Ford Madox Ford," "Skunk Hour"—justify the harshness and violence, the barbarous immediacy, that seem arbitrary in many of the others. He is a poet of great originality and power who has, extraordinarily, developed instead of repeating himself. His poems have a wonderful largeness and grandeur, exist on a scale that is unique today. You feel before reading any new poem of his the uneasy expectation of perhaps encountering a masterpiece.